JUST ONE MORE HAND

JUST ONE MORE HAND

Life in the Casino Economy

Ellen Mutari and Deborah M. Figart

ROWMAN & LITTLEFIELD
Lanham • Boulder • New York • London

Published by Rowman & Littlefield
A wholly owned subsidiary of The Rowman & Littlefield Publishing Group,
Inc.
4501 Forbes Boulevard, Suite 200, Lanham, Maryland 20706
www.rowman.com

16 Carlisle Street, London W1D 3BT, United Kingdom

British Library Cataloguing in Publication Information Available

Library of Congress Cataloging-in-Publication Data

Mutari, Ellen, 1956-
Just one more hand : life in the casino economy / Ellen Mutari and Deborah M. Figart.
pages cm
Includes bibliographical references and index.
ISBN 978-1-4422-3667-7 (cloth : alk. paper) -- ISBN 978-1-4422-3668-4 (electronic)
1. Casinos--United States. 2. Casinos--United States--Employees. 3. Gambling industry--United
States--Employees. I. Figart, Deborah M. II. Title.
HV6711.M88 2015
795.092'273--dc23
2014030156

∞™ The paper used in this publication meets the minimum requirements of
American National Standard for Information Sciences Permanence of Paper
for Printed Library Materials, ANSI/NISO Z39.48-1992.

Printed in the United States of America

CONTENTS

THE WORKERS

Ally	dealer
Aparna	guest room attendant
Bernice	inspector
Caroline	dealer
Connie	surveillance officer
Dario	inventory clerk
Donna	dealer
Emil	craps dealer
Felicia	slot attendant
Graciela	floorperson
Heather	food server
Holly	dealer
Inez	steward
Isiah	dealer
Jesse	dealer
Keith	waiter
Ken	dual rate pit boss
Laurel	dealer
Lena	poker dealer

Lily	costumed beverage server
Manuela	guest room attendant
Marlene	dealer
Nana	seamstress
Nick	bar porter
Nora	loyalty card representative
Patrice	dual rate floorperson
Peter	waiter
Robin	manager
Ruth	beverage server
Sean	surveillance operator
SueBee	pit boss
Terrence	slot technician
Valerie	slot attendant
Walter	food server
Zoe	beverage server

PREFACE

On a cold winter Wednesday in February 2014, 1,300 people showed up for an "emergency job fair" at the Golden Nugget casino in Atlantic City. They had heard that fifty job openings were going to be filled immediately. With local casino employment levels at their lowest point in thirty years, the shutdown just one month earlier of another casino that put 1,600 employees out of work, and New Jersey's unemployment rate stubbornly above 7 percent, hopeful applicants lined up in droves for a chance to win one of the positions. The queue snaked around one floor and down the stairs to another floor. The odds of actually landing a job made slot machines look like relatively good investments. Yet, the job fair still seemed like a rare silver lining amid cloudy skies: Executive Vice President and General Manager Tom Pohlman had told the media that the Golden Nugget was seeing a spike in customers following the closing of local competitor Atlantic Club casino. It was looking to hire additional dealers, as well as front desk attendants, cocktail servers, valet attendants, and more.

Then came the heartbreaking announcement from the Golden Nugget's corporate office in Las Vegas: "While our gaming revenue has been reported as slightly up in Atlantic City, the comparative increase in business is off [of] a low base and not the reason for the job fair."[1] Instead, applicants were asked if they would relocate to a newer Golden Nugget casino in Lake Charles, Louisiana, that wasn't scheduled to open until the end of the year. They were also told that the Atlantic City property still might hire—but not until warmer weather increased seasonal summer business.

Hard-working people desperate for jobs and being told they had to transplant themselves away from family and community to get them. A recession compounding the long-term loss of business to newer competitors. Where had we seen this story before?

In 1995, we moved to southern New Jersey from southeast Michigan. Teaching economics in Michigan in the early 1990s had allowed us a front-row seat to watch how the economic restructuring of the U.S. economy away from a manufacturing base was transforming people's lives and livelihoods. Southeast Michigan is dominated—economically, culturally, and politically—by the dynamics of the U.S. automobile industry. In 1990, Deb had landed a tenure-track job in economics (and was subsequently tenured) at Eastern Michigan University in Ypsilanti, Michigan. Ypsilanti was the site of Ford Motor Company's Willow Run bomber factory built during World War II; the plant was shifted to auto production under several owners after the war, eventually becoming a General Motors (GM) facility. While working on her dissertation, Ellen spent several semesters as an economics instructor at Mott Community College in Flint, Michigan, the city made famous in the 1989 Michael Moore documentary *Roger and Me*. Many of the students taking community college classes in Flint were laid off GM workers whose tuition was subsidized under a union-negotiated agreement. Although our own research during this period focused on issues facing working women, particularly pay equity, flexible working time, and the feminization of work, we often taught and learned from students who were raised in the shadow of the local industry. Any time we needed to illustrate a concept in class, we relied upon examples from the auto industry, knowing that every one of our students would "get it."

Using the auto industry to teach economics was germane because it was such a crucial industry in shaping the concepts and language that we use to talk about economic life. *Fordism*, for example, is a term that describes the political economy of the mid-twentieth-century United States. The term honors Henry Ford, the automobile industry executive who pioneered the "Five Dollar Day." In simplified terms—far more simplified than the actual historical record of whether, how, and why Ford paid relatively high wages to his workers—auto workers who made good wages could afford to buy cars. The Fordist era of U.S. economic history was a period marked by mass production (assembly line manu-facturing) and mass consumption (the rising living standards of middle-class Americans). Keynesian economic policy was the consensus ap-proach, since the oligopolistic manufacturing industries of this era needed to maintain demand for their goods and services in the domes-tic market.[2]

Hard work became a badge of honor and a marker of masculinity.[3] Strong labor unions offered workers—particularly male workers—the kind of job security and good wages that supported escalating consump-tion standards, even as they also afforded employers a respite from strife on the shop floor. While many working families outside of the dominant economic sector were left out of this "Golden Age" of American capitalism and the unpaid work of homemakers that sus-tained the market economy was rendered invisible, it was nevertheless a period marked by income convergence and relative prosperity.[4] And since middle-class families were doing well, they tended not to be-grudge the social safety net that was provided to catch those on the outside.

Starting in the 1970s, however, the institutional foundations of Ford-ism began to unravel. The Michigan we moved to in 1990 was going through hard times, even as other parts of the United States were pros-pering in the so-called new economy. Globalization—that shorthand term for the process that resulted from technological changes making it cheaper to communicate information and ship goods across borders—was, of course, one instrumental factor in this shift. Manufacturing, especially the less-skilled, routinized jobs on assembly lines, was in-creasingly outsourced overseas. As manufacturers produced and traded across borders, their workers did not need to be their customers. The virtuous circle of Fordism was broken. Manufacturing workers were losing their jobs or facing stagnant wages and decreases in benefits. Consequently, our students and their families were watching good jobs slip through their fingers.

When we moved "back east," we landed in another area dominated by an industry. In 1995, Atlantic City's casinos were flourishing. Bus-loads of patrons arrived daily to play the slots or some cards. Couples would be dressed up in slick suits, ruffles, and sequins, excited to leave their normal life behind for a while. Small groups of women heading down after work would book a cheap motel room to take a nap and change clothes before a night of partying. Regulars just wore their street clothes, and restlessly fidgeted during the ride. In those days, the bus fare was free or minimal because the casinos would reimburse the cost of travel for gamblers whose round trip was initiated in places like the Port Authority Bus Terminal in New York City. We sometimes rode the bus with them—but as paying customers because our trip was the reverse, originating in Atlantic City.

There was a charge of anticipation in the air as the bus full of gamblers pulled into the casino garage or parking lot. A casino greeter would get on the bus and give everyone their paper voucher, to be exchanged at a cashier's window in the sponsoring casino. Each bus stopped at one or two casinos when it arrived, and patrons chose buses that went to their favorites. An escape from their dead-end jobs with minimal pensions or no pensions at all, and from fretting over the rising balances on their credit cards, the casinos beckoned gamblers with the possibility of a new kind of American Dream—a dream of quick riches for a lucky few. The atmosphere tended to be much more subdued on early morning return trips back to Manhattan. This was partly due to the time of day, but the quiet also seemed to occupy the gap between dreams and reality.

Our move from Michigan to New Jersey followed the same trajectory as the economy. Services—especially the selling of intangible experiences—were replacing the manufacturing workplaces that were so critical to the livelihoods of previous generations of workers, including our students back in Michigan. We had left the rustbelt behind, and, like Dorothy, found ourselves in a sparkling and colorful new land.[5] New and newly renovated casinos promised adventure and excitement. Advances in technology spurred progressive jackpots linked across casinos. Customers watched professional poker on television and demanded it in the casinos.

Not to say that we were wearing green glasses that made everything in this peculiar industry look like emeralds. *Financialization* was replacing the manufacturing giants of the Fordist era with the Wizards of Wall Street.[6] Making money with money was the order of the day. Middle-income and even lower-income households tried to jump in on the action during the stock market bubble and the housing bubble. Casino gambling is an even more accessible way to participate in this world where you could become wealthy as pieces of paper changed hands.

Not interested in gambling ourselves, we were intrigued by casinos as workplaces. After all, we are labor economists. We are fascinated by how people earn a living. The germination of this book came from wondering how jobs in the casinos compared with the old manufacturing jobs. Could you build a life working in Atlantic City's booming casinos?

The idea for this study sat in the back of our minds for years, as we gradually settled into life in South Jersey. We were diverted into other projects, but kept thinking that someday we really needed to take up the challenge of investigating the work lives of casino employees. When we finally initiated this project in 2006, we now had new students, new neighbors, and new friends. In Atlantic County, almost everyone's life is touched by the casinos. Once we decided to do a study interviewing casino workers about their jobs, it was hard to separate fieldwork from everyday life. If we mentioned what we were doing, everyone had a story to tell, a person who might be willing to participate in an interview, an opinion on the state of the industry.

Which was in flux. We quickly found that we were no longer focusing on an isolated case study. As we describe in subsequent chapters, the now-global casino gaming industry has expanded rapidly. Many folks who used to ride the bus to Atlantic City have more accessible places to gamble up and down the East Coast. The success of two casinos on Native American reservations in Connecticut spurred a new wave of expansion in the mid-to-late 1990s focused on slot parlors and "racinos" (racetracks with slot machines). Gradually, one state after another has tried to upgrade to full-service commercial casinos. As we write, states such as New York, Massachusetts, and Florida are hotly debating whether or how to expand the number of large-scale casinos with table games and resort amenities. At the same time, gambling revenues are falling in many of the earlier gaming states, including Mississippi, Missouri, Illinois, and Michigan.[7] Atlantic City's casinos—and most of the locales offering casino gaming in the United States—now operate in a saturated market. Three more Atlantic City casinos are projected to close by the end of 2014, with a potential loss of over 6,000 more jobs in the industry and ripple effects on local businesses, real estate values, and the tax base.

Why do they keep building? Each time states decide to build more casinos to boost tax revenues, casino companies risk losing market share to a competitor if they don't bid on the project. The philosophy seems to be to keep moving to avoid sinking. On the other hand, the local communities placing all their chips on casinos as an economic development strategy face increasingly long odds. The driving distance to the closest casino is getting shorter and shorter. Each locale has to find new ways to draw in customers or else they have to rely on revenue from gamblers in their own backyard. And even if the casino is profitable, the larger question for economic development is whether the casinos promote rising living standards. The definition of economic development is not simply the proliferation of businesses. Good jobs are therefore critical to economic development because most peoples' income derives from wages, not profits.

Our situated study of jobs in the new economy of casino gambling therefore has broad implications for citizens weighing whether the promises offered by casino development are likely to be realized. The answer to this question is not simple. We found an industry that traditionally offers higher wages than many other service-sector jobs, but the recent introduction of cost-cutting practices is making it harder to find full-time jobs with benefits. We met folks who loved their jobs, others who couldn't wait to leave, and still others who were let go. We heard happy stories about a job where every day is different and horror stories about abusive customers and unhealthy working conditions. Yet even those who loved their jobs felt the best days were a thing of the past. While longtime employees are fighting against concessions and wage stagnation, younger workers juggle multiple part-time and seasonal jobs at several casinos. Listening to their struggles, over and over we heard a dynamic story of change rather than static judgments about good jobs or bad jobs.

The individual experiences of the study participants who sat down for interviews about their work lives were shaped by trends in the political economy of the gaming industry and the U.S. economy as a whole. And the changes casino employees are facing are familiar ones for contemporary workers in many industries. The changes we witnessed in Michigan as the old Fordist regime unraveled are rippling through the rest of the economy. As the world economy slowly recovers from the Great Recession, the long-term trend toward increasingly precarious employment has accelerated. Secure jobs with benefits are scarce for everyone but the most privileged.[8] Deep-rooted unemployment and underemployment undermines the ability of families and communities to sustain themselves.

Casino gaming is an apt lens for viewing this new economic order. Today we are surrounded by risk—the risk of losing our jobs, losing our benefits, losing our homes, losing our credit ratings, and losing our economic footing. Our study participants are living in a casino economy. But, increasingly, so are the rest of us.

Many people are deserving of appreciation for their assistance as we journeyed through the casino economy. They hold no responsibility, however, for our conclusions. Our employer, Stockton College, provided us with research support including a sabbatical, additional release time, and funds for the interview transcriptions. Stockton students who participated in a Research Experience for Undergraduates and a Summer Intensive Research Experience include Bradley Hartman, Gregory Novakowski, Brian Foglia, and Peter Salerno. Joan Frankel, the curator of the Atlantic County Historical Society, located archival materials from the casino gaming referendum campaign. Susan Allen from Stockton's Office of External Affairs photographed images from the society and Margot Alten from Stockton's Graphics Department prepared the images for publication. Other friends and colleagues who helped along the way by suggesting contacts or other resources, reading drafts, or sharing insights include Jean Abbott, Randy Albelda, Lee Badgett, Ben Begleiter, Oliver Cooke, Shawn Donaldson, Betsy Erbaugh, Phil Friedman, Barbara Hopkins, Elaine Ingulli, Rob Jaeger, Maritza Jauregui, Nathan Long, Jon Luoma, Max Lyons, Alex Marino, Tony Marino, Elaine McCrate, Linda Nelson, Suzi Odlen, Adam Patten, Anne Pomeroy, Marilyn Power, Steve Pressman, Yana van der Meulen Rodgers, Lisa Rosner, Jeffrey Waddoups, and Chris Walker. Israel Posner, Brian Tyrell, and others involved in the project to produce *Casino Gaming in Atlantic City: A Thirty Year Retrospective, 1978–2008* shared their experiences and insights. Tina Keck ably and efficiently transcribed most of the interviews from digital recordings. Our interview transcribers also included Maritza Rodriguez-Smith, Anne Waginger, Claire Crawford, and Megan Lindsey.

Papers based on our research were presented at conferences of the Labor and Employment Relations Association, the Allied Social Sciences Association, and the International Association for Feminist Economics. The other participants and attendees at these sessions gave us valuable feedback. This project would have been much more difficult without the resource of a strong local newspaper, the *Press of Atlantic City*. Our editor, Suzanne Staszak-Silva at Rowman & Littlefield, supported our project with enthusiasm. Laura Reiter, our production editor, smoothly guided us to the finish line, assisted by the careful and thoughtful work of copyeditor Jo-Ann Parks.

Most importantly, of course, we are grateful to the anonymous study participants who took time from their busy schedules to answer our questions and tell their stories, stories that are much fuller than we portray here. We enjoyed every minute we spent getting to know them. Our research would not be possible without their trust, intelligence, and patience. This book is dedicated to them.

1

STORIES FROM A CASINO ECONOMY

It's a unique industry because you're basically, it's a factory job because you're producing, but you're not producing a product. It's open 24/7, which most business aren't. You're dealing with the public constantly. You're being watched constantly. You come into contact with the very rich to the very poor; every nationality walks through the doors. You never, it's like live theater because you never know what's going to happen. You think it's going to be a normal day, and somebody comes walking through and does something just so bizarre that, it's like you can't even make it up. It's just like . . . it's like . . . it's so . . . it's never the same.
—Ken, Dual-Rate Pit Manager

The excitement of participating in a perennial party and the adventure of meeting people from every walk of life—from NBA basketball pros and Hollywood producers to gypsies in town for a funeral. A winning player tosses a $1,000 chip onto the serving tray of a cocktail waitress. Regular customers become like family, sharing major life events. The challenge of spotting cheaters. The pride of learning how to handle people when they are at their worst. Walking away at the end of the shift, knowing you made good money for yourself and your family.

And yet. . . . High rollers whose every whim must be gratified and whose abuse must be deflected. Slot machine players who refuse to leave a machine they expect to pay off any minute, so they urinate right where they sit. Exhaled smoke directly aimed at your face because you dealt a losing hand. Or being hit with a drink, or even worse, spit. Being called every possible vile name or swear word. Con artists who advise players and then ask for a piece of their winnings. Prostitutes hanging on the arm of a "whale," with sexual acts performed as if they were hidden from view under the gaming tables. Job auditions requiring a bikini or a short, revealing uniform, and "Please bend down and pick something up off the floor." Constant noise, noise, noise. More drinking. More smoke. More abuse. More unhappy losers.

Sound like a typical day at your job? It is life on the job in a casino.

People construct lives and identities in a particular context that is profoundly shaped by the economic structures in which they work. Workers in Atlantic City's casinos do this in an unusual environment. Gamblers come to hit the jackpot that will transform their lives, or at least to escape their daily routine for a short time. The physical environment of the casinos is designed around escapist fantasies of other places and times—from generic visions of opulence to specific daydreams of a nineteenth-century frontier saloon (Bally's Wild West Casino), ancient Roman bacchanals (Caesars Atlantic City), or a Maharajah's palace (Trump Taj Mahal). Time is supposed to be suspended. Casinos are open twenty-four hours a day, seven days a week, and fifty-two weeks a year. The gaming floors typically have no windows and no clocks. But within these self-contained environments devoted to risk and reward, the diverse employees who make up the casino workforce are also seeking to create their lives. They punch time clocks, serve cocktails and meals, deal cards, spin wheels, deflect complaints, make beds, wash dishes and laundry, observe customers, monitor employees, fix plumbing and slot machines, and perform a myriad of other challenging, mundane, and sometimes curious tasks.

The fact of near-chronic losing influences the interaction between the service provider and the consumer, making gambling distinctive as compared with other experiences for sale in the leisure and entertainment sector of the economy. Gamblers generally lose, and the games played against the house are structured to ensure this is the case. The carrot of "comps" (rewards based on the amount a player bets) and free drinks offered to customers while gambling further complicate the transaction. Graciela, a former pit manager with over thirty years of experience who shifted to a part-time supervisor in order to go to college, compared the casinos with another popular entertainment option: "What makes a difference is because people expect something back.

When you go to Disney World—I'll just use Disney World, I love Disney World—you go there, you're thinking, 'I'm gonna have a great time.' You're not expecting Disney to give you something at the end of your stay." She eloquently observed a few minutes later that "The truth of the exchange is less clear, it seems like, because you know you're just going to get a movie or you know you're gonna get a dance floor to dance on and other things. And in gambling, you don't know what you're getting back as the customer, and customers may have unrealistic expectations about what they are gonna get back." The free alcohol that lowers inhibitions doesn't necessarily mix well with losing money. A relatively new dealer, Ally, noted when asked what makes casinos different as workplaces, "I guess probably the biggest comparison is that most people in the workplace don't have to tolerate smoke and drunks. If a drunk came into an office he'd be tossed out. . . . That's probably the biggest thing—the drinking. Alcohol changes personalities—let's face it."

In important ways, working in casinos is not much different than working in other industries in a market economy. There are bosses, good and bad, who affect your daily experience on the job. There are rules and regulations for job performance—especially strict ones in the gaming pits. There are uniforms to wear and roles to play. There are unionization campaigns and management memos about teamwork. There are conflicting demands from work and family life, and creative ways to solve the conflicts. There are people and policies that make the job better, and others that strip away one's dignity. But central to our study is a story that workers all over can relate to: a workplace in an industry that seemed to promise a solid and stable livelihood is being transformed by competitive pressures, causing employees to lose their economic footing. What seemed like a good job one day becomes a bad job the next. So the experiences of Atlantic City's casino employees are in many ways illustrative of what workers are facing and how they are coping throughout the contemporary political economy.

In a postindustrial United States, casinos have become both a metaphor for a roller-coaster economy and a key service industry selling experiences and dreams. As various economic bubbles have burst, the U.S. economy since the start of the new millennium has seemed to be more of a casino than a factory: a place where you put down your money and cross your fingers. Buying a home, saving for retirement, getting a student loan, starting a business, or even accepting a job seem like risky ventures rather than sure bets. In such turbulent times, we all seem to be gamblers, even when we do not intend to be.

But actual gambling is big business. Thirty-nine U.S. states have commercial casinos, tribal casinos, racetrack casinos, card rooms, and/or electronic gaming devices.[1] (We are not including states that only operate lotteries.) For a decade, gambling has been a form of entertainment with greater consumer expenditures than movie tickets, video games, theme parks, recorded music, and spectator sports combined. Commercial casinos alone earned over $37 billion just from their gaming operations in 2012. Casinos are major entertainment venues. The American Gaming Association reports that 34 percent of Americans visited a casino in 2012. Young adults (aged twenty-one to thirty-five) are even more likely to go to casinos; the same survey found 39 percent had visited a casino. Moreover, the casino industry is emblematic of a relatively recent wave of service industries that sell a form of experience as their product.

Casino billboards advertise: "Easy Street. It's Only a Play Away." Or "How Far Will You Go to Win Big?" And "Are You Ready to Play?" If you can get the customers in the door and into the gaming pits, these businesses guarantee revenue for "the house." The casinos' "edge" is improved by "payment of less than true odds to winners (out of the losers' pool)."[2] Gambling, for casino operators, was a sure bet.

It is no longer a sure bet. The enormous growth of recent decades has reached the point of market saturation. That is, when new markets and new casinos open, they try to "cannibalize" the customer base of their predecessors. Even prior to the economic and financial crisis that began in 2008, the growth pace of gaming across the United States was slowing. During the Great Recession and its aftershocks, revenue plummeted while casino operators found new profit centers overseas. Macau, a city in southern China located on a peninsula, surpassed Las Vegas as the world's largest gaming market in 2006. Less than one-fourth of the gaming industry is now centered in the United States. The global casinos and gaming sector grew at the same time the industry was shrinking in the United States. The average annual decline in U.S.

gross gaming revenue (or "win"), a key indicator used to gauge profitability, was 0.6 percent from 2006 through 2010.[3]

Atlantic City's casinos faced even worse conditions. For example, Atlantic City experienced the country's largest percentage decrease in gross gaming revenue in 2010, over 9 percent.[4] Despite the opening of a new casino in town, gross gaming revenue declined 8 percent in 2012.[5] Once the shiny new attraction that lured gamblers from all over the East Coast, if not the world, Atlantic City today is scrambling to find a formula that can restore its edge, providing lessons for policy makers and others committed to economic development and sustainable livelihoods.

Atlantic City's efforts to restore its position as a destination resort demonstrate the difficulties for local communities that are building new casinos in the hopes of luring tourists. Las Vegas has successfully supplemented gambling with a broader appeal, but copying their model in today's market is challenging. As casinos proliferate and gambling is more and more convenient, it ceases to be special. Why plan a vacation to gamble when you can just drive a few miles to indulge? The voices of Atlantic City's casino workers also show that a casino economy is increasingly a tough way to build a life. Though the jobs can seem fun and glamorous, gambling culture can grind you down. And, as the employers in the industry feel competitors and creditors breathing down their necks, a short-term focus on the bottom line is eroding those aspects of the jobs that were once valued by employees. But this undermining of job quality is not unique to casinos. The U.S. economy has lost its edge in many industries and regions. Businesses are trying to survive by trimming, then cutting, then slashing costs. As they do, good jobs are harder to come by.

The initial puzzle that prompted us to undertake this project was a concern with whether the casino economy was providing employees good jobs. We decided that it would be important to listen to what casinos workers said about what constituted a good job and what they viewed as the positive and negative qualities of their own working lives.

Of course, we brought our own standpoint to this process. We view paid work as more than simply a means to material ends like buying a house, paying your bills, or saving to retire. Work, both paid and unpaid, is part of a complex economic process that can be referred to as *social provisioning*.[6] An economy, from this perspective, is how society organizes these provisioning activities, mediated by culture, ideology, and institutions. The processes involved in social provisioning, according to economist William Dugger, "produce goods and services, but they also produce people."[7] People, as we see it, are the whole reason to have an economy. Their well-being is the most important end product of all. Sometimes policy makers, business analysts, and economists lose sight of this, and talk about people, especially workers, in terms of what they must sacrifice for the good of the economy, treating individuals as means rather than as ends in themselves.

Our lens on paid work differs from the standard economics model. In labor economics textbooks, paid employment generates what economists call *disutility*, meaning dissatisfaction. It is not something that we do voluntarily. This dissatisfaction has to be compensated by paying us to do something that has no intrinsic value for us. Our pay is then used to purchase goods and services that do bring us satisfaction. Work does not provide meaning in this view; "meaning" in economic life comes from the satisfaction of wants through consumption.[8] So when economists and others started doing research that categorized some jobs as "good jobs" and other jobs as "bad jobs," they initially focused on how much the jobs paid, along with other monetary benefits. Bad jobs were jobs that did not allow someone to achieve the material standard of living that a particular society considers normal.

The literature on good jobs and bad jobs took off in the 1970s, as the U.S. service sector was rapidly expanding but the manufacturing sector was still seen as the nation's economic heart.[9] Political economists such as Peter Doeringer and Michael Piore introduced an approach that they called *dual labor market theory*.[10] The idea behind dual labor markets was that the job market was divided between jobs in what they called the primary sector and the secondary sector. In the primary sector, good jobs were well paid and had career ladders. Secondary sector jobs were low paid and had lots of turnover and few opportunities for advancement. Economic restructuring, specifically the declining share of employment in the manufacturing sector and the increase in service-sector employment, was depicted as a declining primary sector and expanding secondary sector. This research was intended to correct an overemphasis on individual worker characteristics (supply) by analyzing the employer (demand) side of labor markets. In other words, how much you earn is not solely determined by how hard you work or the education and skills you acquire. Structural factors like the profitability of the industry, the degree of competition your employer faces, and whether the industry is unionized are equally important.

Over time, scholars came to recognize that many industries, especially in the service sector, include both high-wage and low-wage occupations. Attention turned to good jobs versus bad jobs within industries. Research on job quality also gradually moved beyond a narrow focus on financial compensation to explore other job characteristics. As more studies asked workers to rate what they valued in a job, investigators found that people themselves place tremendous value on job aspects such as autonomy, fulfillment, and ability to balance work and family—in addition to pay. Yet it seemed that the good characteristics clustered together in some jobs and the bad characteristics clustered in others. And it appeared that job quality was declining in the United States and other postindustrial economies.[11]

The focus on clustering of job characteristics led to the argument that jobs are *segmented* by race and gender. That is, good jobs and bad jobs are often allocated to individuals on the basis of the gender, race, and ethnicity of the worker.[12] Good jobs were still defined as breadwinner jobs with full-time pay and benefits that enabled the employee to support a family. These jobs were disproportionately allocated to white males. White women were channeled into jobs that supported mothering while racial and ethnic minorities found employment in jobs that required co-breadwinning because they did not pay family-sustaining wages. Eventually, feminist scholars challenged the idea that this was a two-step process: first a job is created and then there is a hierarchy in job allocation. Instead, feminists argued that job characteristics are shaped by employers' expectations about the potential job-holders—that some jobs are created as male breadwinner jobs while others are designed for workers with family responsibilities, for example.

Dramatic changes in the U.S. labor force at the end of the twentieth century helped contribute to more rethinking about job quality. The workforce became increasingly diverse. Women, especially mothers with young children, were far more likely to be on the job due to a range of factors that pushed them and pulled them into paid employment. Discriminatory barriers to entry into nontraditional occupations were reduced—though of course not eliminated—for many groups of workers. New immigrants came in search of employment as well. The assumption that certain job characteristics are good regardless of who holds them was increasingly problematic. Instead, there was more attention to the differences among workers and their needs, dreams, and desires. Workers may hold different values, and social values may themselves change over time. Our interview informants confirm that job quality is a multi-dimensional concept and diverse employees define a good job in terms of their own life perspective.

Most importantly for our study, these diverse transformations have led scholars to conclude that job quality is not static. There are no intrinsically good jobs or bad jobs.[13] Jobs are continually in the process of being developed, defined, merged, and at times eliminated. Every time there is a change in job responsibilities, working conditions, the number or types of employees collaborating to accomplish a set of tasks, and, of course, the pay and benefits, a job is reconstructed. Even static wages, in a world of rising prices, change job quality. Jobs are shaped and reshaped by individuals, collective behavior, and institutions.

Business owners and their managers play a pivotal role in this process through all the decisions they make about hiring, promotions, and working conditions. They have to be attentive to the economic environment in which they operate, including competitors, financial markets, conditions in related industries, and their customer base. But they also make decisions on the basis of prevailing social norms, and sometimes even their own ethical standards and beliefs.[14] Employees themselves are not passive in this process—either as individuals or as members of unions. Politics and public policy also shape job quality. Employers and employees both jockey for influence in a political world where employers have more funding but employees have greater numbers. Citizens and broader communities view themselves as stakeholders in the kinds of jobs available, so they also seek a voice through political channels. All of these dynamics have played out in Atlantic City's casino economy.

We met Laurel, a young grandmother in her fifties, through mutual friends. Laurel, a white high school graduate, has spent most of her career as a dealer at Caesars, after beginning at another casino. Her employer, Caesars Entertainment, is the second largest global casino operator, and currently the owner of four Atlantic City casinos (Caesars, Harrah's, Bally's, and Showboat). Like others in the industry, she was drawn in through family connections; her cousin was a dealer. Her first employer told her to attend dealer school and then tested her for assignment to the gaming floor. She remembers her first day: "They tell you to come in with black pants and a white blouse . . . then you go to the benefits office where you apply for the job and they take you to the casino floor and whatever games you have they'll tell you, 'Okay, jump into that game' and they'll watch you. Then you'll do whatever other game you deal and they watch you and that's how you get hired." In casino parlance, it's called an audition. They watch how you deal the game and how you deal with customers. Laurel wanted to deal craps because of the exciting, high-stakes action. Management told her she was too short for the craps pit and sent her to roulette at first. At that time in the early 1980s, it was more likely that they didn't think a woman dealer belonged in craps. Think of the names of the dealers in any craps pit: a boxman, a stickman, and one or two base dealers, often called "croupiers" in European casinos.

When she moved to Caesars in the early 1990s, it was because Caesars had the best toke (tip) rate in town. To keep herself from being bored, Laurel learned new games and rotated among them, what are referred to as "carnival games" such as three-card poker, four-card poker, Let It Ride, Texas Hold' Em, and Caribbean stud poker. These tend to have a higher edge for the house than regular games like blackjack or baccarat. She did not get paid a higher base wage for knowing more games, yet they made her a real asset to the casino. When we interviewed her she said, "so tonight, I'm going to Asia Poker in pit twelve." Caesars promoted Laurel to a floorperson who watches or supervises games, but the job didn't earn tips. She suffered a loss in income without tips, so she gave it up to return to full-time dealing "because I'm making more money dealing."

There were some very good years for Laurel and other dealers in the industry. For example, she worked part-time for several years because she had young children, and her employer at the time offered benefits to part-timers. The flexibility helped her balance work and family. "It's different now," she said, referring to the aftermath of an acquisition of her longtime workplace, as well as Bally's Atlantic City, by Harrah's Entertainment in 2005. (The name of the parent corporation was changed to Caesars Entertainment soon thereafter because it had better brand appeal.) These days, it is difficult to secure a full-time dealer position at all if you are a new employee, because part-timers no longer get benefits. And casinos have been cutting benefits for full-timers, too. Venting her frustration with the new management dictates when we interviewed her in 2007, Laurel said: "They made our benefits horrible. I never had such bad benefits, like if you have to go in the hospital now it's like you have a $1,500 deductible." She added that the company also charged a lot more for benefits through paycheck deductions: "They went up sky high." "And plus another thing they were doing is [the parent company] tried to weed away people that are making the most money," meaning the senior, full-time dealers. Like Laurel. She was at the top rate of $8.50 base pay per hour and the rate for new hires was $4.00 per hour. Corporate, she felt, wanted to replace her with a lower-paid part-time employee. But when we spoke with her again in 2013, she was holding onto her job despite the pressure. In fact, she had become active in the new dealer's union, and felt the grievance procedure was helping protect jobs. And get her more money, as she is now up to almost $10.00 an hour plus tips.

Zoe laughed as she repeated a line that she has uttered many times before: "I am fifty-two years old. I am not what corporate would think is the ideal cocktail waitress." "Corporate," in this case, also refers to Caesars Entertainment. A white woman who was born and raised in Atlantic City, Zoe is a "Day-Oner," meaning that she helped open Resorts Casino Hotel in 1978, directly after graduating from high school. Her jobs, at various casinos and family-owned restaurants throughout the city until she settled at Showboat over twenty-five years ago, have helped her, along with her husband, raise three children. It has been, in her words, a "great job," particularly for a working mother. While she joked about the fact that "To get the job you had to show up in a bikini," she recognized that any job working with the public requires a lot of hidden skills: "You have to be able to talk to all sorts of people. You have to kind of head off conflict if you can, and not make conflict."

Her job security, she said, has come from being a union member (Local 54 of UNITE HERE). Being a union member, however, has not prevented major changes in the way she does her work. Nor could it prevent Caesars Entertainment from announcing its intention to close Showboat one year after our interview, abruptly forcing her to look for a new line of work. As she took one of her rare days off in 2013 to talk with us, she observed that "One of the reasons why I've always done the job and liked the job and been involved in the job is because I liked interacting with the customers. I like, that's part of, and I could always get a bigger tip out of somebody because I could schmooze them or whatever. And now that's not . . . because I'm timed. I only have six minutes from the time the drink is ordered from the iPad to the time I deliver it—only six minutes."

About three years ago, she indicated, management introduced a new system for ordering and serving free drinks for gamblers—the "iApp" system. The casino hired new employees, mostly younger, to walk up and down the casino floor with iPhones (now iPad minis) and take drink orders. Zoe described the process: "They'll go up to you and say 'Would you like a drink?' And they would punch in the drink and I'm to wait in the bar, and the drink [order] is shot into the bar. The bartender makes the drink and it's put in a row. And if it's my turn, because I no longer have a station—it's called the next tray where everybody just waits for their turn. . . . I take the next seven drinks out to the casino floor and serve them whether they are anywhere on the casino floor." Because the customers for these seven drinks are spread out, "you are kind of like ping-ponging around a little bit instead of the traditional, the older way, where you would just go up and down your aisle or up around your one pit. Now you're kind of like, darting around, kind of like *The Hunger Games*." The new system saves the casino money: "What it's done is shrunk the staff down. They don't need as many people any longer. They don't need as many cocktail servers." Conversations with customers are eliminated. Not surprisingly, tips—which cocktail servers keep rather than pool with the others—have declined. And the cocktail waitresses, who used to be trained to monitor customers' alcohol intake and cut them off when they had imbibed too much, can no longer keep track of how many drinks someone has had.

Terrence, a middle-aged African American man, also helped raise a family with his casino job. He is a huge fan of late senator and vice president Hubert Humphrey, especially because of the Minnesota senator's work in developing the Comprehensive Employment and Training Act (CETA) program. After dropping out of college in the 1970s, Terrence found himself, in his own words, "poor and destitute." He did not have meaningful skills or experience, so he found himself in a

"Catch 22 situation. Employees didn't have the training to get the job, and the employers didn't want to hire you because you needed experience." CETA paid for job training while he worked in a public service job, but to qualify he had to go on public assistance which was a blow to his pride. Once in the program, he was faced with a choice between learning to deal blackjack or to service slot machines. Terrence chose to become a slot machine technician because he had read Alvin Toffler's books, *Future Shock* and *The Third Wave*, and believed it was important to become comfortable with technology and technological change: "Primarily the thing I did the most, I think, for myself is I helped myself to feel comfortable around high technology."

As Toffler would have predicted, the technology that Terrence was initially trained to fix has become obsolete. Slot machines no longer accept coins. Terrence described the changes on the job: "Well, day-to-day, right now, a typical day for me in a casino now, is almost kind of boring, as a matter of fact. Because the fact that [pause] due to the nature of the slot machines, right now, as they exist today. I theorized years ago, about fifteen or so years ago—I talked to one of the chief technicians—I told him that the slot machines of the future, or the casinos of the future, will require fewer and fewer technicians to service more and more slot machines." He continued, "Why is that? Because of automation."

Terrence graphically described the old system:

> Okay, imagine if you will, a customer, here's a typical customer walking through the casino. They're walking through the casino; they pull money out of their wallets. They look for a change person who then sells them coins, from a cart, or from a booth. And then they put the coin, they got the coins, they start playing. They put the coins in the slot, they pull the handle. One, two, three, four. If [the coins] get stuck, you have to call somebody to unstick them. When they get a pay up, it pays out in coins. If that gets jammed, you get that. Most of the work that was done was done because it was a coin—basically, it's a metal wafer that has to go inside the machine. It's a bucket inside the machine, a hopper, that pays out a little hole in the bottom of the slot machine where excess coins go. . . . But it used up a tremendous amount of manpower, because somebody had to sell the coins, someone had to collect the coins. Someone had to pay the jackpot. Some-

one also had to fill the machine with money when it ran out. And it employed a tremendous amount of people.

In contrast, he described the current, coinless slot machines as akin to an automated teller machine at a bank:

> Okay, now we're gonna skip, go from that to what it is now. So, the customer puts a bill inside the machine, the machine gives them credits, they play, they get done, it spits out a ticket, you go to a window, you either get your cash or go to a machine and then use that. It eliminates the need to have a hard count team who collects the coins at the end of the night, a cashier who sells the coins, an attendant who has to attend the problems with the machines, and technicians, who fix the machines. Now there are fewer and fewer technicians. Hardly any slot attendants—where you used to have 130 slot attendants, now we have thirty. We used to have, at our place, about, at least 200 slot cashiers. Now we have maybe twenty. We used to have thirty-seven technicians; now we have maybe nineteen. But we still have 2,700 slot machines.

In order to appreciate the individual stories that casino workers tell, we need to better understand the industry and the city in which they work. The changing fortunes of casino gaming in the local and national economies are profoundly shaping the opportunities and experiences for the 30,000-plus workers in Atlantic City's casinos and their compatriots across the United States. Changes in job security and job quality, such as the changes described by Laurel, Zoe, and Terrence, are often wrought by *macroeconomic* fluctuations of the nation's economy that impact specific industries or groups of workers. Tight labor markets (meaning low unemployment rates) boost employees' bargaining power while recessions and unemployment give employers the upper hand. Product demand is also affected by the macro economy. Gambling was long touted as a recession-proof industry, offering relatively cheap entertainment akin to movies during the Great Depression. The economic crisis of 2008, however, disproved this contention. Weighed down by debt and losing their nest eggs (house values and retirement accounts), middle-class consumers cut back. In an industry where line workers depend on tips for a good livelihood, shrinking demand has a direct and profound impact on living standards.

There are also *microeconomic* dynamics within particular industries, as businesses strive to increase their market power and operate as oligopolies or monopolies. Textbook economics extols models of "perfect competition," that is, markets for products where many sellers compete to produce identical low-cost goods or services as efficiently as possible and sell them to buyers with perfect information about prices and quality. A rational business owner, however, abhors perfect competition. Political economists since Karl Marx have observed the constant striving for market power that leads businesses to consolidate and merge, differentiate their products, and externalize costs. In the mid-twentieth century, Joseph Schumpeter, who was both a champion of free-market capitalism and an admirer of Marx, embraced this dynamism, coining the term "creative destruction" to describe the process of innovation that can threaten the position of mature industries.[15] As entrepreneurs continuously seek to be the first out of the gate with the next new thing, they render existing product lines and production processes—or older casinos—obsolete. In contrast, Paul Sweezy and Paul A. Baran, radical critics of market economies, suggested that maturing industries will tend to concentrate in order to preserve their market power.[16] The consolidated market leaders use strategies such as cost cutting, product diversification, and lobbying for government favors to retain their position. Baran and Sweezy spurred a line of research starting in the 1960s on the economic and social impact of this drive toward monopolization, focusing on capitalism's tendency toward stagnation and an incessant downward pressure on wages.[17]

These dynamics are clear in the contemporary casino gaming industry. But we need to review how we got to this point in the history of the industry. Nevada pioneered the modern era of casino gaming starting in the 1930s. Las Vegas, its casino mecca, was isolated in the desert, built relatively from scratch, and did not spark an immediate wave of imitators. Then Atlantic City ventured into the industry in the 1970s as the U.S. economy shifted from the Golden Age of postwar prosperity to the recent era of sluggish economic growth, deindustrialization, and income polarization. Atlantic City's gamble with gaming was viewed as a success story that inspired other economically depressed areas. Casinos, it was thought, would bring jobs and tax revenues and enhance the economic development of surrounding communities.

Expansion of the industry nationwide started around 1989, about a decade after Atlantic City opened its first casino doors. Initially, gaming operations outside of New Jersey and Nevada were mostly situated on Native American reservations and riverboats. For example, the Indian Gaming Regulatory Act, passed in 1988, created the structural framework for the operation and regulation of Indian gaming through the National Indian Gaming Commission and the U.S. Department of the Interior. Though Native American casinos are owned by the tribes, the day-to-day operations are often under contract with a commercial casino company.[18] Iowa's riverboats started cruising in 1991, followed quickly by Illinois, Mississippi, Louisiana, and other states on the Mississippi River. Many of these casinos were positioned to draw revenue (for state governments as well as casinos) from population centers in neighboring states. This pattern drove the escalation in riverboat casinos, as states tried to recapture lost revenue.[19]

Sensing a new revenue stream, more and more states beckoned the industry onto dry land. A 1999 report by the National Gambling Impact Study Commission (created by the U.S. Congress) helped legitimate the industry, even as it pointed to the need for regulation and possible ensuing social problems. In its recommendations, the Commission noted that "especially in economically depressed communities, casino gambling has demonstrated the ability to generate economic development through the creation of quality jobs." The Commission contrasted the job creation impact of casinos with the lack of economic development fostered by lotteries, Internet gambling, and non-casino electronic gaming devices.[20] Low- and middle-income communities latched onto the Atlantic City model. Casinos, racinos, and slot parlors gradually expanded into urban areas such as Detroit, Michigan (in 1999); Philadelphia, Pennsylvania (in 2010); and Cleveland, Ohio (in 2012).

Equally important for our study, ownership within the industry changed. Discovering a viable profit stream, non-gaming corporations absorbed casinos and casino companies starting in the 1990s, streamlining processes and changing the culture of these workplaces. The industry "moved out from the gray shadows of illegitimacy and [became] a major and visible presence on Wall Street and Main Street," according to William Eadington, director of the Institute for the Study of Gambling and Commercial Gaming at the University of Nevada, Reno.[21] First firms from other hospitality sectors, including hotel chains like Hilton, moved into the casino gaming industry. Eventually, as with other sectors of the U.S. economy, private equity firms and other financial speculators sought a stake in this booming business. Table 1.1 lists the twelve casinos in the Atlantic City market and their ownership in 2013.

Table 1.1.   Atlantic City's Twelve Casinos and Their Ownership as of 2013

Name	Ownership
The Atlantic Club Casino Hotel	Colony Capital LLC
Bally's Atlantic City	Caesars Entertainment, Inc.
Borgata Hotel, Casino, & Spa	Marina District Development Company, LLC
Caesars Atlantic City	Caesars Entertainment, Inc.
Golden Nugget—Atlantic City*	Landry's, Inc.
Harrah's Resort Atlantic City	Caesars Entertainment, Inc.
Resorts Casino Hotel	DGMB Casino LLC
Revel	Revel AC, Inc.
Showboat Atlantic City	Caesars Entertainment, Inc.
Tropicana Casino and Resort	Tropicana Entertainment, Inc.
Trump Plaza Hotel and Casino	Trump Entertainment Resorts
Trump Taj Mahal Casino Resort	Trump Entertainment Resorts

*The casino now using this name is unrelated to the Golden Nugget that opened in 1980. Source: New Jersey Casino Control Commission website (accessed June 4, 2013).

Employees felt the change. Ken, a dual-rate pit manager who has worked in the industry in Atlantic City since he got a job soon after graduating from college in the early 1980s,[22] responded to a question about ownership changes:

> Claridge is a very small, tight-knit community. It was the smallest casino in town. When we were first taken over by Bally's, we were merged with them, and Bally's was such a large property, it's like going from working at Wawa [a regional chain of convenience stores] to working at Walmart. There is so many people, and it's such a large operation. It's just like you come from everybody knowing who you are to nobody knows who you are. So it was quite a culture shock.

Because I worked with most of these people for over twenty years. . . . Lately the changes have been bad.

Echoing Laurel, Ken complained that the "faceless" corporation was cutting corners and squeezing workers at the lower levels while upper-level managers kept their perks and bonuses. In his words, "now the bean counters are running the corporations instead of actually casino management."

All of these macroeconomic and microeconomic forces have shaped the work experiences of the workers we interviewed. The full force of these macro and micro shifts are generally experienced at the *meso* level, the analytical level of organizations, institutions, and social practices.[23] As we saw above, Ken feels the microeconomic changes in ownership in his daily life in the organization. So do Laurel, Zoe, Terrence, and the other workers we interviewed. This level of analysis is too often ceded by economists to other social sciences such as sociology and anthropology. Without understanding the meso level—the lived experience of an economy—we have an incomplete picture. Most crucially, an overemphasis on political and economic dynamics can risk overlooking the collective and individual agency of those working inside the casino economy. The folks we spoke with were not passive victims of impersonal forces. They were actively building lives and constructing meaning out of the raw material provided, in part, by their jobs.

Meso-level analysis informs this study. In order to examine the lived experience of working in a casino economy and how these jobs and these workers have been affected by and responded to macroeconomic and microeconomic trends, we conducted two waves of in-depth interviews with thirty-five current and former employees in Atlantic City's casinos. Collectively, the employees have amassed over 550 years of experience in the Atlantic City casinos. The first wave of interviews took place from late 2006 through the summer of 2008, the period leading up to the Great Recession. We returned to interviewing in 2011,[24] and completed the second wave of interviews in 2014. A few interviewees were revisited to update their experiences as the industry and their lives changed. The interviews were supplemented by extensive reading and monitoring of journalistic accounts of the local and national industry, a review of research about the casino industry by scholars, industry ana-

lysts, and policy advocates, and hundreds of informal conversations with
local residents, as well as our own theoretical and empirical understanding of labor market dynamics.

As is typical for qualitative research, we did not commence the study
with a set of hypotheses to test, but rather a general sense of themes
and questions based upon extensive prior research. The interviews were
loosely structured around a set of open-ended questions.[25] The questions in our survey instrument reflected our reading of the interdisciplinary literature on job quality.[26] The first assumption we made was that
work itself can be a source of satisfaction. In fact, meaningful and challenging work can enhance one's identity, self-esteem, and dignity as
well as intellectual and creative development, and establish a sense of
community—an esprit de corps—at the workplace. The second, related
assumption was that employees, through their time and effort, are not
simply inputs into the production process. We construct our lives and
our identities partially through the (paid and unpaid) work we do and
how we do it. The well-being of the people is just as important an
output as the goods and services being produced.

The interviews were digitally recorded and then transcribed, changing the names of the participants and omitting names of coworkers (but
not casino owners) and customers. Occasionally, we have altered or
obscured biographical details in order to protect the confidentially of
our sources. Our aim was not to generate a random sample but rather to
target representative constituencies. We sought to include employees in
a variety of occupations, emphasizing the key frontline workers with
direct contact with casino customers. We balanced our sample with
employees from different casinos that had various marketing strategies
and types of ownership, people from key racial and ethnic groups in the
Atlantic City population, and men and women with different household
structures and sexual identities.

In New Jersey, about 40–45 percent of casino employees work exclusively on the gaming floor—dealers, their direct supervisors, slot technicians, and casino hosts. Security and surveillance constitutes another
7–10 percent. The term "casino key employees" refers to most managers, another 3–4 percent of employees. Casino employees and casino
key employees must be licensed. Back-of-the-house employees do not
need a license or regulatory approval. Casino service and back-of-the-
house jobs, serving the gaming floor in restaurants and bars and in the

hotels, are roughly another third of total Atlantic City casino employees. The remaining jobs are in maintenance and construction, entertainment, administrators not on the gaming floor, and other miscellaneous positions.

Early on, we determined that our participants would be more comfortable if we could clearly indicate that we had neither sought nor received cooperation from their employers. We did, however, contact staff and activists with two of the key labor unions, Local 54 of UNITE HERE (representing employees involved in hotel and restaurant services) and United Auto Workers Region 9 (representing dealers at three casinos) for background information including contract language. A few interviews were with union activists, balanced by one dissident activist and many other employees with little direct union involvement. Interviews were conducted outside of work hours, in participants' homes or at a neutral site. We never approached anyone at their work. Supplemental stories gathered from public sources such as newspaper articles use real names if they were printed in the story.

All of the interview transcripts were printed and then coded by the coauthors. The coding focused on identifying extracts that articulated perspectives on key issues related to the broad themes. As we read and coded, the scope and stance of the research was continually refined. The result was an iterative process of synthesizing our primary and secondary sources. In particular, we benefited by comparing our own findings and interpretations with other second-hand accounts of casino employment. We quote and paraphrase from the interviews throughout these chapters. When we do, we have tried to retain the original phrasing and sentence structure, while eliminating linguistic fillers such as "um" and "eh." Punctuation denotes our best representation of the length of pauses and other verbal signals.

Starting from our own view of the economy as a system for providing for well-being and listening to our participants, we developed a broad definition of job quality:

> A good job is one that helps you create a life and reinforces a positive sense of identity.

Creating a life includes provisioning for the material needs of an employee and his or her family through wages and benefits. This aspect of job quality is commonly the focus of most economists. The *Final*

Report of the National Gambling Impact Study Commission in 1999 noted that, "resort, hotel, and commercial casinos"—the sector of the legalized gaming industry most closely identified with Atlantic City— "provide jobs with good pay and benefits."[27] The extensive testimony gathered by the commission went on further to declare: "Hundreds of employees in several cities described the new and better jobs they had obtained with the advent of casinos. Some described relocating from other states to the sites of new casinos; others spoke of leaving minimum-wage jobs in which they had no benefits, to accept unionized jobs at the casinos at higher compensation and with significant employment opportunities."[28] The majority of casino jobs are open to workers without a college education, providing an important opportunity in the contemporary economy where it is harder and harder to earn a living without some postsecondary schooling.

In terms of job quality, the commission found that casino jobs in destination resorts were "better than comparable service sector jobs."[29] This is borne out by local data as well. According to a New Jersey Department of Labor 2013 fact book about Atlantic County,[30] a county that includes Atlantic City and its surrounding communities, "Interestingly, leisure and hospitality is the only sector where Atlantic County's average annual wage significantly exceeded the statewide average annual wage ($29,173 vs. $22,265 respectively) in 2011. The county's higher annual wage can be traced to the gaming industry's unionized hotel and restaurant workers, higher tipping rates and a greater proportion of higher paying jobs compared to similar nongaming establishments." Many participants in our study indicated that they were gratified by the financial opportunity the industry provided—especially at the entry level. Over time, however, some people became frustrated by truncated career ladders and stagnant base wages. The fact that so many workers' income relies upon tips (pooled among dealers and individually for most servers and housekeepers) means that their take-home pay is particularly vulnerable to shifts in demand for their employers' product. And, as we have seen in the stories above, the working conditions and benefits are deteriorating as Atlantic City's casinos respond to competitive pressures from other jurisdictions.

Beyond wages and benefits, good jobs support workers' family and community activities. "Work-life balance" and other popular catchphrases are meant to capture the attention of policy makers and advocates. Because workers have a variety of living situations, family responsibilities, and ties to volunteer, religious, union, or other social networks, the relationship between their paid employment and the other facets of their lives is very complex. And, as we found, these living situations and priorities can change dramatically over the arc of a career. The dominant work-life issue among our participants was the difficulty of synchronizing schedules in a twenty-four-hour service economy. Further, a good job cannot diminish your life, meaning health and safety can also be seen as job quality dimensions. Many of our participants' nagging health problems such as sore feet, bad backs, carpal tunnel syndrome, and maladies related to second-hand smoke meant that their job was encroaching on their enjoyment of life.

Finally, we note that a good job is one that reinforces a meaningful identity. No one we spoke with viewed their job as only a means to a paycheck. At minimum, the people we interviewed valued work situations that afforded them respect and dignity as individuals. They wanted to be recognized when they did their jobs well. Some found meaning in their relationships at work—either the process of collaborating with coworkers or ongoing interactions with regular customers who recognized their hard work. The casino workers who enjoyed their jobs emphasized their ability to bring excitement into the lives of their customers. Nevertheless, some casino workers struggled uncomfortably with their feelings about the industry, particularly with the problem gamblers they saw and came to know. The increased sexualization of employees in recent years also made it difficult for some to maintain their sense of dignity. These factors ultimately led a few to make casino work a temporary means of furthering their education so that they could enter other fields where they felt they could contribute to society. Others felt trapped with little to no way to effectively exit.

The three dimensions of job quality identified—pay and benefits, work-life balance, and building an identity—are further illustrated as we explore how our participants are building their lives in an industry experiencing dramatic changes. Their keen insights and articulate observations provide a richness to the narrative within each chapter. In addition, between each chapter of the book, we will introduce you to at least one of the workers in more depth. In the chapters that follow, we seek to provide context for their stories, relying upon our expertise as political economists. While the resulting account of this changing indus try incorporates facts and figures as well as history and theory, it is the participants' stories that ground our portrayal in the lived experience of working inside a casino economy.

SUEBEE'S STORY

SueBee is a tall, fit, fifty-something woman with pale skin and a gentle soul. She invites us to her home to talk about her life and her work. She started working at the Golden Nugget casino as a dealer in 1980 and left in 2007 when she took a severance package to retire from her position as a pit boss. We take off our shoes as we enter, then she guides us into her cozy living room with a Ganesh mural on the wall. These days, she is a yoga instructor and massage therapist. The entry to the massage room just off the living room welcomes you with a piece of framed art: a black-and-white charcoal of a young woman in a yoga pose, "the dancer" (natarajasana).

As we settle into comfy chairs with cups of herbal tea and turn on the digital recorder, SueBee begins her story of how she came to work as a dealer: "Prior to [working in the casino], I had lived in Bucks County, Pennsylvania, where I had a multitude of different jobs, from a baker to stonemason, to food server—let me see—lab technician, a multitude of jobs. And I was tired of working two to three jobs and not making any money; and the casino industry opened, and my younger sister's boyfriend at the time had gotten a job and was working at Resorts when Resorts first opened. So, in 1978, I started to travel down and look at the city and look at the job situation and go into Resorts and see what it was like. And I decided that I needed to do this." She relocated to New Jersey and moved in with a sister who lived within commuting distance of Atlantic City. To support herself, she worked as a waitress while attending gaming school. Once she obtained her blackjack license, SueBee tried for a job at the newly opened Caesars, but they would not hire her as a dealer. To get her foot in the door, she took a job selling change around the slot machines.

When the Golden Nugget was ready to open, she went for three auditions and failed each one: "I don't know what their criteria was but I had the same guy audition me every single time. So I was adamant that I can do this job. I don't understand why I'm not getting hired, and I made an appointment with the . . . casino manager, VP, something like that. I walked into his office and I said I have had three auditions. I don't understand what the problem is. I know I can do this job. I know I'm going to be a great employee for you. And we sat and had a forty-five minute conversation. He was very receptive. And he said, 'OK, no problem, show up and you've got the job'. So, he hired me on the spot."

At the time, the Golden Nugget was owned by casino pioneer Steve Wynn. He was a good employer. She was acutely aware that the casino job offered her good wages, especially for someone who started working right out of high school: "Oh, I made more money than I ever thought I would ever make in my life. I was a high school graduate. . . . My parents could never have afforded to send me to college, and I just wanted to go out and explore the world. I wanted to go and live a life and get out of school." One evening, SueBee went out with a bunch of friends from work and met up with employees from other casinos. A workmate whispered in her ear: "Don't tell them you work at the Nugget because these people are really jealous; everyone wants to work at the Nugget." She laughs as she tells the story, saying at the time she was oblivious to that kind of energy. But she realized it was true. They were making the most money, were treated the best, and, "obviously, had the most fun."

As she talks, she remembers the hectic early days of opening the new casino and the positive relationship between management and the newly hired staff: "In the beginning, it was really hard. You didn't get a day off. Some people worked sixty days in a row without a day off. It was only twenty [operating] hours [per day] when we first opened, so we were working ten- and twelve-hour shifts. So it was not uncommon to work sixty-two hours in a week or more. You know, it was pretty intense." The hard work didn't feel like work, though, because they were all in it together. And they felt appreciated.

Within two years, SueBee was promoted to a supervisor, a full-time floorperson. Soon after, Steve Wynn gave everyone in management a brand-new car. As she recalls, it had to be American made and she could spend up to $10,000. "I forget how many cars he bought, but there was a fleet of cars that went out, and I know some people who wrecked their cars and he gave them another one." We pause her story to ask her who was eligible for the cars: "Supervisors. Floorpeople, supervisors from 'floor' up. And I'm sure that the amount of money that you could spend on the car went up with your position and salary. . . . Oh my God! It was a gift! It was such a gift! I never owned a new car. I kept that car for almost twenty years." She reminisces more about how it felt to be treated like a valued employee, to bond with her coworkers, and to experience new things.

SueBee relates the details of her daily work life. But as the interview moves into the second hour, the tone of the story subtly begins to shift. It was clear that the party atmosphere wore thin over time, and the downsides of the job began to weigh on her being: "I was thinking, as everybody else was thinking, that this place is killing me. And it wasn't just the cigarette smoke. If you go into a casino, back then, there was a lot more business on the casino floor. But your senses, all of your senses, were being bombarded. There was no natural light, there were no windows to take your attention away, there was a slot machine noise that was deafening—not just the coins falling into the metal tray, which was purposely done, but the music that each little slot machine would play. Even when you pulled the handle, there was noise with the reel going around. And then there was the music that they played over the loudspeaker system. And then there were interruptions in that, with the operators calling for somebody to pick up the phone. It was constant. So, it was a really caustic place to work. But when you begin, all those things are there, and all those things are put into play to create an atmosphere of excitement. So when you first start to work, it's exciting: 'I'm at the party; I'm at the disco; I'm at the place where everything was happening.' I mean, I remember it would take me ten minutes to get from the baccarat pit, to the door, up to the second floor, to get to the break room—because you would have to fight your way through the crowd on the casino floor to get to that door. It was amazing! It was just not like a walk. You didn't just walk; you were, like, thumping into people, shoulder to shoulder, getting around people, weaving in and out, and you had to stop and take your time."

There were other stresses in the work environment for her as a self-described naïve young girl from a farm, and they affected her perceptions of the job. As the years passed, she witnessed changes in herself. When she arrived, she "Never drank, never smoked, never cursed, you know, was not around rude, ignorant people. So, it was a big eye opener." She recounted sexual harassment experiences by some of her supervisors that upset her. "I remember standing at a blackjack game, and I had a skirt on. It was not short. I was not promiscuous. My skirt was like Catholic school; if you kneeled on the floor and your skirt touched the floor, you were good. That's how I wore my skirts. And I had a supervisor and I dropped a card, I dropped a chip, I dropped something. And the supervisor bent down to pick up the chip and had my leg, around my ankle, with his other hand. And as he stood up, he rode up my leg with his hand, and I was frozen. I was just, I was on a live game, I was dealing and everything just kind of stopped. And I froze, and he stopped when he got to my knee and threw the chip on the table and said something about what great legs I had or laughing and . . . I was just like, I couldn't speak! I was flabbergasted! I was like, 'Did that guy just do that?!' I was stunned. I was stunned. I didn't know what to say or do." Blatant sexual advances were common. As she notes, half of the come-ons were from married men. She had grown up in a family of mostly women so for her "men were always an education." SueBee viewed these experiences as part of her education process, part of coming of age as a woman. Other casino women we spoke with coped with overt and subtle harassments from customers, supervisors, and coworkers in different ways, but most tended to downplay their experiences—perhaps because they needed to in order to survive.

As SueBee tells her story, she describes the transformation she has witnessed to the industry, both while she was there and since she left. She is particularly struck by the effects of deregulation, cost cutting, and cutbacks. Just the previous week, she read a newspaper story about a problem at an Atlantic City casino where cards were being counted by players. Casinos had taken to purchasing pre-shuffled boxes of cards to speed along the games. In this case, the card manufacturer had not pre-shuffled the cards. The players caught on and took the casino for a lot of money. SueBee is horrified at such practices, which she takes as an affront to the professionalism of dealers: "That's hard for me to believe that the card company shuffles the cards and they come that way in the box? Never." With pride, she details the intricacies of shuffling back in her day. Listening to her, it is clear that the pursuit of efficiency is contributing to "deskilling" the job—a process that political economists have long argued undermines job quality.

As she puts it about her career at her own "house," "I never actually left the building; other owners bought the building and came in. . . . It definitely changed after Steve Wynn left. It was not [one big happy family anymore]; you were part of a big corporation." Cutbacks in supervisory employees had started even before she left. Supervisors who once watched two to four games were responsible for six to eight or even more. By the time she left her job as a pit manager, there were periods, if only half an hour, that she was watching the whole casino floor because the shift manager had pulled the other pit manager to do something else. As she was called upon to supervise a larger area, she felt the work suffered. "You couldn't watch the games, which was really something that I enjoyed doing when I first got my pit job. And I can't tell you how many people I caught cheating, how many dealers were caught taking money off the tables, how many card counters, how many mistakes you can catch when you are walking around as a pit manager." In her mind, cutting back on supervisors is a short-sighted managerial practice. "To know where the money is" was the most important part of the job, critical in order to keep good faith with the customers. Without such assurances, "the quality of customer service, the integrity of the games, is just disappearing," she asserts. This will backfire, she argues, as customers will eventually perceive the difference. "And evidently, the companies that own these casinos aren't really concerned about that."

Once earnest and anxious to go for promotions to higher-level jobs, SueBee found that the changing corporate culture affected her own aspirations. In her words, she didn't "feel safe" with the new owners (Bally's, which was later purchased by Hilton). She was also relatively newly married and did not want to be forced to change her shift or be on call as it would interfere with her routine dinners and private time with her husband. Eventually, the job insecurity brought about by multiple ownership changes coupled with the accumulated wear and tear on her well-being led her to leave.

When asked about moments on the job when she felt proud, she comes up with a notable act of bravery: "It's really hard in that business to, for me personally anyway, it was a really, there was nothing socially redeeming about the job—nothing! I guess after about ten years it really started to get to me as far as what I did for a living—how I was not really contributing to the betterment of humanity, how I was really working all of the time with the dregs of the earth. And gosh, my proudest moment was probably, oh boy, I hate to say, when I raised my hand in a meeting and said I would take a retirement package and started to progress to really leave my job. Because as difficult as that was to do, I'll never forget it."

As SueBee describes her last day at work, she begins to choke up— about the coworkers she was sorry to leave and the new managers that she wasn't going to miss: "But the day that I, the last day I was there, that was really emotional. It was very—and it was so funny to watch people around me. The dealers and the floorpeople, some of them would just walk by the pit crying and they, like, wouldn't come in. Others would come in and hug me and give me presents. (I'm getting emotional.) I mean, I walked out, there was so many beautiful gifts and heartfelt cards and words and a lot of disbelief. Literally, people couldn't speak to me. But when I left, I didn't—everyone was like, ah you should go around to all the pits. And, I was like, 'Aw, please, it's all I can do to get out the door!' There was not a shift manager, there was not a casino manager: no one in upper management to say goodbye. I just walked out the door. I remember I got out the door and I was standing at Boston and Pacific [Avenues] and I thought, oh my God I've done it [laughing]. And it just, I took the deepest breath and I remember it was a gorgeous day. It was a September day and it was just so beautiful. And I stood on the corner and waited for the Jitney to speed in front of me and try to kill me with its rear-view mirror. And I just laughed and crossed the street, went to my designated parking spot . . . and pulled out and left and just breathed an exhale and I never looked back. I've never regretted it and I don't think I ever will."

2

A CITY BUILT ON SAND

Unlike many formerly industrial cities of the northeastern and midwestern United States, Atlantic City has service in its bones. Located on a relatively thin strip of barrier island—Absecon Island—off the coast of southern New Jersey, the so-called Queen of Resorts was created and marketed as a beach resort. The Philadelphia–Atlantic City Railway Company started bringing Philadelphians to the shore after the Civil War, back when "seabathing" was a radical new pastime. Tourism has been at the heart of the economic health of Atlantic City ever since. In 1870, an innovation in publically funded infrastructure was born with the installation of a mile-long walkway of wooden planks on the sand for visitors—the first U.S. boardwalk. A more permanent version was built twenty-five years later, and its street name—Boardwalk—became official. Boardwalk eventually became venerated as the most valuable of the twenty-two colored streets in the original version of the board game of Monopoly, streets whose names all came from the famous resort (or nearby towns).

A growth spurt ensued. Boardinghouses were followed by elegant resort hotels. The population grew from 2,000 in 1875 to almost 30,000 by the turn of the century. The bulk of the service work for tourists was performed by African American workers who initially migrated from nearby southern states only during the summer months. In *Boardwalk Empire,* first published in 2002, Nelson Johnson wrote that "While the money to build a national resort came primarily from Philadelphia and New York investors, the muscle and sweat needed to keep things going was furnished by Black workers."[1] Foreshadowing the first Great Migration, African Americans started immigrating to Atlantic City in the 1870s, and by 1915 the resort had became the most "Black" city in the north, according to Johnson. Hotel and restaurant work paid better wages (and tips) than the private domestic service employment that most African Americans found in northern cities. They were quickly joined by Irish, Italians, and Jews, who came for jobs in construction as well as tourism. Sicilians settled in Ducktown, a neighborhood around St. Michael's (Catholic) Church, when they were hired following a strike by African American waiters in 1906. Jewish and Irish families were less ghettoized, gradually settling in the South Inlet and other neighborhoods.[2]

Atlantic City took pride in its growing hospitality industry. The resort became popular with working- and middle-class whites who could act out rituals of prosperity as they dressed up to stroll the Boardwalk or ride in rolling chairs pushed by African Americans. The city and its workers took care of a customer's wants and desires, even during Prohibition (1920–1933): bathing on the beach during the day and cavorting at clubs late into the night. Hollywood portrays this golden age in the HBO television series *Boardwalk Empire*, with protagonist "Nucky" Thompson, based loosely on the real-life Nucky Johnson described in Nelson Johnson's (no relation) book of the same name. The revelry continued after ratification of the Twenty-First Amendment once again legalized sales of alcohol, and Atlantic City became known for its nightlife.

The city began a long-term economic decline following World War II that accelerated in the 1960s. As tourism slowed during the war, Atlantic City housed (single male) soldiers between deployments overseas who were, as historian Bryant Simon noted, "hard on the hotels."[3] Local lore tends to place particular blame on bad publicity following the August 1964 Democratic National Convention at Boardwalk Hall. Folks who came to town to nominate the incumbent President Lyndon B. Johnson found that hotels were not kept up to high standards. What was once the city's strength in meeting customer needs was now its weakness. The city found it very difficult to stem the tide of reporters spreading the word in print and informally about the city's urban decay and poor services.

The decline of the Queen of Resorts as a favored tourist destination was, however, years in the making and can be attributed to many factors, from the rise of air travel and air conditioning to a suburbanization of vacation destinations that mirrored white flight from urban living.[4] These factors explain why the hotels were not renovated once the soldiers left. Gaming analyst Michael Pollack (managing director of Spectrum Gaming Group) refers to this period from the 1940s through the late 1970s as an "Age of Divestment," as local business owners saw little prospect of return on any capital improvements.[5] While the industrial Midwest—and with it, much of the U.S. economy—was enjoying unprecedented prosperity due to the dominance of U.S. manufacturing, Atlantic City was falling behind. Atlantic City was not unique; many of the processes that fed its decline also affected non-tourism–related urban areas in the 1960s and 1970s. Jane Jacobs was already describing urban decay as early as 1961 in her landmark book *The Death and Life of Great American Cities*.[6]

Major changes in tourism were nonetheless key. With more middle-class wives employed, leisurely summers spent "down the shore" (with Dad commuting to visit on weekends) became a relic of the past. Air conditioning made cool ocean breezes less imperative. Meanwhile, tourists in the postwar period had new alternatives for their vacation dollars. The affordability of the automobile and policies promoting suburbanization, while a boon to the U.S. economy as a whole, sucked the life out of many cities.[7] Our growing car culture meant that tourists could take to the open road and vacation wherever their automobiles could take them. And their cars could take them further than ever before, thanks to the national Interstate Highway System created with passage of the Federal-Aid Highway Act of 1956. By the time a new expressway from Camden County, New Jersey (across the Delaware River from Philadelphia), to the southern New Jersey shore was completed in 1965, it was too late to resurrect the resort to its heyday.

Americans also increasingly took to the air to get to their leisure destinations. With the development of pressurized and heated passenger cabins by the airline industry, air travel became more accessible in the 1950s and 1960s. "Out" was Atlantic City. "In" were Florida and California, including Disneyland; the theme park opened in Anaheim, California, in 1955. In the words of Bryant Simon in his book *Boardwalk of Dreams*, "Disneyland's fantasy world centered on Main Street, a less urban, small-townish version of the Boardwalk."[8] Overseas getaway destinations included Bermuda, the Bahamas, Acapulco, Hawaii, Europe, the islands of the south-Asian Pacific Ocean—basically wherever Pan Am and TWA (Pan American Airlines and Trans World Airlines) flew.

Just as Joseph Schumpeter would have predicted, the maturing industry, resting on its laurels, was pushed aside by emerging enterprises: The creative entrepreneurship of Walt Disney, Conrad Hilton, and others contributed to Atlantic City's "destruction." There were not enough consumer dollars to maintain Atlantic City's great hotels. As a result, many of them closed or were converted to boardinghouses. By the time visitors arrived for the Democratic National Convention in 1964, Atlantic City, no longer enticing and exotic, seemed past its prime.

The economic stagnation affecting the United States, including New Jersey, from 1970 to 1975 further impacted Atlantic City. According to U.S. Census data, the city was becoming ever more black and elderly. Income was falling, and it was income that was needed to generate local spending and jobs. In addition to declining income and job losses, a key barometer is retail activity. According to George Sternlieb and James Hughes, authors of *The Atlantic City Gamble*, dollar sales in the Atlantic City central business district fell 12.4 percent from 1972 to 1977 and 119 retail establishments closed.[9] French director Louis Malle filmed the best picture Oscar-nominated movie *Atlantic City*, starring a young Susan Sarandon and the seasoned actor Burt Lancaster, partly on location in 1979. By then, Atlantic City's old resorts and piers were in conspicuous disrepair. Some had already seen the wrecking ball and others would soon, making way for new casino properties.

In the early 1970s, New Jersey leaders began to strategize to bring Atlantic City back, and proponents of gambling as a means to do that lobbied for some kind of exception to New Jersey's constitutional gambling prohibition. Proponents promised new commercial and residential construction and, with it, economic development and jobs. They faced some significant obstacles. Long before the television shows *The Sopranos* or *Boardwalk Empire*, New Jersey was associated with organized crime in the public imagination, and so was Las Vegas gaming.[10] It took two tries to get approval from New Jersey voters.

In the first proposal to legalize casino gambling, there would have been state-owned casinos rather than private businesses. This version also incorporated a local option, meaning any of New Jersey's twenty-one counties could have chosen to permit casino gambling.[11] But many citizens were not immediately open to the idea. There was great trepidation about the social costs of gambling. The New Jersey Council of Churches rallied in opposition. New Jersey voters defeated this first referendum at the polls on November 5, 1974, with only 40 percent in favor and 60 percent opposed. Industry analyst Michael Pollock, author of the book *Hostage to Fortune: Atlantic City and Casino Gambling*, puts it this way: "New Jersey's voters were frightened of casino gambling in 1974. They feared a long, dark association between casinos and organized crime."[12]

Gaming proponents, under the auspices of the Committee to Rebuild Atlantic City (CRAC), redoubled their efforts. The second time, a revised proposal would allow privately owned casinos, but in Atlantic City alone. Generous donations to the cause came from Resorts International and other powerful economic interests.[13] Resorts had already purchased the old Chalfonte-Haddon Hall Hotel in anticipation of converting it into a casino. In a more polished and professional campaign that followed the initial defeat, there were bumper stickers, pennants, lapel pins, postcards, and other giveaways urging voters to approve casinos. One campaign button read: "Help Yourself. Vote 'Yes' Casinos in Atlantic City Only."

Strategists attempted to convince voters that "The acceptance of the casinos in the city was . . . a matter of urban life and death."[14] A brochure promised that a "yes" vote would help:

> balance taxes
> create jobs
> boost the economy
> cut down on street crime

Job creation was pivotal. "The need for more and better jobs is critical throughout the State of New Jersey, a State with a 12% unemployment rate," states the brochure. According to a 1983 study, "The promise of employment played the largest part in winning endorsement for casino gaming."[15] Local residents campaigned vigorously for the initiative, believing in the promise of good jobs. Zoe, still in high school at the time, remembers that her stepfather, who worked at a local hotel,

Figure 2.1.   Casino Referendum Campaign Items. Courtesy: Atlantic County Historical Society; Photo credit: Susan Allen

was very anxious for the referendum to pass. The revised referendum also specified that tax revenues raised through gaming would be allocated to programs to benefit New Jersey's senior citizens and the disabled. New Jersey voters anticipated lower taxes due to the revenues that casinos would generate. Yet, by geographically segregating the casinos in a largely African American city, voters in the rest of the state could minimize social costs to their own communities.

New Jersey's policy makers determined that casinos would be highly regulated, in part to alleviate concerns about organized crime. Two state agencies were created, each with distinct regulatory responsibilities: the Casino Control Commission (to approve and issue licenses) and the Division of Gaming Enforcement (to investigate violations of the Casino Control Act). Casino operators and their vendors needed licenses, with the burden of proof on the operator to demonstrate their lack of ties to corrupt individuals. Nelson Johnson, in his evocative style, compared the licensing process to a proctology exam.[16] Holding a casino license was treated as a privilege, not a right. Originally, all employees needed to be licensed by the Casino Control Commission. (Today, only casino managers and employees directly involved with gaming operations, as opposed to hotel or restaurant services, undergo licensing.) Details of casino operations were controlled as well. Initially, for exam-

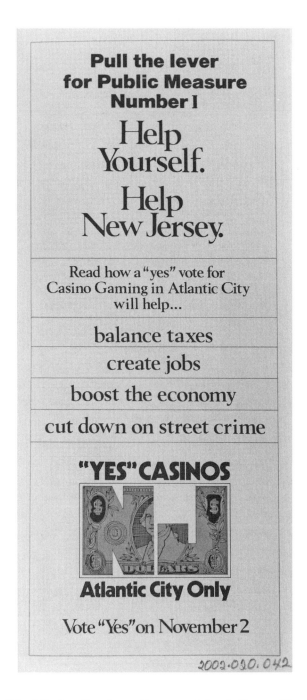

Figure 2.2. "Yes" Casinos Brochure. Courtesy: Atlantic County Historical Society; Photo credit: Susan Allen

ple, state regulators restricted gambling to only eighteen hours per day during the week and twenty hours during the weekend; these restrictions were gradually loosened and the casinos have operated 24/7 since 2002.

There would be minimum hotel size requirements, unlike in Las Vegas, so that investors and entrepreneurs would only erect glitzy gaming halls with hotel rooms, dining, and entertainment for visitors.[17] New Jersey policy makers viewed their approach as distinct from that of Las Vegas, which they viewed as "tacky" and singularly focused on gambling. According to gaming attorney Nick Casiello, Jr., "Casinos were intended to be an *additional element in the hospitality industry* and not just *the industry unto themselves.*"[18] A phrase that dates back to the Casino Control Act—and that labor leaders cling to today—is "first class": Atlantic City's casinos were supposed to be first-class operations that offered diverse entertainment options and quality accommodations that created middle-class jobs and that helped develop the city beyond the walls of the casinos. The second time, in 1978, proved to be the charm. The referendum passed with 56.8 percent voting in favor.

Resorts International Casino became Atlantic City's first legal casino, opening with great fanfare on May 26, 1978. Anticipation had built for months. The city had 8,000 hotel rooms at the time and they were fully booked. There was a long line outside after Governor Brendan Byrne—a major proponent of Atlantic City gaming—cut the ribbon. During that opening Memorial Day weekend, Resorts booked entertainers Steve Lawrence and Eydie Gormé as headliners. A bit of trivia: Steve Lawrence opened the craps table at Resorts with a $10 bet on the pass line and rolled a five; next he rolled a seven and lost. By all accounts in the media, Atlantic City's gamble would be more of a success.

People jumped at the chance to land the new jobs. Caroline quit college when Resorts opened to become a dealer. Her family's business had just gone under. Caroline recollected, "I thought I would just do it for a while and then I would go back and get my accounting degree. . . . I'm still there." She married a casino worker and her son is now in the industry. Zoe had just finished high school when Resorts opened. Her whole family was excited about the prospect of working in the new casino. They sat down as a group to complete the lengthy sixty-page application to become licensed to work in the casino. Her mother, stepfather, older brother, and older sister all got licenses and jobs in the industry. Starting in a job in "soft count" (i.e., counting cash or banknotes), Zoe's mom became a dealer, then a waitress, then a coat checker. The job as a "coat check girl" was "Mom's" favorite because the tips were good and she was laid off each summer when no one wore heavy coats. As happens when someone is a cop or a carpenter or a coal miner, family members helped usher other relatives into the new gaming houses. This practice has continued, even as the mostly Italian, Irish, Jewish, and African American workers from the early days have been joined by Latino and Asian immigrants and their families. [19]

Job seekers soon had other opportunities besides Resorts. As conveyed by Michael Pollock, Resorts' corporate profits increased 1,600 percent in the first seven months of operation. He adds: "The race was on. Old hotels went down and steel frames went up. Atlantic City glowed with the flushed face of a gambler holding four aces."[20] Nine casinos, including the majority of properties still in operation, opened between 1978 and 1981: Caesars and Bally's, the next to open after Resorts, in 1979; the Brighton (which became the now-imploded Sands), Harrah's, and the Golden Nugget in 1980; and Tropicana and Claridge in 1981. Even Playboy had an Atlantic City casino for awhile, opening one in 1981. The initial investment of the first nine Atlantic City casinos was well over $1 billion;[21] this is equal to almost $2.9 billion in today's dollars. Economist Oliver Cooke, writing in a 2009 retrospective on *Casino Gaming in Atlantic City*, notes that this initial build-out phase "was marked by rapid job, income and population growth," strong enough that the Atlantic City economy significantly outperformed the state and the nation in the midst of a five-year period of macroeconomic growth. Employment in the city grew 21.7 percent from 1978 to 1980, far more than the 4 percent growth rate in the United States and New Jersey as a whole.[22] (We present a detailed timeline of the Atlantic City casino industry in an appendix in the back of the book.)

After the initial burst from 1978 through 1981, erection of new casino properties slowed but did continue. During the U.S. macroeconomic expansion of 1982 to 1990, Atlantic City saw the opening of the Trump Plaza (in 1984), Trump's Castle (in 1985), Showboat (in 1987), and Trump Taj Mahal (in 1990). After the opening of the Trump Taj Mahal, referred to as "the Taj," no new casino properties were built in Atlantic

City for more than a decade; only renovations occurred. The energy for new construction shifted to new opportunities in other states. The majority of the changes within the industry in the 1990s were ownership changes and several casinos were reorganized following bankruptcy filings—trends that would continue into the 2000s and 2010s.

Many of the first casino executives were large personalities, and longtime employees still talk about key figures from the old days, contrasting them with today's corporate management. "The whole Atlantic City was run by guys from Vegas. They were cowboys. They were old-school cowboys," exclaimed SueBee, who worked briefly at Resorts before opening the Golden Nugget. Her boss, Casino mogul Steve Wynn, was an early entrant into the Atlantic City market with the Golden Nugget in 1980. He later sold it to Bally's in 1987 and left Atlantic City to develop the new wave of mega-casinos in Las Vegas, Macau, and elsewhere. Describing the changes she saw in the building she worked in for twenty-eight years, SueBee recalled, "It definitely changed after Steve Wynn left. It was not, you're part of a big corporation. . . . Steve Wynn—this was *his* casino in Atlantic City. This was *his* diamond."

Hugh Hefner's Playboy Casino had to take on a financial partner before the Playboy Bunnies could open the casino's doors in 1981. Nana, whose job was to dress the Bunnies and take care of their costumes, remembers the atmosphere as fun and exciting, and quite a contrast with her former jobs in Philadelphia factories and laundries. Donald Trump expanded his business as a hotel developer and came to Atlantic City in 1984, eventually building three properties that bore his name. His relationship to the casinos fluctuated with his economic circumstances, but two of them continue to use the name "Trump" even though "the Donald" is no longer an owner. A Day One employee, Donna, identified Ivana Trump (former wife) as taking a strong role in guiding Trump Castle/Marina in its early days. Ivana was "meticulous"; in later years, Donna claimed, the property became "Trump's Dump."

These years represent the strong initial spurt of a relatively infant industry and mirror strong growth rates in the service sector nationwide. Only the second location in the United States (not including Puerto Rico) to legalize casino gaming, and the first near the major population centers on the Eastern Seaboard, Atlantic City was an industry innovator. Employment grew almost every year during the first twenty years of legalized gaming and peaked at 49,123 employees in

1997. As shown in figure 2.3, growth was most notable during the years when new casinos opened; however, employment declined in three years (1989, 1991, and 1993). The 1990–1991 recession brought the only year of appreciable decline, as employment fell 2.9 percent in 1991. Optimism was so high that in 1998 the New Jersey Casino Control Commission predicted an increase to 75,000 full-time and part-time jobs in the industry by about 2003.[23] Such estimates, as the figure also demonstrates, were vastly overconfident.

Despite the promise of economic development beyond the walls of the casinos, many analysts and critics concluded that the initial wave of casinos did not reinvigorate the city.[24] Ironically, the requirement that casinos offer diverse entertainment options may have contributed to the problem. Few casino patrons left the buildings to visit local restaurants and shops. The casinos provided gourmet dining on site. They kept the customers inside, in a controlled playland without windows or even clocks that told time. There were no views of the Atlantic Ocean, the beach, or the renowned Boardwalk. Visitors arriving by bus or car and disembarking in garages could have been anywhere. Local businesses

Figure 2.3.   New Jersey Casino Employment, 1978 - 2013 (at year end). Note: Casino work that is outsourced (e.g., an independently-owned restaurant) may not be included in these totals even though the employees work at the casino property. Source: New Jersey CCC annual reports until 2010, then DGE website.

and local residents generally missed out on gains from the gaming operations. Zoe, whose family worked on the campaign to pass the casino referendum, voiced her disappointment with the outcomes for the city: "My thought on Atlantic City is: they came in and kind of robbed it for what it was worth and then left. They built these boxes and put everything that they wanted inside the box and they wanted you to stay in the box. And they didn't care if the Boardwalk fell apart; they didn't care if everything around them was parking lots with litter. . . . The more, the better, because then you were going to stay in the box. They provided everything you could possibly need in the box so, 'Don't go out there; you don't need to go out there!' So, the vision that my family, my mother, thought was going to happen with casino gambling—that they were going to bring in and revitalize Atlantic City—was nothing. They did nothing."

There were winners, however, particularly business owners in the nearby suburbs. The powerful construction industry benefited from new construction and periodic renovations. Ancillary businesses that provided services to the casinos also flourished.[25] Unfortunately, as noted by anthropologist Joseph Rubenstein in a 1984 article, "most of the money is obviously being spent outside Atlantic City. For example, of the 383 businesses that list themselves as food suppliers to the casinos, only 75 have Atlantic City addresses, and most of those are small sandwich shops rather than large-scale purveyors. Of the 221 office supply and furniture dealers, only 16 are local."[26] Reflecting back on the period from 1977 to 1980, Oliver Cooke echoed that it was the larger metropolitan area that "gained 0.7 jobs for every one hotel (casino) job generated during this period," outperforming the state and national economies.[27]

In response to concerns about the lack of spillover effects on the Atlantic City community, the Casino Reinvestment Development Authority (CRDA) was formed in 1984. This agency, unique to New Jersey, channels a portion of casino revenues (state-mandated taxes and/or investment in CRDA bonds) into local redevelopment and directs some monies to other areas in the state.[28] CRDA (pronounced by locals as crē'da) also provides tax incentives for entertainment and retail development in Atlantic City. CRDA has funded numerous urban revitalization projects since its founding, within Atlantic City and across the State of New Jersey. From 1984 to 2012, it reinvested $1.5 billion in Atlantic

City—in areas such as housing, public recreation and entertainment, education, and infrastructure improvements. Still, much of CRDA's investment activity today is aimed at maintaining the gambling industry's competitive position, as elaborated in chapter 7.[29]

Employees who reminisce about the early days describe a period when Atlantic City attracted high rollers from all over. They bet large pots, dined extravagantly, and tipped generously. One waiter described serving a meal worth $20,000, including $2,000 in food and most of the rest for an obscure wine ordered to impress other guests. The gossip about particular gamblers was passed around to coworkers and friends. "Oh, you must have heard the story about 'So-and-So,'" we were told. "No?!? Everyone knew him back in the day!" The patrons who could afford to lose money—or who were at least determined to look like they could afford to throw money away—sustained a shared fantasy with the employees about the glamorous pleasures of gambling.

The reality, however, was that high rollers could not sustain the casinos by themselves. Unlike Las Vegas, Atlantic City never took off as a market that draws gamblers by air. Atlantic City's comparative advantage was its location on the densely populated East Coast. While some private planes brought high rollers and casino performers to Bader Field—a small airport within the city limits—or to the larger Atlantic City International Airport ten miles outside the city, most casino traffic came by automobile and bus. (Bader Field closed in September 2006.)

Bus patrons were generally not wealthy gamblers. Bus patrons from major cities were often given vouchers that could be refunded for part or all of their fare, making the transportation costs of an excursion free or extremely cheap. These rebates were originally given in cash, but this meant that riders did not have to gamble once they arrived. Eventually, as technology shifted, the rebates could be given in "slot dollars" (credit on a casino's loyalty card that can only be used to gamble). The train from Philadelphia, popular earlier in the twentieth century, accounted for less than 1 percent of total visitors during the casino era, according to data from the South Jersey Transportation Authority (SJTA) analyzed by Anthony Marino.[30] Philadelphia is only 62 miles away. New York City is 126 miles north of Atlantic City. Baltimore is 154 miles south. The 45-mile-long Atlantic City Expressway, with two or three lanes in each direction, proved to be the fastest and most inexpensive way to reach the city. Thus, any gambling competition within Atlantic City's "market," a 100-to-300-mile radius driving distance, or less than a one-day drive, would strike a blow. And it did.

Starting in 1989, Nevada and New Jersey lost their status as the only places in the United States where people could gamble in a casino. Iowa, Louisiana, and South Dakota legalized casino gambling that year, followed by Colorado, Illinois, and Mississippi a year later. The opening of the Mirage casino in Las Vegas, also in 1989, marked an era of renewed investment in that city. Mirage, created by former Atlantic City casino executive Steven Wynn, became the first casino "destination resort," with more than 3,000 hotel rooms and non-gaming attractions. Illusionists Siegfried & Roy opened their act at the Mirage with exotic white tigers and lions onstage and played there until an injury forced their retirement in October of 2003. While none of these competitors were on the East Coast—yet—they were a harbinger of the end of Atlantic City's near monopoly.

In 1992 and 1993, table games and slot machines were added to a bingo hall founded by the Mashantucket Pequot Indian Reservation in central Connecticut; Foxwoods Resort Casino was now in competition for the East Coast market. Mohegan Sun was opened by the Mohegan Indians in 1996. Dover Downs in Delaware, a harness racetrack 130 miles southwest of Atlantic City, installed slot machines in 1995. Horse and greyhound tracks in Pennsylvania and New York followed suit, becoming "racinos," a hybrid term of casinos and racetracks. Once table games such as blackjack were added to racinos, it further blurred the boundaries between a casino and a racetrack. In fact, the lines have become so blurred that beginning with the *State of the States 2011* annual report, the American Gaming Association aggregates data from racetrack casinos and stand-alone casinos.

Not surprisingly, the growth of Atlantic City's total casino revenue slowed in the 1990s relative to the growth observed throughout the 1980s. But it is important to remember that the new casinos elsewhere were frequently owned and/or developed by the same companies that operated in Atlantic City. So while the city was facing more competition, the industry itself was growing and consolidating. The nature of the owners was, in fact, changing as well. Once the profitability of casinos had been demonstrated, corporations in other leisure-focused industries moved in. Hotel chains such as Hilton bought gaming-oriented companies like Bally's Entertainment. Wynn's company, Mirage Resorts, was purchased by MGM Resorts International; it is now one of the dominant companies in the global gaming industry.[31] As competition increased, the casino industry increased its lobbying efforts to modify New Jersey's stringent regulations. Since they were diverse companies with properties in multiple locations, they were well positioned to make demands on local policy makers. At minimum, they could threaten to divert resources and investment into their newer properties; at worse, they could threaten to exit the state altogether.

The impact on casino employment is clear. As figure 2.3 illustrates, the local industry began a secular (long-term) decline in employment in 1997, pausing only when a new casino, the Borgata, opened in 2003. Other factors contributing to this change—from the development of labor-saving technologies to work intensification—are discussed in later chapters. Loss of market share to other locales that offered the same slot machines and table games was critical, and only worsened in the new millennium. Looking at figure 2.3, we can see that the recession and slow recovery since 2007 deepened job losses, as casinos scrambled to cut costs. The opening of Revel in 2012 provided only a slight boost to employment numbers.

Atlantic City was literally built on sand. The city's founders—innovators in the relatively new industry of middle-class tourism—laid down some planks on a stretch of beach real estate and encouraged visitors to come enjoy the ocean air. But the tourism industry also rested on a soft foundation, as travelers' tastes and options evolved over time. By the 1970s, a new wave of innovators hatched a plan to bring back the tourists: casino gaming. Once again, Atlantic City pioneered a new kind of leisure activity. These trendsetters and their hard-working employees collaborated to make the party come to life. Despite some efforts of policy makers and activists to ensure that the city around the casinos shared in the prosperity, spillover effects were limited. The gamblers stayed inside the boxes built on the sand. The success of Atlantic City's casinos attracted established corporations drawn to the industry's profitability. Eventually, they adapted the model to other locations. As gamblers had more convenient alternatives to Atlantic City, local industry promoters and political leaders realized that they needed to differentiate their product and/or cut their operating costs. Their efforts to do this are detailed in what follows.

CAROLINE AND RUTH'S STORY

Caroline and Ruth have a very special, atypical, friendship. One is Irish Catholic. One is Jewish. They both fell in love with the same man, one and then the other, in different decades. All three have been casino employees. Caroline met and married Tommy first, but they eventually parted ways. When he later met Ruth on the job and they fell in love and married, Caroline decided there was no reason for drama. So they coparented Caroline's children, sharing custody between the two households. Ruth and Tommy were happily married for over twenty years. Unfortunately, he died suddenly. Since Tommy's passing, the two women have remained close friends, seeing each other at least weekly. In some ways, the bond is even stronger now, as there is only the two of them to look after each other and the now-grown kids.

We talk with each of them on different days in the tidy mid-twentieth-century bungalow where the recently widowed Ruth has been struggling with her loss. A short tour of her small home reveals creative use of space. Ruth swapped the dining room and living room in her open floor plan. This allows her to have bookshelves from floor to ceiling, lining two walls of the dining room, so it can double as a library and large workspace where she writes. We sit in the living room, which also served as a family room and den. Ruth says when the kids were young, they all slept in sleeping bags on the floor, while she supervised from her nearby bedroom.

Caroline is a longtime dealer, a "Day-Oner" at Resorts in 1978. While Ruth was not a Day-Oner, she too was employed at Resorts early on before transferring to another casino. Together, Caroline and Ruth have nearly six decades of experience in Atlantic City casinos. Ruth was a beverage server until her back and her feet refused to let her continue. Caroline soldiers on. Both unreservedly love their jobs in the casinos. They are apparently great at what they do.

Ruth's path to becoming a cocktail server was circuitous. She grew up in the suburbs outside Philadelphia in a solidly middle-class family and taught school there after college. Unhappy in the classroom, she got a master's degree but still wasn't satisfied. As she puts it, "Now I know this sounds goofy because who, with two degrees at age thirty would, you know, decide to be a waitress." But she thought it would be a stopgap job until she could "figure this out." She lied about having waitressing experience to get her first job in Philadelphia, working from 10:00 at night to 2:00 in the morning. And she took to it, as she says, "like a duck to water."

Her concerned parents initially thought she was crazy. After such an investment in her education, she was throwing her life away! But her father wound up being the one who suggested she work in the casinos. He loved to play blackjack at the newly opened Resorts. The family already had a vacation condo in one of the shore towns near Atlantic City, and he started slipping off to gamble. At the tables, he saw how much money the cocktail waitresses were making. Voicing her father's advice, Ruth recalls, "As long as you're going to be a waitress (the worst thing he could imagine), why don't you at least move to Atlantic City?" She was shocked by the suggestion, mostly because of the revealing outfits the casino waitresses had to wear. It wasn't how she was raised to look. But she adored her father and took his advice, heading down to the Local 54 union office for help in applying.

As it turned out, Ruth loved waitressing. She felt she had a knack for the job. Responding to the judgmental voices she still heard in her head after all these years, she is adamant that serving people didn't make her feel "subservient" at all. She knew how to treat the customers and how to get tips, sharing some of her secrets: "I carried a lighter, I lit every cigarette, I clipped every cigar, I had little mints on my tray, do you know what I mean? I did this for other people. If I saw you were hungry, let me run down to the gift store, I'll put down a pack of peanuts next to you. It came so naturally to me; it was like taking candy from a baby. It's like I just knew what to do. . . . I never went and served a drink in front of a losing hand. I stood back and waited. If the guy was going to lose the hand, I'd come back in a second and serve somebody else first. It's a matter of focusing, paying attention to what's happening." This is actually very skilled work when put this way, not rote, not machine-like, but rather custom work for each and every customer.

Being a dealer was also an unintentional career for Caroline. She used to keep the books for the family business and originally dreamed of becoming a CPA (certified public accountant). But she had to pitch in and support her family when her father had a heart attack after the business collapsed. She was the one who suggested dealer school to her parents, putting her plans for college aside. Decades later, Caroline is a seasoned dealer. Despite the oft-reported 20 percent or 25 percent turnover rate in the casino industry across the United States, she and many of her coworkers have stayed around and turned a job into a long career. Maybe they tried "dual rate" jobs for a while, to get a (dis)taste of lower-level management in the gaming pits. Maybe they switched casinos in town. But they're still there.

Also like several women we interviewed, Caroline stepped away from her paid job for a few years when she had very young children. When she returned to the labor market, she was offered and accepted a job as a floorperson. She hated it! "I'm not meant to be a floorperson," she asserts. Why, we ask? Hourly pay plus overtime, but no more tips. Not enough contact with people. Too much worrying about player ratings for comps, too much responsibility for supervising other dealers at gaming tables in the pits. "Instead of having my seven players, because you had four games you had to watch, now I had twenty-eight people that I had to comp, rate—boom—didn't have time to talk and have fun." After a few years, she went back to full-time dealing, though she would be asked repeatedly to consider flooring again.

Caroline deals baccarat, blackjack, all the carnival games, and roulette. She loves dealing tournaments, even taking a different or extra shift for a day to work them. And she is not afraid—in fact she relishes—being pulled off her regular games to handle the hundreds of thousands of dollars that pass through the casino with high rollers. Many dealers are intimidated by the high-action pits. Ruth, interjecting from the kitchen where she is having a cigarette, even comments to us about Caroline's skill: "When you see these kind of mega bets, where she is good enough, dealer wise, not to make a mistake. Most of them are terrified of that. So that's a huge asset; they can use her for the high-action pits." Caroline shares her secret: simple division. For instance, once a whale (high roller) bet $10,000 in three-card poker and won a straight flush, 40-to-1 odds. The payout and bonus were huge. When the shift manager asked her how she was able to push the chips to the player so quickly, she said that she treated $50,000 as if it were $5 in her head. She broke down large sums of money simply by dividing.

Caroline has lots of whale stories. She reminisces about one who flew in regularly from out of town. The casino had set up a separate room for him with blackjack, roulette, and craps. And he got to pick his dealers. When whales like him come into the casino, dealers are allowed to "drop orange," or put $1,000 chips into the tip box. The whale bet $60,000 on just two hands, and he did toss her an orange even though he lost. The player ordered a water and also gave the beverage server an orange chip. Paraphrasing one manager to us, Caroline mimics, "What are you doing? You lost. You tip too much." It was as if they were saying, use and lose the money at the table; don't share it with the staff. After a few other games with Caroline dealing, the whale threw her a gray chip (worth $5,000). She "cut it down," gave him five orange for change. "I push it to him, he gets it, pushes it back, and says 'that's for you.'" Looking at the pit boss, he adds, "Don't ever tell me how to spend my money." Naturally, we ask Caroline how she feels about having to pool her tokes with other dealers rather than keeping her own (as the server who brought the water could do). Sometimes it bothers her, especially in situations like this, when the whale lost boatloads of money and dropped over $100,000 in tips to the dealers he selected to play with him.

While an orange chip tossed on a server's tray is rare, an average senior beverage server delivering free drinks on the gaming floor could easily take home $500 per week in tips. Ruth was no average server. She worked extremely hard, explaining "And the only way to make money at the job is to go back and forth, back and forth even with one drink on the tray so you never miss a customer . . . for six hours straight." In good years, Ruth was proud of her take-home pay. She maintained meticulous, "precise" in her words, records for tax purposes. The biggest tip she ever got was $3,000. She remembers it vividly: "He was playing blackjack and he was up a million dollars and he picked up, I saw him reach into his stack and put his hand on a group of chips, I had no idea how many, but when he picked them up, he took my hand and put them in my hand. I was literally shaking. I ran into the bathroom with a hand full of chips and they were all $500 chips, purple chips, and there were six of them. I ran upstairs, left the floor, and called my parents at 3:00 in the morning to tell them. I was like, 'Oh my God!'" No wonder it was hard to walk away from these jobs to go back to college or begin college or look for something different. When the casinos were busy and business was thriving, dealers and servers could sustain a middle-class lifestyle and support a family.

We learn from Ruth and Caroline that for every generous whale there are multiple with bad reputations. Caroline has dealt to many of them. The worst offenders have been so drunk that they have turned their head, vomited on the casino floor, and turned back to keep playing. They have thrown cards at her face. They would call her names. Regular gamblers, too. They would get into fights. One fistfight was so bad that two blackjack tables got turned over. Each one weighs at least eighty pounds! Ruth has also served these more malicious gamblers. Cocktail servers are trained to cut customers off from alcohol if they are drunk. But who is going to cut off a high roller who gambles hundreds of thousands of dollars in a sitting?

Regrettably, too, for every player who comes to the casino for entertainment and who can afford to lose money, there are others who cannot. Gambling addiction is a serious problem. Ruth and Caroline have seen more than their fair share. Some are regulars. Others are not. Like a college student. Caroline sighs remembering a story: "Oh, it breaks your heart. Especially when you see the young kids that, you know, a young kid comes in on spring break a lot, and they'll say '[Caroline], you gotta help me out, I'm down.' And you know they don't know me, they just look at my badge and they'll be in on spring break. 'This is all I got left; I spent all my money for the semester.' I'll say, 'Why don't you go home with that?' and it's like you pray that they win. The one guy lost, he had a bet up, and it was $100. He lost it because I flipped over like twenty winners. He put his hand on the bet and started crying." They also tell us of suicides that don't always make it into the local press. Some addicts feel there is no other way out.

With the repetitive motion of dealing night after night, Caroline developed severe pain in her hands. "Some days I'm hurtin' so bad, I can't shuffle the cards." She doesn't know whether it is carpal tunnel syndrome or arthritis. The pain forces her to take early outs, being tapped out of her game early to go home. Ruth, too, suffers from the ailments that come from working on your feet throughout a career. "What happens to your body is almost incomprehensible," exclaims Ruth. "I mean constant pain, bordering on unbearable, where, on your days off, you want to lie in bed, where you don't want to get out of bed." She is a petite woman, and very agile on her feet. She estimates that a full cocktail tray weighs about fifteen pounds; she carried that tray over her head and served about 200 customers per shift, five shifts per week, for over twenty years. Naturally, Ruth discloses, a lot of the girls had foot and shoulder problems. If it weren't for the pain, Ruth would still be swerving around the casino floor, serving tray after tray of drinks.

As business got worse, even before the Great Recession, and as her nagging pain for at least five years had become more magnified, Ruth quit—suddenly. "I was on my last legs," she professed, "and I one day woke up, I called them up and I said, 'I hate to do this to you after twenty-five years later, not to give you a two week notice, but when you saw me yesterday, that was my last day.' I didn't even tell my husband for two days. And he thought I was kidding when I told him. I said, 'I quit.' He said, 'You can't be serious!' I said, 'I'm telling you, I quit.' He said, 'Oh my God!' I said I could not walk one more step. One more. I had lost it."

Caroline and Ruth have mixed feelings about the current state of the industry. The decline in business and subsequent cutbacks have made it hard on the workers on the floor. They have not received an increase in their base pay in six or seven years. Declining business with competition from nearby Pennsylvania has meant declining tips. The double dose of competition and the recession have forced Caroline, Ruth, and other casino working families to curb their expenses. While families were once excited to have large numbers of their siblings and children join the industry, now there is more skepticism. One of Caroline and Ruth's shared children is in the industry, in a relatively rare full-time job in the back of the house. Caroline's sister is also in the industry. In general, though, they would not necessarily recommend that their children, nieces, and nephews seek employment in the casinos. Ruth explains why, especially the odd hours and the gambling culture: "Number 1: you are never going to have a normal life. You are going to be working every holiday, every evening. You are never going to be home to raise your kids. You are going to want to be there at night where the money is when you should be home with your teenage kids. The kind of person you meet, whereas I enjoyed them, most of these people if you get to know them, they are troubled people. They've got a gambling addiction. . . . And the drinking, no." Ruth's idiom to describe a typical casino was "a den of iniquity." In retirement, she has turned to writing short stories about her experiences, trying to bring a sense of closure to everything she's seen and been through.

3

GOING UPSCALE IN AN ERA OF INCOME POLARIZATION

Atlantic City area locals still refer to day trippers as "shoobies," a term that dates back to when Philadelphia families traveling by train to the Jersey shore for the day would carry their lunches in shoe boxes. When the casinos came to town, a new type of shoobies did as well. Visitors arrived by car or bus for the day, mostly to play the slot machines.[1] The cliché customer was a senior citizen with limited mobility planted in front of a whirling display of flashing lights and dinging sounds. In the words of one Showboat executive, "people in the industry thought of Atlantic City as nothing but a bus market for blue-haired nickel-slot players."[2] For a long time, the casino owners and managers seemed content.

But as gambling venues on the East Coast multiplied, it became clearer that Atlantic City needed to differentiate itself as a destination resort. Las Vegas, which had transitioned to the era of megaresorts, became a source of envy rather than scorn. One problem facing the local industry was that 90 percent of revenues came from gambling, in contrast with Nevada, where approximately half of the dollars spent went toward rooms, food, and entertainment. In describing the differences between the two gambling centers, entertainment industry analyst Harold Vogel observed how much Atlantic City had been left behind in the evolution of the industry during the 1990s: "while Las Vegas truly became a global entertainment capital—a citywide theme park in itself—Atlantic City casinos remain largely a collection of slot-machine malls attracting primarily day-trip visitors."[3] Those day-trippers now had slot parlors closer to home. And, given the economic squeeze that middle-class Americans were facing, they had less and less disposable income for gambling. As noted by a Credit Suisse analyst in a 2014 article on the industry's troubles in *Bloomberg Businessweek*, "Gaming can skew a little more blue-collar and middle-income, and if you look at the national economic statistics, that's a subset that remains challenged."[4] In the same article, the general manager of an Ohio casino observed that the weak economic recovery since 2009 had squeezed the budgets of the key demographic playing the slots—women over fifty. To survive, Atlantic City had to attract new customers.

In response, New Jersey's policy makers and civic leaders have tried, haltingly, with some successes and some failures, to lure a new wave of redevelopment that would bring overnight guests seeking multiple distractions. Convention business, which had shriveled up following the 1964 Democratic National Convention debacle, was actively solicited, and accompanied by building sprees to add hotel rooms to accommodate larger groups.[5] The beach and the Boardwalk, the sand and the surf, ignored for several decades, were once again touted as selling points to prospective visitors.

There is economic logic behind this strategy. Any student studying supply and demand in introductory microeconomics will tell you that an increase in the number of suppliers in a market puts downward pressure on equilibrium prices. Lower prices are supposed to boost the quantity demanded for your product. The product that the casinos sell, however, is extremely intangible. The sunk costs in capital equipment are incredibly high. Substituting "nickel slots" for machines accepting quarters in order to "lower prices" is not an easy fix. Minimum bets on table games can be lowered as a marketing ploy. Whether such price changes boost revenue depends upon a concept that economists call *demand elasticity*. If consumer demand is elastic, a small change in price will cause a significant increase or decrease in their willingness to buy. In this case, lowering the price will draw in new customers. But if demand is inelastic, consumer demand is relatively stable and inflexible, so price decreases will not motivate buyers; instead, a price decrease will reduce total revenue. At least one study indicates that demand for casino gambling is, in fact, inelastic.[6] Further, the routine price adjustments that economists expect in competitive markets do not always occur as neatly as they do in supply and demand graphs. Prices can be sticky, especially in a highly regulated industry where new firms have to be licensed in order to enter the market and casino operations are subject to review. The licensing requirements serve as barriers to entry. An alternate economic strategy for larger firms is to try to increase the demand curve itself, keeping prices stable while attracting new customers.

Political economists have long studied the ways in which businesses attempt to shift demand and increase their market power using strategies other than price adjustments. Casino operators can try to *increase their market share* compared with their competitors, a common strategy in oligopolistic industries. As casino management is increasingly coordinated by large corporations or hedge funds with multiple holdings, the market structure is more clearly that of an oligopoly, that is, dominated by a few firms. The American Gaming Association reports that mega-mergers of casino companies became the norm as early as 2005, when MGM Mirage acquired Mandalay Resort Group (April 2005) and Harrah's Entertainment, Inc. acquired Caesars Entertainment (June 2005).[7] Even in Nevada, where barriers to entry are far lower than in New Jersey, megacorporations dominate the casino landscape.

Oligopolies are also cemented by differentiating products so that customers make choices on factors other than the cheapest deal (that is, price). Customer loyalty and brand identification are critical in this process. One change was the advent of electronic "player cards" that track when a customer visits, how much they gamble and on which games, and even which other amenities they use. Since players accumulate points on the card for a particular casino (or casinos with shared ownership, such as the Caesars Total Rewards card) and the points earn them "comps" (cash, goods, or services), the rewards programs incentivize loyalty. In effect, they make player demand more inelastic, since they are more likely to return to the same casinos.

Lifestyle branding emerged as an identifiable trend in the United States and other postindustrial countries during the 1990s. Naomi Klein, in her book *No Logo*, portrays branding as an effort to sell "meaning" through products.[8] Customers purchase goods and services only partially for their use values or functions. A more important motivation is that the products we use—and people see us using—signal the type of person we are or aspire to become. Branding is a perfect match for casino gaming since the industry has always marketed fantasies and experiences rather than tangible products. In Atlantic City's casinos, brand identification attracts customers by marketing the casino as appropriate for a particular demographic group or by focusing on aspirational desires to act out a particular lifestyle. Several casinos, for example, market to Asian American communities with familiar amenities including pits focusing on specific games such as Pai Gow and Pai Gow poker and noodle bars and other appealing food options; they have also recruited Asian dealers. While Bally's Wild West Casino plays country music and evokes nineteenth-century saloons, Showboat has a New Orleans riverboat theme and even a House of Blues. Other casinos opt for less specific symbols of luxury, from marble columns to ornate chandeliers. In recent years, as we describe below, such segmented marketing has increased.

As part of their branding strategy, two newly constructed casinos (Borgata in 2003 and Revel in 2012) as well as several existing properties have targeted new demographics, especially upscale consumers with greater disposable income. Entertainment, nightclubs, beach bars, and dining have been redirected toward a youthful market. The new marketing strategies make sense in an era of increased income polarization. Documented by Robert Frank in his book *Luxury Fever*, rising incomes for the wealthy combined with stagnant incomes for the middle class have contributed to a surge in consumption and marketing of luxury goods and services.[9] Like the bank robber Willie Sutton (in a possibly apocryphal story), the casinos started "going where the money is." New technologies, especially magnetized customer loyalty cards, have also enabled casinos to more precisely target their high-spending customers and to deemphasize the gamblers who travel by bus. "Those customers who arrive by car are much more profitable," observed Mark Juliano, then-Trump Entertainment Resorts CEO, in a local newspaper article on the shift in strategy.[10]

In sum, casinos in Atlantic City have responded to competition by trying to boost demand (the demand curve) and thereby bring in new customers. Managers have also sought to retain the customers they have. In economic terms, they have tried to reduce demand elasticity for their own house, making demand for their casino more inelastic. This chapter will explore these efforts in more detail.

On the supply side of the picture, another possibility is to concentrate on *cutting costs* and crossing your fingers that you do not lose customers. Competitors in the same industry may merge to try to lower costs through economies of scale. Businesses can cut costs in a labor-intensive industry by (1) incorporating labor-saving technologies, (2) reducing customer service in order to cut down on the number of employees, and (3) reducing labor costs by cutting wages and benefits. Deregulation is another cost-cutting tactic, since regulations intended to keep the games honest or to assure quality in other ways can increase the cost of operations.

In casino gaming, market saturation and pressures from debt holders have led casino management, in critical instances, to shorten their time horizons. The problem with this strategy is that it may restore profitability to the corporations and private equity interests that own the casinos without improving the well-being of the employees and the local community.[11] As we have already seen in the stories of employees in chapter 1, many cost-cutting measures such as the elimination of coins, reorganization of work processes, and cuts in benefits have been implemented.[12] Overall, the level of customer service has declined, especially for anyone who is not a high roller, and some of the employees we interviewed indicated that the cuts and looser regulations have increased the amount of cheating that goes undetected. Chapters 4 and 5, which focus on the characteristics of frontline jobs, elaborate on the impact of these cost-cutting efforts. Chapter 6 examines the pushback from organized labor, specifically the two unions representing frontline casino employees in Atlantic City.

Politically connected business leaders have other ways of restoring profitability that cannot be neatly categorized as supply or demand factors. Government helps provide the physical and social infrastructure that enables businesses to function. The difficulty comes in discerning the difference between appropriate public initiatives to improve broadly shared economic well-being, on the one hand, and corporate welfare or bailouts, on the other. Dean Baker, director of the Center for Economic Policy Research and author of *Taking Economics Seriously*, argues that much of the debate over economic policy is really over the *type* of economic regulation, not its *extent*; in his words, "In the

U.S. economy, there is no free market."[13] Rather there is a tug-of-war over policies that primarily benefit corporations and policies that promote shared prosperity. One of the critical attributes of government, from this perspective, is that it enables corporate interests to lobby for subsidies, regulations, and other policies that *externalize their costs*, meaning the public pays some of the costs of doing business. When underpaid workers collect food stamps, when the Environmental Protection Agency cleans up toxic waste sites, or when banks pay zero interest on funds from the Federal Reserve, government is absorbing some of the costs that businesses would otherwise pay. In chapter 7, we explore recent initiatives to save Atlantic City's casinos that have increased public subsidies and involvement in the fate of these private-sector businesses.

All three of these types of strategies—product differentiation, cost cutting, and externalizing costs—have been adopted in Atlantic City. The relative balance and the way they are implemented varies by property and property owner. And the composition of the mix has a profound effect on the workforce and the surrounding community. Therefore, cost-cutting strategies have generated tensions between labor leaders who adhere to a "high-road" model of casino operation and some, though not all, of the new corporate owners who are viewed as importing a "low-road" strategy from other jurisdictions. Policy makers and political leaders are being pressured to pick sides.

Economist David Gordon succinctly summarizes the distinction between these approaches in his book *Fat and Mean*: "The 'high road' seeks to build economic growth and prosperity through cooperation and strong worker rewards, including relatively rapid real wage growth. The 'low road' relies on conflict and insecurity, control and harsh worker punishments, and often features relatively stagnant or even declining real wage growth. Both are coherent strategies, both can conceivably work."[14] Even though both strategies are plausible in the abstract, Gordon argues that habits and structural incentives tend to make low-road strategies more attractive for individual firms in the short run. For example, declines in the real value of the minimum wage, policies that make unionization difficult, and a tattered social safety net since the 1970s have signaled a new set of institutional structures in the U.S. economy that have seen rising productivity without wage growth. In an era in which financial markets respond favorably to labor discipline, individual corporations face shareholder pressure to cut labor costs.

Efforts to implement the first strategy, product differentiation to attract new customers, are explored in more detail in this chapter, as we examine the peaks and troughs of the casino economy starting in 2003. We identify two waves of efforts to rebuild Atlantic City in the image of Las Vegas. The first swell crested in the period immediately following the opening of the Borgata, but crashed along with the rest of the global economy by 2008. This was followed by a smaller breaker, as more of the existing properties pursued variations on Borgata's successful attempts to bring in more prosperous demographics. By 2014, however, few of the copycats could claim the kind of success that Borgata enjoyed.

The grand opening of the Borgata, a $1.1 billion casino, during the Fourth of July holiday in 2003, marked a turning point after years of stability in the number of Atlantic City casinos. Much excitement ensued during construction of a fresh new property. Borgata emphasized table games over slot machines. Because a player can lose money quickly at the tables, they tend to draw higher-income customers. The casino's developers were seeking to capitalize on the growing popularity of poker rooms, especially among a younger crowd who plays online. Poker differs from blackjack, baccarat, and other typical casino table games in that gamblers play against each other instead of the house; casinos, then, garner revenue through seat/table fees. Borgata also pioneered completely cash-free and coin-free slots. It reduced the need for slot machine technicians and cashiers in "cages."

In the most significant departure from past practice, Borgata emphasized a hip, youthful image by offering trendy nightclubs (including one with bottle service) and restaurants associated with celebrity chefs such as Bobby Flay and Wolfgang Puck. (Las Vegas had already become known for fine dining.) Like the other two properties that are in the back bay Marina District rather than on the famous Boardwalk, Borgata does not have a program for gamblers to arrive by bus. While older casinos lured regular customers with comps—freebies such as buffets, show tickets, or prizes based on how much the player had gambled— Borgata drastically cut back on such marketing. The casino looked beyond day-trippers. Starting a trend, Borgata was one of the first Atlantic City properties to incorporate a spa offering massages and other treatments, as well as a small set of luxury shops. Commercials for the newly opened casino showed a group of stylish twenty-somethings arriving on motor scooters. According to Nora, a fresh college graduate who started at the Borgata as her first full-time job, the casino recruited a younger labor force in customer service positions. Over time, marketing utilized Facebook and other social media tools.

Borgata was deluged with employment applications from experienced staff at other casinos, quickly developing a reputation as a relatively good place to work. Patrice, a dual rate floorperson at one of the Trump properties, applied for a job when Borgata opened. At the time, she was forty-two years old, with fifteen years in the industry. She brought photocopies of her employee-of-the-month certificates and other recognitions. But the manager who interviewed her just wasn't interested. Even though he reportedly commented that she looked nice in her black slacks and shirt, she left with the impression that "if I was a lot skinnier and I was lot younger, I wouldn't have anything to worry about." The new casino seemed to be looking for a younger clientele, and hired employees to match.

Drinks are served by "Borgata Babes" in skimpier-than-ever uniforms who helped market the casino by posing for an annual pinup calendar. Lily, a twenty-something college student paying her way through school by working as a Babe, described her first attempt to audition for a better position in a different club—one with bottle service. She compared the elimination of candidates in various rounds to the television show *American Idol*. Wearing a costume that she described as looking like it "could fit a twelve-year-old," she and the other "girls" were brought into the audition room one by one. "We walked into this room and there were three big beverage managers and they were sitting at a table just like this," she explained, as she gestured to the table that we were using for the interview. Her story continued: "We had to stand a couple of feet away from them and there was a light directly on us. So they're sitting at the table and there's a light directly on us. They were looking at us and they said, 'Why do you want to work at the Borgata?' And I'm just standing there, like, this is absurd. I just want to serve drinks. It was like a judge panel—judging who I am. . . . I gave them the usual B.S.—'I love working here!' I turned around and I went back. And it was interesting because after all the girls had done that, they came back and asked two girls to leave. So right off the bat, just from them telling their names. I can only imagine that they did it only based on appearance."

Buffeted by its successful branding, Borgata quickly became the local front-runner, topping the city's casinos in gross gaming revenue. At its tenth anniversary in 2013, it was still #1 atop the revenue charts. As the busiest casino, its toke (tip) rate is also the highest. Borgata initially built and still holds the largest poker room in the city. Reflecting upon the first ten years, a local newspaper reporter summed up the Borgata brand and results: "its mix of South Beach hipness and Las Vegas-style glitz has allowed it to remain the city's dominant casino."[15] Borgata's success did not prevent loss of casino business to other nearby states, but it probably lessened it.

Other casinos tried to rebrand and remarket themselves to set themselves apart from the competition. Over time, more casino marketing departments incorporated use of Facebook and other social media tools. The year after the Borgata opened, Tropicana added a separate building called the Quarter, an "Old Havana" (meaning pre-Fidel Castro) themed shopping and dining complex with an Imax theater and comedy club, but no slot machines. Once the Atlantic City Council passed an enabling ordinance in 2002, several Boardwalk casinos set up beach bars during the summer months, finally capitalizing in a big way on their oceanfront locations. Restaurants were reconfigured to add windows offering ocean views. Non-gaming attractions were added outside, as well as inside, the casino walls. The first stage of the Walk, an outlet mall owned by Tanger Factory Outlet Centers, opened the same year as Borgata. The Walk has been praised for bringing tourists out of the casinos to walk the streets of downtown Atlantic City, while giving locals access to reasonably priced retail shops as well as entry-level retail jobs.

In 2005, the Atlantic City casino industry celebrated when gross gaming revenue topped the $5 billion annual revenue mark. A record number of visitors, 34.9 million, came to Atlantic City in 2005. And 2006 was the twenty-ninth consecutive year (1978–2006) of positive revenue growth for Atlantic City gaming. A forced shutdown of the casinos three days at the start of the state's fiscal year in July of 2006, a casualty of a budget battle in Trenton, the state capital, did not prevent 2006 revenue from growing 4 percent over 2005 figures. However, the rate of change in the increase in revenue had been decreasing for some time. That means gaming revenues were growing, the slope was still positive, but it was leveling off. While not yet saturated, the Atlantic City casino industry was maturing.

Plans for more new casinos, however, were in the works. Pinnacle Entertainment bought the Sands Casino Hotel in 2006 and imploded it to build a $1.5 billion megaresort. By mid-2008, there were rumors that Coastal Marina and Jimmy Buffett were planning to purchase the Trump Marina and convert it into a Margaritaville-themed casino. Another international company, Penn National Gaming, investigated property on the outskirts of the city, either on one of the causeways onto Absecon Island or the former municipal airport, Bader Field. Perhaps the most critical project involved MGM Mirage, under the helm of pioneering Atlantic City developer Steve Wynn. The company planned to build a $5 billion megaresort and convention center in the Marina District near Borgata. It was anticipated to have 3,000 hotel rooms and the largest casino floor in the city, as well as upscale shops, restaurants, and entertainment. If successful, the project would have eventually incorporated on-site condominiums, a unique feature for the city.[16]

Most of these dreams of an upscale destination resort were shattered by early 2009. Competition from Pennsylvania, coinciding with the onset of the Great Recession, proved lethal. Pennsylvania regulators granted permanent casino licenses to six racing facilities in 2006. Further, four stand-alone casinos were licensed and opened in Pennsylvania, spanning from Philadelphia to Pittsburgh, between 2007 and 2010. Then came the worst recession in the United States since the Great Depression. Consumers held onto their wallets. And the associated financial crisis triggered a credit crunch in late 2008, strangling most of the new development on which gaming advocates had pinned their hopes for a revival.

At first, it was difficult to disentangle the impact of short-term cyclical economic fluctuations—the recession—from longer-term, secular trends like market saturation. Atlantic City's gambling revenue hit a peak of $5.22 billion in 2006. Then, the casinos registered a revenue decline of 9.9 percent in the first quarter of 2007. The skid continued in the second quarter, suggesting that the first annual decline in history was likely. Summer business was no help. Competition from neighboring states and a slowing national economy began to take their toll. Sands became the first East Coast casino to be imploded. Both gambling revenue and casino profits dipped in 2007.

As the United States plunged into the Great Recession, gambling revenues continued steady annual declines. During the economic crisis, southern New Jersey residents learned that casinos are not a "recession-proof" industry, in Atlantic City or elsewhere. Gaming revenue fell by 8.5 percent in 2008, 12.4 percent in 2009, and 9.6 percent in 2010 (our calculations based on annual reports from the American Gaming Association). Atlantic City was not alone. As a result, from 2007 to 2009, for the first time ever, U.S. casino revenues nationwide experienced decline. Casino stock prices dropped. The industry saw bankruptcy filings followed by restructurings, consolidations, and mergers. For example, Harrah's Entertainment, Inc. (later renamed Caesars Entertainment Corporation) was acquired by two private equity firms—Apollo Global Management and Texas Pacific Group (TPG Capital)—in a $17 billion leveraged buyout during 2008, assuming a massive amount of new debt in the process.[17] At the same time, casino gaming as a global industry continued to prosper and expand.

Locally, casinos laid off employees or cut their workforces through attrition. Thousands of Atlantic City casino workers lost their jobs, about 10,000 from 2006 to 2013, despite a slight uptick following the opening of Revel in 2012 (see table 3.1). The gradual trickle of jobs leaving the industry—around 1 or 2 percent per year following Borgata's 2003 opening—turned into a cascade. If we look at employment per house, it peaked in 1997 and has fallen dramatically. Casino hotels were closing off some of their rooms and services mid-week. The impact was broad—a ripple effect—as casino vendors saw their business dwindle.

As Pinnacle, the owners of the gigantic hole where Sands once stood, announced delay after delay in breaking ground on the new casino that was supposed to rise from the dust, the empty lot seemed to taunt the local community. One city council member vented that "They had an operating casino running. They buy it, crush it and take all the jobs away. Now they can't build."[18] The loss of so many jobs was devastating, and sent a large supply of workers into the local labor market precisely when jobs were scarce. The bargaining power of the workers

Table 3.1.   New Jersey Casino Employment and Employees per House

Year	# Casinos	Casino Employment	Employees per House
1978	1	3,226	3,226
1979	3	11,301	3,767
1980	6	21,151	3,525
1981	9	27,842	3,094
1982	9	28,093	3,121
1983	9	30,197	3,355
1984	10	35,968	3,597
1985	11	37,004	3,364
1986	11	37,262	3,387
1987	12	38,829	3,236
1988	12	42,134	3,511
1989	12	41,627	3,469
1990	12	45,241	3,770
1991	12	43,910	3,659
1992	12	44,240	3,687
1993	12	44,111	3,676
1994	12	44,894	3,741
1995	12	47,286	3,941
1996	12	48,956	4,080
1997	12	49,123	4,094
1998	12	48,542	4,045
1999	12	47,366	3,947
2000	12	47,426	3,937
2001	12	45,592	3,799
2002	12	44,820	3,735
2003	13	46,159	3,551
2004	13	45,501	3,500
2005	13	44,542	3,426
2006	12	42,456	3,538
2007	11	40,788	3,708
2008	11	38,585	3,508
2009	11	36,082	3,280
2010	11	34,145	3,104

2011	11	32,823	2,984
2012	12	34,726	2,894
2013	12	32,427	2,702
2014 (March)	11	30,380	2,762

Note: Data is as of December 31 each year, except as noted. Sources: New Jersey Casino Control Commission, annual reports until 2011; thereafter, New Jersey Division of Gaming Enforcement website, casino hotel employment statistics.

at the remaining casinos diminished. No one wanted to risk joining the burgeoning ranks of job hunters. One floor manager we spoke with in 2009 described the chill brought about by a combination of limbo over ownership changes, a spate of firings, and increased supervisory responsibilities for remaining staff. In an e-mail two years later, her brother told us that her workplace continued to resemble a "ghost town."

Macroeconomic recovery for the U.S. economy, however, did not turn the trend around. Atlantic City's gambling revenue fell to $3.05 billion by 2012—a 42 percent drop from the peak six years earlier. In fact, according to the American Gaming Association's *2013 State of the States* annual report, Atlantic City was the poorest performing casino market in 2012. What was even worse news is that in the AGA report— for the first time ever—New Jersey fell out of second place in terms of gross gaming revenue. Instead of being second to Nevada, Pennsylvania was second and New Jersey was now third. By 2013, eleven casinos operated in Pennsylvania, with two more planned. Delaware had three with two more planned. New York had fourteen (nine racetrack and five Native American). Annual visits to Atlantic City casino properties had fallen off. The winning streak was over.

The crisis intensified underlying weaknesses in the local gaming industry as the short-term recession undermined efforts to turn around the longer-term problems. Economic conditions weakened the incentives for would-be casino ventures by entrepreneurs. Gradually, most of the projects—Pinnacle, Bader Field, and the MGM Mirage complex— dried up along with their financing. The profits for the industry in Atlantic City no longer seemed to justify the high cost of capital attributable to building and maintaining a new casino. The Revel project, whose financing was hamstrung by the credit crisis, was the only new casino to emerge from the rubble.

In late 2012, Atlantic City casinos, still hemorrhaging from a weak economy and competition from neighboring states, suffered another severe blow—this time from Mother Nature. Hurricane Sandy, a Category 3 hurricane, battered the Eastern Seaboard for two days, affecting twenty-four states from Florida to Maine. Atlantic City was in the large eye of the superstorm at landfall on Monday, October 29, 2012. Governor Chris Christie ordered the casinos closed the day before as Absecon Island was evacuated. Five days later, the order was lifted, but the casinos were left with cleanup and remained closed for a week. Hourly workers were laid off and were not allowed to use their vacation time during the closing. Salaried workers sustained days or even a week without pay. Collectively, casinos lost $5 million per day in gaming revenue. The superstorm's water damage was extensive near the coast and the back bays throughout Atlantic City and the rest of the barrier island. Even upon reopening after Sandy, casino business was slow to recover. And less than two years after Revel opened, the Atlantic Club Casino—the property that once housed the much admired Golden Nugget—went into bankruptcy and closed its doors, sending 1,600 workers scrambling for jobs.

As of mid-2014, there are eleven casinos operating in Atlantic City. By the time this book is published, there are likely to be fewer. The current properties are listed in table 3.2 along with their market shares. Borgata is in many ways the market leader, with over a fifth of total casino revenue, not just gaming revenue. The picture becomes more complex, however, when we remember that many of these properties are owned and/or operated by larger corporations and other entities with diverse holdings.[19] Even within the Atlantic City market, for example, Caesars Entertainment Corporation and its private equity owners hold four of the eleven properties, including the second- (Harrah's), third- (Caesars), and fifth- (Bally's AC) ranked properties. Trump Entertainment Resorts Holdings still owns two properties, "the Taj" and Trump Plaza. The third Trump-named property was sold off and given the revived name Golden Nugget. Table 3.3 shows that Caesars Entertainment is actually the largest firm in the local market with 41.0 percent market share in 2013.

So how much competition is there really in the local industry? How dominant are the top firms? Economists and antitrust lawyers use two measures to assess how competitive or anti-competitive an industry is:

Table 3.2.   Atlantic City Casino Market Shares at End of Year 2013

Casino	Total Revenue ($ in thousands)	Market Share	Rank
Borgata	$913,516	23.5%	1
Harrah's	$530,881	13.6%	2
Caesars	$444,295	11.4%	3
Trump Taj Mahal	$353,932	9.1%	4
Bally's AC	$346,399	8.9%	5
Tropicana	$318,194	8.2%	6
Showboat	$275,351	7.1%	7
Revel	$250,426	6.4%	8
Golden Nugget	$177,769	4.6%	9
Resorts	$176,547	4.5%	10
Trump Plaza	$104,685	2.7%	11
Totals	$3,891,995	100%	

Note: Atlantic Club is omitted because the casino closed in January, 2014. Source: New Jersey Division of Gaming Enforcement, quarterly financial reports from casinos, Fourth Quarter 2013

the concentration ratio (CR) and the Herfindahl-Hirschman Index (HHI). These two measures shed light on the nature of a market. How concentrated an industry is can be measured by the simpler four-firm concentration ratio, the percentage share of total sales/revenue of the four leading firms. Isolating the Atlantic City market, the four-firm concentration ratio is 84.5 percent (see table 3.3). Such a high CR means that the Atlantic City casino industry is one of most concentrated markets in the United States, on par with beverages (Coca Cola as leader) and tobacco (Philip Morris as leader).

A weakness of the CR as a measure is that it does not give us information about the competitiveness of the rest of the industry. For example, do one or two firms in the top four hold the lion's share, or are the four relatively equal players? Beyond the big players, are there only a few other firms (think Atlantic City) or hundreds of other small firms that would give consumers a choice (think Las Vegas casinos)? The Herfindahl-Hirschman Index (HHI) named after its developers, economists Orris Herfindahl and Albert Hirschman, is a more sophisticated measure of market power and thus possible anti-competitive behavior.

Table 3.3.   Atlantic City Casino Concentration Ratio and HHI in 2013

Corporation	Market Share	Square
Caesars Entertainment [Caesars, Harrah's, Bally's, Showboat]	41.0%	1,681.0
Marina District Development Company, LLC [Borgata]	23.5%	552.3
Trump Entertainment Resorts Holdings, LP [Taj Mahal, Plaza]	11.8%	139.2
Tropicana Entertainment, Inc. [Tropicana]	8.2%	67.2
4-Firm Concentration Ratio	**84.5%**	
Revel Entertainment Group LLC [Revel]	6.4%	41.0
Landry's Inc. [Golden Nugget]	4.6%	21.1
DGMB Casino LLC [Resorts]	4.5%	20.3
Herfindahl-Hirschman Index (HHI)		**2,522.1**

Source: New Jersey Division of Gaming Enforcement, quarterly financial reports from casinos, Fourth Quarter 2013

It is the sum of the squares of the market shares of the fifty largest firms, or all of the firms if the number is less than fifty. This measure better accounts for the relative sizes of firms in the industry. The HHI can theoretically range from 0 to 10,000 with 10,000 for a monopoly: 1 firm with 100 percent of the market, (100 x 100) or 100^2. The U.S. Department of Justice Antitrust Division uses the HHI to evaluate proposed mergers for possible anti-competitive effects. The Justice Department considers a market with an HHI higher than 2,500 points to be "highly concentrated."

As shown in table 3.3 (organized by firm ownership), the HHI for the Atlantic City casino market is 2,522.1. This means that the casino market in Atlantic City is highly concentrated. Eleven casinos have only five owners. The arithmetic of the HHI is driven by Caesars, by far the dominant firm. This dominance presumably was a factor in the company's seemingly anti-competitive recent behavior. Caesars and Tropicana swooped in and bought the closed Atlantic Club, with Caesars purchasing the building and physical assets. Then Caesars turned around and sold the building with a deed restriction that prevents it from being used as a casino in the future.

But Caesars is not exactly a firm, in the conventional sense. As noted by Eileen Appelbaum and Rosemary Batt, authors of *Private Equity at Work*, the primary shareholder in Caesars Entertainment is a fund controlled by two private equity firms, TPG Capital and Apollo Global Management. The buyout of Caesars was one of the largest in the history of private equity, and burdened the company with billions of dollars in debt. To manage the debt, the private equity managers "cut staff, reduced hours, outsourced jobs, and scaled back operations," as well as "cut dealers hours and benefits." And, they engaged in the type of behavior that Appelbaum and Batt warn about in the conclusion to their book: "all too often private equity owners have engaged in financial engineering . . . to maximize their own returns while putting operating companies and their stakeholders in jeopardy."[20] In fact, Caesars' employment policies in recent years have been particularly draconian, raising concerns that other gaming houses will follow the market leader.

We chose to complete this mathematical exercise for the Atlantic City gaming market. If we were to perform the same calculations for another jurisdiction—a city or region—we would find that the gaming marketplace is similarly concentrated, even when measured nationally or internationally. Excluding casinos owned and operated by Native American tribes, the global gaming market is comprised of oligopolies. In other words, large firms under few corporate owners are the market leaders and powerhouses.[21]

It is not surprising, then, to see market dynamics common to oligopolistic industries, where a few market leaders set the trends and most competition is focused on grabbing market share from other firms. Borgata's rise to the top of the local market based on this new managerial strategy made it a model to be copied or surpassed. Many of these efforts overtly focused on marketing strategies to appeal to a more affluent customer base.

Economic revitalization needed a spark. The existing Atlantic City properties, along with local political leaders and policy makers, pushed even harder to remake the city's image into a regional destination resort. Yet policy makers rarely mention the underlying political economy forces driving the strategy of appealing to young, hip consumers in their twenties, thirties, and even their forties who have higher levels of disposable income. Casinos are not the only U.S. industry that has targeted the luxury market in recent years, and with good reason.

Income inequality in the United States has been rising since 1979. Timothy Noah points out that while similar trends can be observed in other advanced industrial economies, "the level and growth rate of income inequality in the United States has been particularly extreme."[22] In 1928, on the eve of the Great Depression, the richest 1 percent in the United States earned 24 percent of the income; by the 1970s, at the end of a period that economists Claudia Goldin and Robert Margo label the Great Compression, the share of the "1-percenters" was down to 9 percent. Incomes stagnated for the wealthy as well as the middle class during the 1970s, according to Noah. The Great Divergence, a term coined by Nobel-winning economist and *New York Times* columnist Paul Krugman, brought the income share of the top 1 percent back to 24 percent by 2007, the onset of the Great Recession.[23] During the entire period from the 1980s to 2005, Noah observes, "*80 percent* of the total increase in Americans' income went to the top 1 percent."[24]

Those earning just below the wealthiest also did quite well. After-tax income for the top 20 percent—what economic analysts refer to as the top "quintile"—rose 65 percent from 1979 to 2007, compared with a 37 percent increase for the households in the middle-income ranges. Stagnant wages, erosion of the social safety net, outsourcing of living wage jobs held by those with less education, lower union density, and other trends slowly undermined middle-class incomes. During the same period, financial bubbles and favorable tax policies concentrated income and wealth at the top of the ladder.[25] Economist Robert Frank noted as early as 1999 that luxury spending was growing four times as fast as overall spending, fueled by "unprecedented prosperity" of top earners.[26] Frank documents the explosion of conspicuous consumption on larger homes, yachts, high-end watches, professional cooking ranges, cosmetic surgery, premium wines, and other luxury items, as well as the impact of luxury markets on middle-class aspirations.

Conspicuous consumption, including glitzy décor, lavish buffets, and the affectation of carelessness with money were always part of the image that casinos and their customers projected. But the new expansion wave has amped up the signifiers of luxury. High-income consumers need to be attracted by more than the dream of hitting it big at the slots. Atlantic City has tried to give them what they want. For example, in 2008, Harrah's, long associated with the low end of the market, built a more luxurious set of rooms called the Water Tower, outfitted with a

40,000-square-foot space that includes a massive pool and Jacuzzis as well as an Elizabeth Arden Red Door Spa. Adding to the burgeoning nightclub scene, "The Pool After Dark" becomes a Vegas-style nightclub with poolside cabanas offering bottle service and the chance to rub elbows with various celebrities—from reality television standouts to other pop culture icons—while dancing to the beats supplied by famous deejays. Marketing of the pool was separated from general marketing of the casino property in order to draw a younger crowd.[27] As a unique attraction, Harrah's Water Tower also introduced the only Viking Cooking School in a casino. Capitalizing on the popularity of television cooking shows, the Viking schools offer classes where participants prep dishes under the guidance of a chef, then dine on and drink their output, all while using Viking's professional-grade kitchen products and appliances. Casino houses also tried offering indoor surfing, trapeze lessons, and other attractions to draw customers.[28]

In 2010, casino manager Dennis Gomes, who had built the Quarter when he was at Tropicana, became CEO of Resorts when he and business partner Morris Bailey purchased it. Gomes had started his career in Las Vegas working for the Nevada Gaming Control Board as a regulator; his major case investigating organized crime was the basis for the 1995 Martin Scorsese film *Casino*. He also worked for New Jersey's Division of Gaming Enforcement before going through the revolving door from casino regulation to casino management. Under his leadership, Resorts was rebranded with a Prohibition speakeasy theme, seizing on both the popularity of the HBO series *Boardwalk Empire* and incorporating architectural elements from the 1920s-era building's former life as the Chalfont Hotel and Hadden Hall. Female cocktail servers wearing plunging backless flapper costumes became a prime feature of casino marketing on billboards and other advertising. They were following the trend set by the Borgata Babes. Back in 2007, a *New York Times* article about Atlantic City's casinos observed, "These days, cocktail waitresses working the flashier casinos show more skin and are younger and more buxom than they used to be, and a few years ago the city adopted a new advertising slogan: 'Always Turned On.'"[29] Controversy surrounded some of the casino's rebranding efforts. Hundreds of former employees lost their jobs or took pay cuts.[30] This included a number of middle-aged women who had worked as cocktail waitresses before the ownership change at Resorts. Nine of the waitresses charged that they lost their jobs when they had to audition with a modeling agency to wear the skimpy new uniform. The waitresses were offered alternative positions in the company but declined to take them, opting to initiate an age and gender discrimination lawsuit.

On a more positive note, the new Resorts also broke new ground by being the first casino to explicitly target the gay, lesbian, bisexual, and transgender (GLBT) community. Atlantic City had once had a lively gay bar scene centered around New York Avenue, dating back to the 1920s, but the casino era along with other trends had displaced the once-thriving culture. Resorts opened the first GLBT-oriented dance club inside a casino, then added a drag show (that attracted straight audiences as well) and a piano bar. Other casinos have also sponsored drag bingo events to raise money for the South Jersey AIDS Alliance or hosted special weekends with circuit parties. The two developments are, in a sense, intertwined. As the casino deliberately sought to market itself as a hot destination, it signaled this by ramping up markers of sexuality, both heterosexuality (skimpier costumes on waitresses) and homosexuality. Gay men are viewed as trendsetters by some heterosexual consumers. Gay marketing frequently reflects common assumptions (often myths) that the GLBT community consists of relatively privileged and hedonistic consumers with few family responsibilities,[31] and this may have influenced the strategy as well.

Yet Gomes's sudden death in February 2012 caused turmoil for a company that largely drew upon his vision and expertise. By the summer of 2012, Resorts announced that it had turned to Connecticut-based Mohegan Sun to become a minority owner and to manage Resorts' operations. The deal gave Mohegan Sun its first inroad into the Atlantic City market and marked another step toward industry consolidation. Loyalty points earned at any of the three Mohegan Sun casinos (in Connecticut, Pennsylvania, and Atlantic City) are transferable. Less than one week after the agreement was made public, the new management team announced its intention to construct a major expansion in front of Resorts, where the old Steeplechase Pier once existed. The new complex built out over the beach would have a "Jimmy Buffett's Margaritaville" theme, resurrecting the concept once intended to remake Trump Marina. The sprawling Connecticut Mohegan Sun complex already had a Margaritaville component that is popular with "Parrotheads" (the moniker for Buffett's fans). The local news coverage noted that "Margaritaville customers are generally between the ages of 35 and 64 and are split evenly between males and females. More than 60 percent have college or graduate degrees, and 39 percent have household incomes greater than $100,000." The article also indicated that the project was supposed to "generate 238 construction jobs, 45 professional temporary jobs, and 162 permanent jobs."[32]

Resorts was able to secure some brand protection for Margaritaville, specifically, that it would be the only operation within 200 miles of the Atlantic City location, keeping the brand out of eastern Pennsylvania and Delaware. Ribbon cutting was Memorial Day weekend in 2013. A portion of the Resorts casino floor is now bright turquoise. Palm trees and surfboards abound. Just across the Boardwalk is the Landshark Bar & Grill, occupying the once-decaying pier. Roughly one year later, Resorts announced that it would stick to one principal theme: the Roaring Twenties was out, including the flapper uniforms, and Margaritaville was in. Also "out" (ironically) was gay marketing, including the drag show and bars. According to local casino consultant Michael Pollock, "Margaritaville represents a very desirable demographic. It's a combination of young people and people who don't realize they are no longer young."[33]

Pursuing a different strategy for marketing and branding, several casinos are emphasizing the locals market. "Industry nights" target workers during their off hours who often are not permitted to patronize their own casino but can party at others. Tropicana introduced a "Tropicana Loves Locals" program as early as 2002, but interest in the approach has increased. The struggling Atlantic Club, in a last gasp before its demise, heavily marketed to locals starting in 2012; they lowered prices on meals, offered free parking, and gave gamblers comps they could use at local small businesses. In 2014, Caesars Entertainment introduced "Local Perks" at all four of their properties as part of their Total Rewards program. Customers have the option of using their comps at shops at the Walk, local restaurants, and even a nearby grocery store. The idea is to bring in customers from the surrounding suburban and exurban communities, especially on weeknights. One local restaurant owner who participated in the rewards program praised the strategy, noting, "Now that times are tough, you have to look in your back yard."[34] Even Borgata offered weeknight discounts at their high-end restaurants, noting "We have some affluent customers locally."[35]

If you can't beat 'em, join 'em. Convenience gambling is undermining the usual emphasis of a tourism economy on bringing in money from other locations. As more people in surrounding states can gamble closer to home, Atlantic City's casinos are seeking survival by sucking in dollars from locals rather than outsiders. This scenario has implications beyond Atlantic City, raising questions about the viability of casinos as a local economic development strategy. As casinos proliferate, each locality is more and more likely to draw its customer base from a smaller and smaller geographic radius. In a telephone conversation we had with John, a Massachusetts activist who worked to oppose the establishment of casinos in Holyoke and Springfield, he shared concerns that casinos located a mere sixty miles apart would primarily draw upon a radius of only thirty miles. Rather than bringing money into any particular local economy, the fear among gambling opponents like John is that casinos will be likely to divert local consumer spending to the corporate coffers of the casinos—to then possibly be reinvested elsewhere, anywhere but the community.

When the Atlantic City Sands Casino was imploded on October 18, 2007, it was a figurative ending of an era in Atlantic City. It took just less than twenty seconds. Then it was dust. Gone with it were the entertainment venues that hosted Frank Sinatra, Sammy Davis Jr., and other members of the "Rat Pack." Gone, too, was the security of knowing that Atlantic City had an edge—a comparative advantage—in gambling. One strategic response has been an upsurge in branding, especially marketing to younger and more prosperous customers or other niche markets. With assistance from the Casino Reinvestment Development Authority and state officials, Atlantic City is trying to rebrand itself, with efforts to draw visitors to leave the casinos for shopping, clubbing, dining—and even to spend time on the beach and famous Boardwalk. Some of these economic development strategies seem to be successful, especially the non-gaming ventures. In fact, the Division of Gaming Enforcement now tracks gross operating profit as their primary indicator of the industry's health rather than the more narrow gross gaming revenue.

But as every economics student knows, demand is only one half of Alfred Marshall's famous "scissors." Casino management has also pursued strategies to reduce costs on the supply side. While the specific strategies and approaches have varied across houses, owners, and management teams, the general trend has been a reduction in job security, hours, and benefits, especially for employees without union representation. As we will see in the upcoming chapters, even workers who loved their own jobs are increasingly wary of recommending the casinos as good places to work for the next generation. The promise of first-class jobs that would allow workers to support themselves and their families seems to be slipping through their fingers like sand. In the long run, cost cutting may restore profitability to the powerful owners. But without good jobs, we argue, this will not constitute an economic success story. The well-being of communities and the provisioning of its members is at risk.

KEN AND MARLENE'S STORY

The contrasts between Ken's and Marlene's stories say a great deal about how the work lives of Atlantic City's dealers have changed over time. Ken is a Day-Oner, meaning he started at one of the casinos when it first opened during the boom years. A white male from one of the suburban towns on the mainland near Atlantic City, being a dealer was always a full-time job with benefits for him, and he was able to work his way up into a supervisory position. Marlene, in contrast, is the daughter of Korean immigrants who started working as a dealer just before the recession hit in 2008. She and her husband both have part-time casino jobs; he has two of them and she has one in order make ends meet. Their casino jobs do not provide a sustainable livelihood.

Ken explains that he actually backed into his career in the gaming industry. Working for Caesars as a security guard while the casino was under construction in 1978 and 1979, he watched the old Howard Johnson's hotel site being completely renovated and reconstructed from his security post. Fresh out of college, he daydreamed about a placement with the Federal Bureau of Investigation (FBI). For the FBI, he was told he needed two years' work experience in a law enforcement agency first. He had an idea. With his baccalaureate degree in hand, he was eligible for a job with the Casino Control Commission (CCC), and the CCC counted as law enforcement. This would be his stepping-stone to the FBI, he thought. Sitting at the dining table of a mutual friend, he describes a lengthy written application and a series of interviews as if it were yesterday. Then Ken was suddenly informed that he could not be hired because of a conflict of interest. What?! "Oh, I was quite irked," he affirms as he recalls the story. It turned out that there had to be a two-year lapse between what was termed a casino job at Caesars and a civil service position at the CCC, even though he was only doing security on a construction site. "It was a new business, and nobody really new all the rules and regulations. . . . If I had [known], I wouldn't have taken the casino job."

After a year on the job in security, Ken took the sergeant's exam and passed it, but he was passed over for promotion. And he was bored. He spoke with his buddy, Eddie, who was on the job with him at Caesars, saying, "We've got to get out of here because this isn't going nowhere." Some of his friends had started working as dealers at Resorts when it opened the previous year. For $1,100 each at the time, Ken and Eddie decided to attend gaming school for thirteen weeks and apply for a craps license. School was a breeze for Ken. He tried for an in-house transfer to deal within Caesars but actually landed a job at an even newer casino in town, Claridge. Thirty-plus years later, Ken is still there, but now he is managing gaming pits in a dual rate position. During his tenure, Claridge was bought by Bally's, became part of Caesars Entertainment, and then Caesars was bought by Harrah's, which changed its corporate name to Caesars again. Riding through the changes, he was promoted, got married, had children, divorced his first wife, shared child custody, remarried, and sent children off to college. Three decades of working weekends, holidays, and unsocial hours has taken its toll on normal family life.

Ken remembers $4.50 per hour in base pay and about $8.00 per hour in tokes as a good wage in 1981. "You could survive on that." Now it is much harder to live on dealer pay. According to the Bureau of Labor Statistics inflation calculator, $12.50 in 1981 would be equivalent to $32 in 2013. At less than $30 per hour with tokes, dealer pay—even for full-timers with seniority—has not kept pace with inflation, as measured by the Consumer Price Index (CPI), especially for new hires. That's why Ken decided to go for promotion to floorperson, the next rung on the career ladder. A decade later, he would be promoted again to dual rate pit manager, the position he still holds today. Ken's typical work day is spent roaming among different tables and different games, with the number of tables and games he is required to supervise creeping upward over the years.

The industry has changed during Ken's tenure. Take the demographics of the labor force, for one. When he started, Ken frankly observes, it was a "majority white industry." Now it is one of the most diverse labor markets within the United States. First blacks and Latinos/Latinas were hired. Then came workers from India. Then the rest of the Pacific Rim: Vietnamese, Thai, Cambodians, Koreans, and Chinese. There are dozens of languages spoken by casino workers. Ken expands on this, "So, when you are trying to deal with these people on a supervisor level, sometimes I had to get an interpreter to explain how to do something or explain what they are supposed to do because of the language barrier. And previously, when the business started, it wasn't that way." The casinos have responded by providing some customer service training and English as a Second Language (ESL) courses on site or through local colleges and institutes.

The workforce has changed markedly in other ways, too. "The full-time staff is shrinking," Ken explains, "and it's part-time that's increasing because they don't have to pay the benefits. So a lot of the—we have part-time dealers, we have seasonal dealers, we have part-time supervisors that only work two days. They pay them a little higher rate, but they pay them no benefits at all." Benefits were cut for full-timers as well. Anything that could possibly be trimmed to pare costs was cut. Ken speculates that such actions by top management helped usher in an environment that was more hospitable for union organizing. And, in fact, dealers at his casino voted in favor of representation by the United Automobile Workers (UAW) in 2007.

Workplaces have their office politics as well. Casinos are no different and may even be worse. As Ken tells it, "Politics in the casino business is horrendous. It's based basically if you're in a clique or you're not in a clique. You could be the best employee, but if so-and-so in charge doesn't like you, you will go nowhere." The drinking and sexual (mis)behavior tolerated among gamblers on the casino floor also seems to be leaching into the professional workplace. Women employees, in particular, would be urged to play along and sleep their way up the career ladder. Annual employment evaluations are based upon his job performance and his extracurricular activities: "'Do you do anything more for the company, or do you just do what you have to do?'" Managers are expected to volunteer off the clock in their communities, like working in a soup kitchen or on a community service project. They are also expected to staff casino-sponsored events such as blood drives. He begrudges doing community service in order to polish the company's image.

If they are called away inside the casino to attend mandatory training, that's on the clock and they are paid for that. Ken welcomes being tapped out for assignments such as staff training away from the casino floor. One time, he was asked to help test fellow supervisors. Coworkers get jealous of these "cake jobs." Naturally, they would, Ken admits: "You know, because I didn't have to deal with the public, which sometimes, you know, it's a nice break being so long working with the public that the last thing I want to do is see anybody. Because you've heard every story, you've seen everything—well, I can't say because there's always a surprise. You've seen some bizarre things that it's just like sometimes it's entertaining and sometimes it's just so frustrating." Like the second-hand smoke blown in your face, or customers, he says, who don't take restroom breaks when they're in the middle of gambling. A maintenance worker will ultimately have to come and replace the gaming chair/seat when this happens. He adds that the craps tables have a thin ledge just under the top surface, and guys have actually urinated into the ledge because they won't leave a hot table. People can forget about normal rules of decorum when they are hooked on the gaming tables.

Even a medical emergency won't stop some gamblers, Ken vented: "I saw somebody die on the casino floor, and he was a shift manager. He was also a friend of mine. And patrons around were acting—they still wanted to play on the games next to him while the EMTs were working on him, trying to get—he had a heart attack—trying to get his heart started. So people were looking by, and they're like, 'Oh, I can't play that slot machine?' Or, 'I can't play on this table?' And you're like—it's just like, you're sitting there staring, and it's like gambling never stops. It's like if we have a fire alarm, you have to pry these people out with a crowbar to get them out. And I'm just sitting there wondering, 'How sick are these people that they're just so focused on gambling that they lose sight of reality?' There was like no humanity, I guess you want to call it." Ken adds, "This is really such a really sick business. This is how I get my paycheck? This is what I'm into? This is my livelihood?"

Marlene is part of the immigrant wave that Ken describes moving into dealing over the past few decades. These new employees often do not have the same opportunities as the first wave of workers. Today's employees on the casino floor are increasingly part-time or seasonal employees. Marlene, a thin, serious young woman with long black hair, has spent three years on the job as a part-time dealer. She went to dealer school to learn the games and started dealing when she was twenty-one years of age. Marlene's mother, Joy, gambles regularly in Atlantic City. Joy pushed her daughter into dealing to earn decent money that she could apply toward a college education. The family is from South Korea, with a mix of Chinese ethnicity. Gambling was entertainment. Education was essential. So Marlene works ten to fifteen hours a week on a grave shift at the Trump Taj Mahal, and attends college in the daytime, squeezing in naps and homework as much as she can in the remaining daily hours.

Like other novice dealers, she started in blackjack. In her audition and interview, she also expressed an interest in dealing craps precisely because it was more difficult for women dealers to break into craps. Not only is Marlene ambitious, but she is a quick learner. Within a year, the casino moved her to baccarat. Marlene loves the pace of the work and the excitement of meeting new people—including her husband Chin, an older casino employee with about twenty years on the job. She chuckles, recalling sage words from her father: "My dad always used to tell me, if you were the manager at McDonald's, who are you going to marry? You're going to marry the manager at Burger King. And so, that's pretty much what happened." Marlene says that she and Chin are very happily married.

But, as with so many of the folks we interviewed, the patina of an exciting new job wore off after a while. Customers and hangers-on include pimps and prostitutes, not just her regulars looking for an evening's entertainment from time to time. Even some high rollers "seemed miserable even though they had hundreds of thousands of dollars." Marlene hated how one player in particular had two women on his arm. All three were playing with his bankroll, but he was grabbing at their assorted body parts and pulling their hair. And the customers who would win for the first time, say $1,000, and then "come back and come back and start losing and losing." She adds, "I would see them coming back with their wives, like this one guy I remember coming back with his wife and, you know, just started losing everything and it's, you know, there were a lot of times where I just want to be like, 'Get out of here!' you know, 'Go and run, take your money and run! It's not, you are not going to hold on to [luck and money]. It's not going to stay with you.'"

Both Marlene and Chin witnessed the severe cost cutting in the 2000s and especially after the 2008 financial crisis. She mentions her employer being fined after a card-shuffling scandal, when the decks of supposedly pre-shuffled cards turned out not to be shuffled at all: "I think a year and a half ago or something like a new manager came and all he was worried about pleasing the, you know, and just having—he was just worried about how much everything costs. He cut back on everything. Everybody hated him. Even with the bac [baccarat] game, you are supposed to shuffle the cards, like washing them. He got rid of that because he said it took minutes away from dealing and so, you know, we all believed that that's one of the reasons that happened." Her base pay is frozen.

Luckily for Marlene, she is pursuing higher education. If the dealing job were full-time with good pay, circa $40,000–$50,000 per year, "good work for a provider," she would recommend dealing as a career. She recognizes that those jobs are hard to find. When we met with her, she was concentrating on finishing up the last two courses to complete her undergraduate degree. And then she stopped dealing when she had a newborn baby. No more second-hand smoke. Her husband, Chin, still holds two thirty-hour-per-week jobs to support the family. That's sixty hours in total. She wishes he could work one forty-hour-a-week job instead. While Chin and Ken seem to be stuck, Marlene is working on moving into real estate and looking into teaching as an alternative to going back to the casino. She is still cobbling together part-time employment, but now it is outside the casino economy.

4

DEALING WITH CHANGE

In the olden days of casino gaming in the city, the message to employees was simple: For the customers to have a good time, you need to have a good time, too. The customers were taken care of by the casino hosts and other frontline casino employees. The frontline employees were taken care of by the shift managers and casino managers, guided by the managerial philosophy of the casino owners and presidents, like Steve Wynn at the Golden Nugget. SueBee remembers getting ready to open up the Golden Nugget. "I will never forget going to a meeting, a general meeting, all of the dealers, everyone, before we opened and Steve Wynn got up on the stage and told us how proud he was of us and told us that he wanted us to go out and have a good time. Just go have a good time. Don't worry about anything. There's nothing you can't do that we can't fix. So don't worry about it. You go out and have a good time. You let people know you are having a good time and you enjoy their company as well." It was a party. Management wanted a party atmosphere.

In fact, Wynn built employee morale by throwing regular parties for employees, parties that lasted twenty-four hours, through three work shifts. "We would have a Christmas party every year and I just cannot imagine the money he must have spent on that," Sue Bee said. "There were Christmas parties. There were Halloween parties. I'm trying to remember what other occasions there were, but maybe he just called them holiday parties. But I remember shrimp bigger than my hands! And when the bowl was getting low, they would just put more in it. I have never experienced anything like that. I had never experienced that kind of abundance for an employee. There were prizes. At the time, I remember the first few parties, everything was open bar, and you are talking about a lot of people in every department—maybe 3,000 people and their spouses, their significant others. It was pretty amazing and this was a party that went on because of the nature of the business; it went on for twenty to twenty-four hours. It was pretty amazing to watch. I won a color TV once at one of our Halloween parties; I never owned a color TV!" Steve Wynn would ensure that he spent some time at the parties, at least once per shift, so that he could mingle and his employees could see him face to face, up close and personal.

SueBee put in almost thirty years working her way up the ladder on the casino floor. After Steve Wynn sold the Nugget property to Bally's Entertainment Corporation in 1987 and it was renamed Bally's Grand Casino Hotel, the job gradually turned out to be far less fun and far more nerve-wracking. The casino was becoming so corporate. Working weekends and holidays had become grueling—too many birthdays, graduations, funerals, picnics, and family events missed. Sex, drugs, alcohol, and offensive customers had taken their toll. Allergies, coughs, colds, lung problems—watching a friend die from COPD (Chronic Obstructive Pulmonary Disease). The hopes for the city of Atlantic City went unfulfilled, she said. When management was cutting staff and offered a $60,000 severance payment in cash, she walked away. After almost thirty years, she just walked away.

Like SueBee, many casino employees we met now have a love-hate relationship with their jobs. But when the longtime employees talk about the old days, they express more love than hate. Early on, the growing casinos enticed job applicants to jump in from other industries and join the party. Employees recruited their own relatives from near and far—from towns in Atlantic County to cities in Latin America and Asia—to join the "family business." With only about one in five Atlantic County adults possessing a college degree, the money was good for workers with a high school diploma or some college. That's what we heard over and over again. In the early days, it was a living wage. Think about comparable entry-level service jobs: fast food server, retail cashier, janitor, and home health aide. These jobs pay very low wages. For the first generation of dealers and other casino employees in Atlantic City, real income increased for many years, even in the face of declining real income for service sector workers throughout the state and the nation.

Now, second generation descendants of casino employees have been joined by new immigrants. After three decades of gaming, Atlantic City area residents no longer believe the rosy depictions of job opportunities offered by casino work. Business is down. Employment has been falling. With less business, dealer income has suffered due to a huge loss in tips. And the work process has sped up, as fewer employees are covering more and more gaming tables. Casinos are hiring fewer full-time dealers to avoid paying benefits at all; in fact, some casino houses are trying to replace their more senior, higher-paid, full-time dealers with part-timers. Several employees relayed frustration that long-established benefits were being taken away. Dealers, like workers in other industries, are paying a rising share of their health care costs. Contributions to retirement plans are declining. Penalties for taking sick days (based on a disciplinary point system) were increased. The rate of increase in annual raises has declined.

In what follows, we describe the working lives of dealers and their supervisors in the gaming pits. The employees we interviewed told us about the qualifications and hiring process for the jobs, opportunities for career mobility, daily job tasks and working conditions, compensation and benefits, and interactions with customers and coworkers. The unique aspects of dealing poker are covered separately. Then we turn to the maze of thousands of dinging and flashing slot machines and video poker machines that take up much of the casino floor and account for the majority of gaming revenue. Employees who tend to the machines are less visible than dealers, but no less important, despite their dwindling numbers. We highlight the impact of cost-cutting measures in transforming job quality for these employees.

The table games on the casino floor are staffed and run by a team of dealers and other licensed casino employees. The teamwork among competent coworkers is one of the best parts of the job for many. In addition, they get to meet people from all walks of life and from all over the globe. Each dealer's work is overseen by several layers of supervisors as well as the security staff who monitor the surveillance cameras. Until recently, teams of state regulators were also a visible presence, but their numbers have been cut drastically. While the dealers staff the front line, interacting with gamblers—taking bets and giving payouts—supervisors watch for problems and help customers with issues related to comps.

The jobs that comprise the typical career ladder on the casino floor are displayed in figure 4.1. Upon a successful audition, you start as a dealer. Progression was more streamlined in the earlier days of casino gaming, as there were fewer increments. You could get promoted directly to floorperson (or floor supervisor, as they are called in some casinos), an entry-level supervisor of table games. Once a floorperson, you gave up tips. As you moved up, you sometimes had to sacrifice income in hopes of upward career mobility.

Casinos invented "dual rate" positions as a hybrid job between job rungs. Job ladders now progress from dealer to dual rate floor, a position in which the employee is a part-time dealer and a part-time floorperson watching over the games. The term dual rate signifies different hourly pay for shifts dealing or on the floor. When dealing, you are eligible for tips. When "flooring," you are not. Your work week, or even

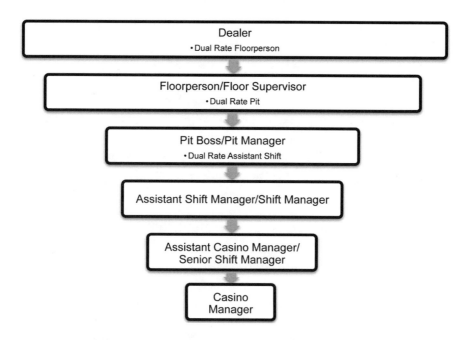

Figure 4.1.   Typical Career Ladder for the Casino Floor

work shift, can be split between dealing and flooring. Dual rate workers are included in the bargaining units; in other words, in a unionized workplace, theirs are union jobs. This arrangement enables the casino to try out a dealer's supervisory skills, and a dealer to try moving up without giving up tips completely.

The next rung on the ladder is pit boss, although once again it is possible to work as a dual rate pit, spending part of your week flooring. Pit bosses supervise entire gaming pits where dealers and floorpersons work at eight to ten tables each. Rating players for comps is also the responsibility of the pit boss, though the system is now more automated than it was when the casinos first opened. Consequently, some casinos have completely eliminated the pit boss position, removing a key rung in the career ladder and heaping more work on the floor supervisors. Looser regulations made this possible.

Each work shift on the gaming floor then has two or three shift managers and assistant shift managers, depending on the size of the casino. Shift managers are the ultimate arbiters of problems on the casino floor: alleged cheating, miscounts, misdeals of cards, and ejecting customers. The job titles above this level vary (vice president or director of this and that) and are held by upper-level managers. At some point in the hierarchy, management of gaming operations includes both table games and the slot machines/video poker. (Hotel operations are separate.) A 2003 study of twenty-four large casinos, including eleven in Atlantic City, found that women had much more difficulty breaking through the glass ceiling in gaming management positions than managerial jobs in hotel or food service operations.[1]

Forgoing tips makes sense only if you keep moving up. Some of the workers we interviewed moved up the ladder to dual rate pit boss or even higher, like Ken, SueBee, Patrice, and Robin. We spoke with other dealers who tried taking promotions to dual rate floorperson or full-time floorperson, but who then stepped back to dealing—not just for the money but to escape the stresses of lower-level management. Laurel, Caroline, and Isiah, for example, decided supervisory work was not for them. Graciela was a dual rate pit boss but returned to part-time floorperson in order to go back to college. Emil eschewed even trying to move up in the first place.

Being a supervisor is becoming more of a hassle. Casinos keep upping the number of tables that floorpersons supervise from two or three at a time to as many as six or eight; some employees even reported ten or twelve. Donna, a floorperson and former craps dealer, insisted that a supervisor can only accurately watch one craps table at a time. "Who can really watch what's going on at all of these tables?" was a common refrain. The unfortunate result, according to one manager we interviewed, is more mistakes and therefore more unhappy customers. The same manager admired the Borgata for not skimping on levels of supervision, and consequently earning higher ratings from customers.

To get a job dealing table games, the casino needs to have a job opening, and then you come in for an audition. A casino manager puts you into various games on the floor and watches you very closely, with another dealer or supervisor nearby. It can be nerve-wracking. "Don't be nervous" goes through your head. "Don't sweat." "Count the cash and chips correctly." You try not to shake, though your hands seem to fumble more than when you practiced at home. Experienced dealers are proud of the way they shuffle cards, spread the deck or decks for view, and reveal the cards. A lot of tension and excitement ensues as cards are revealed. It's called "squeezing the cards." Dealers try to make it fun. And the squeeze is as unique as the dealer, from a simple bend-turn or bend-flip to the more dazzling rubbing-and-rotating, or a pivoting motion. Here's Caroline, describing her baccarat deal: "I have a tendency to be very open with my players. Like when I'm dealing three cards [she rubbed her hands together to demonstrate the start], you know, I'll say 'don't look, see the ace?' and then I'll blow on my fingers. Nobody squeezes and spreads like me. And they get a kick out of it. I have to make them feel they want to be there." She contrasts herself with dealers who seem more like robots than artists. For her, it is an entertainment industry.

Training on specific casino games used to be a formal process that was paid for by the employee. Most of the dealers we interviewed went to dealer school, a six-to-eight-week program offered by a local private academy or, in earlier days, the local county (community) college. Craps is the most difficult game to learn. A craps dealer like Emil would take a twelve-week course (about 240 hours) to learn to deal the game. Regulations have loosened here as well, and now dealers simply have to audition in a game to demonstrate competency. They can learn how to deal from friends or family, or even through the Internet. Caroline compares then versus now: "I had to go [to school] for baccarat nine and a half weeks. [Now] I could go and teach you the game and you could just go and interview, do the audition, and get hired."

Here is what a full-time dealer signs up for: The work schedule is five days a week, forty hours a week. You are required to work weekends because that's when a casino is busiest. Every dealer normally works Saturdays and most holidays. Dealers with the highest seniority are able to pick Sundays as one of their days off, even though Sundays are busy, too. A senior dealer who wants two consecutive days off would choose Sunday and Monday. Dealers with less time on the job might have Tuesdays and Wednesdays off, or Monday and Tuesdays. This work schedule makes it difficult to balance work and family.

Atlantic City casinos are now open 24/7/365, 24 hours, 7 days a week, 365 days a year. An eight-hour day shift normally starts at 8:00 a.m. or later. Swing shift begins around 4:00 to 6:00 p.m., and almost every new dealer starts on swing. Grave shift can start from anywhere between midnight and 4:00 a.m. The dealers we spoke with who had accumulated the highest seniority or tenure tended to opt for the swing shift, the shift spanning midnight because of the action. The day shift on weekdays is least preferred because business is slower and time moves slowly when the gaming floor is quiet. Dealers prefer to work when the action is lively. However, we heard from several employees with children that they actually favored the day shift. Of course, this is a better option for frontline workers who do not rely on tips, or in casinos where tips are pooled across shifts.

One of the benefits of working on the casino floor is access to an employee cafeteria and one free meal per shift. Some dealers arrive an hour early for work to get their employee meal before the shift while others stay late to eat after work. Comments we heard from dealers ranged from how grateful they were for the meal to complaints about the poor quality of cafeteria food. Such complaints have accelerated in recent years.

When you are dealing in a gaming pit on the casino floor, you remain on the floor until your break. You are a performer. You are "on" for the duration, typically one hour dealing followed by a twenty-minute break. A dealer's hands must be completely visible to the customers and the security cameras at all times. Got an itch? Need to scratch your head? Did you sneeze? Need a tissue from your uniform apron? If so, then you must immediately open both hands wide, bring both hands together in a soft clapping motion, and show that they are empty to the eyes in the sky. It's called "clearing your hands." It has become such a habit for dealers to clear their hands that several do it even when they are not at work! Caroline laughed when she remembered, "I would set down my forks for a Thanksgiving dinner and then [clapping motion] clear my hands." Count my money out at the cash register, clear my hands. Receive change, clear my hands. Return a necklace I asked to see up close at a jewelry store, clear my hands. Light my cigarette, clear my hands. It becomes second nature.

Break times away from the gaming tables occur often compared with other frontline service jobs. After an hour, a dealer gets tapped on the shoulder by a relief dealer. It's called being "tapped out." As soon as practicable in a game, you must leave the gaming pit for a twenty-minute break. Even an urge to go to the bathroom needs to wait for a break. Employees risk disciplinary action if they use public restrooms at most casinos. Facilities for their use are provided in the back of the house, but it could be quite a walk. As discussed in the 1998 book, *Void Where Prohibited: Rest Breaks and the Right to Urinate on Company Time*, regulations that require employers to provide bathrooms do not necessarily mandate that they allow employees to use them.[2] The Occupational Safety and Health Administration (OSHA) has subsequently tightened regulations to assert a right to void based on health, but implementation is inconsistent.

Since the dealers we spoke with often have regular customers who may dislike when their dealer leaves the table, a dealer heading off for a break will have an exit line such as "Good luck; see you in twenty." Most dealers go to a break room, the employee cafeteria, or outside for a cigarette. Some may use break time to deliver one or two of their issued uniforms or blouses to the cleaning department, but most employees we spoke with prefer to wash their own uniforms. "If my uniform gets lost, then I have to take a substitute that may not fit me right," we were told often.

Pay is the main reward for working in an environment where you handle thousands of dollars in cash, smoking is permitted, security cameras watch every move, you deal with all kinds of customers, and you feel the wear and tear that comes with repetitive motion work of the hands and arms. Our respondents listed their base wages as approximately $5.00 to $10.00 per hour before tips. Note that entry-level dealers at the lower end do not earn the federal minimum wage as a base wage. At some casinos, dealers improve their base salary by learning more table games, but at others, the incentives for additional training are primarily to avoid boredom and to increase one's value to the employer. "You've got to have more games in order to hold your job," Caroline says. You learn those games on your own time, except maybe the carnival games, the newer niche games. Sometimes managers will have you tap out, go upstairs, and train in-house on these games such as Texas Hold 'Em, three-card poker, four-card poker, Let It Ride, Caribbean poker, Texas Shootout, and Mississippi Stud.

Tips, called "tokes," are pooled among the dealers. They are added to a dealer's weekly paycheck. All tips from players go into a clear, metallic-like box. Dealers must "tap the box" to indicate that a tip is being taken and recognized. A chip that constitutes a tip is received, the box is tapped, and then the chip goes in with a clinking sound. "Ting!" Even an insulting tip of fifty cents or $1.00 needs to go into the box. "Fifty cents. Thank you very much, sweetheart. Oh, I now get to bang my box," was a sarcastic comment uttered by Caroline during an evening shift. It is both an honor and a responsibility to be voted by your peers to serve on the toke committee. All of the boxes with tips are gathered by the committee, opened and spread out across a craps table, and carefully counted. A high "toke rate" for the week is cause for celebration.

In a typical week, the base pay with pooled tokes for an Atlantic City dealer might average $20–$25 per hour. Taking the midpoint of $22.50, for forty hours of work, that is $900 per week, or roughly $45,000 per year. On a good weekend at a busy casino, the dealers can average $40 or $50 in tokes per hour, bringing the annual salary closer to $50,000 or $60,000. Lately, competition from nearby states and a sluggish economy have decreased revenue, and the toke rate has dipped to below $20 per hour. But Borgata dealers have been holding steady at about $27 per hour or more in tokes alone, so full-time dealers at this top-grossing casino in town can earn $65,000–$68,000. Even some part-timers who hustle to get extra shifts are able to make this kind of money. Tips are generally pooled across all dealers for all work shifts during a week, except at the Borgata: Borgata's toke rate is not weekly, but daily. This encourages employees to work weekends for the money. A weekend day or days included in your paycheck boosts your income. Just recently, Caesars also changed its pooling policy from weekly tips to daily tips because too many dealers were calling out of work on Saturdays. They didn't want Saturday call outs to be free-riding on other dealers who did work their weekend shifts.

Because base wages are so low, tips are essential to providing a living wage for dealers. Defining a living wage is complex, but social scientists have calculated it based on the costs of running a household. The Center for Women's Welfare at the University of Washington developed a well-respected standard that provides estimates of the minimum income needed to support families in each of the United States.[3] We used *The 2011 New Jersey Self-Sufficiency Standard* (5th edition), a detailed analysis of monthly costs for over seventy family types in each county. The self-sufficiency standard for a single adult in Atlantic County, New Jersey, would be $21,987 per year. Assuming full-time work of forty hours a week, fifty weeks a year, the hourly wage equivalent is $11. You can see why a dealer job is a desirable option for someone with a high school degree. With tips, the job earns far greater than the state and federal minimum wage, and a more-than-adequate income for a single-person household. But what about, for example, a household with one adult and two school-age children? That self-sufficiency standard in 2011 would be $41,262, requiring an equivalent hourly wage of $20.63. A dealer supporting a three-person family on one income would just barely reach the self-sufficiency standard.[4]

Dealing poker is different from dealing the other table games like blackjack, baccarat, or pai gow poker. Poker players are not playing against the house. There are typically six to ten players at a table competing against each other for pots. A player pays the casino an entry fee for a seat at the table. Or, in lieu of collecting table rent, the casino might take a cut of the pot, called a "rake" or commission; it is usually 2 to 5 percent of the pot, enough to cover the dealer's base salary. Normally, poker dealers keep their own tips unless the individual casino has a pooled tip policy. And unlike other table games dealers, poker dealers do not stand throughout their shift; they sit at the table while dealing.

Poker got hot in the early twenty-first century, fueled by the rise of online poker games, televised tournaments, and pop culture depictions of cool, young poker players. National surveys from the American Gaming Association find that young adults prefer poker and craps more than older gamblers. A new generation of poker players broke the stereotype of working-class men in their undershirts, drinking beer while playing poker around the kitchen table. Once state gambling regulations were revised, Atlantic City responded to the growing popularity of poker by opening separate "brick and mortar" poker rooms. New Jersey casino visitors spent only $32.5 million on poker in 2002. Following the opening of Borgata in 2003, poker spending exploded to over $77 million in 2006.[5] That year, the Borgata went all in on poker and debuted the largest poker room in the city; they immediately captured a large share of the poker market. Other casinos have been dedicating more and more space to their poker rooms. By 2013, nine out of the twelve houses had poker rooms, according to Division of Gaming Enforcement monthly gross revenue reports. In 2014, the World Poker Tour (WPT) championship moved to the Borgata from the Bellagio in Las Vegas—a real coup for the Atlantic City casino.

Casino poker rooms have full- and part-time employees who deal poker exclusively. Those same dealers—or sometimes other table games dealers—can be called in to deal at poker tournaments. For Connie, who dealt blackjack before she got a job in security, dealing poker was a part-time gig at another casino in order to make extra money. "Novice poker dealers always start out doing tournaments, and that's where you got your experience. So, I actually dealt one tournament and I didn't like it. I didn't like it at all," said Connie. To her, poker (and craps) players are the rudest gamblers, the ones with the worst attitudes on the gaming floor. Her first poker tournament was also her last. But Lena spent years dealing in the poker room.

The pressure faced by poker dealers is to move the game or hustle the game, "how fast the deal ends and how many games you can get out there," Lena says. The faster the games, the more pots; the more pots, the more revenue for the casino and the more tips for the dealers. A good dealer can "push" forty or fifty poker hands per hour. With eighty-five poker tables at the Borgata, that equates to roughly 3,825 hands played per hour on a busy Friday night, or over 30,000 hands per eight-hour shift. Besides speed and speed-up, another pressure faced by poker dealers is the intensity of the deal and the play—to never make a mistake: "You make a mistake and they're not gonna let you get away from it. I mean, they are gonna eat you alive," Lena confides about the players. As Connie expressed earlier about poker players, they can be nasty—cursing, name-calling, throwing cards and drinks, and sometimes getting more physically abusive. The latter can mean a call for security.

So that poker players don't get too accustomed to a certain dealer, the dealers rotate among tables. As Lena puts it, "If I'm allowed to sit there for two hours, he'll crush the game because of the way I am shuffling. There's an order to it." Poker dealers also get tapped out for breaks, but not as regularly as blackjack dealers. When you're in the middle of a hand, you cannot leave the table. When the poker room is busy, you may get mandatory overtime. It makes it hard if, like Lena, you have a family, especially one that includes young children. She shares this: "So if we're busy and let's say I start at 10:00 in the morning and I'm counting to be home at 6:00 [p.m.], and I have a babysitter or I have to be home by 6:00, 6:30, and the room gets backed, I'm not leaving."

When business slowed after Pennsylvania opened its casinos, and then even more during the Great Recession and its aftermath, Lena lost a lot of income. The full-time dealers collaborated and cooperated, choosing to engage in a kind of work-sharing program, with each voluntarily reducing the number of hours in their shifts to five or six hours (with early outs) in order to preserve full-time jobs.[6] Also, overtime used to be calculated daily. As soon as you exceeded your eight hours, you received overtime pay. Now it is tallied weekly. A slow five-hour day with an early out and a busy eleven-hour day average to eight hours, with no overtime pay. Such employment flexibility, averaging hours over a longer period of time, favors management, not workers.

Significant square footage of a gaming floor is set aside for slot machines. That's where the money is. The maximum edge for the house, set by state regulation, is more favorable to the casino than table games. Sometimes the slots are "looser" than that. By 2012, Atlantic City had 26,883 gaming machines, second only to Nevada among commercial casinos in the United States.[7] Electronic gaming machines such as slots and video poker are the most popular with casino visitors, according to the American Gaming Association's annual reports. In Atlantic City, slot machine revenue overtook table games relatively early in the city's casino history and slots have stayed as the overwhelming number one ever since. In calendar year 2012, for example, slot machine win was 72 percent of total casino win.[8] Besides raking in money for the gaming halls, slot machine manufacturing is big business. A new commercial slot machine typically costs no less than $10,000. Companies are continuously trying to bring newer games to the consumer. New games require new or repurposed machines from the manufacturer.[9]

"Perhaps nothing has so profoundly impacted the nature of gaming operations in Atlantic City as much as technology innovation," writes Jane Bokunewicz, a hospitality professor with industry experience.[10] Especially slot machines. Once mechanical slot machines were called "one-armed bandits" for the black handle one would pull on the right-hand side of the machine after inserting coins into a hopper and hearing them drop; next came watching the wheels spin and praying for a win that would dispense by coins in a tray near the bottom. Customers collected the coins in large plastic cups featuring the casino's logo. The early machines didn't even require electricity.[11] Employees transported hundreds of thousands of dollars in coins to the "hard count room." According to Bokunewicz, "The weight of the trolleys that transported coin from the slot floor to the count room often caused the marble floors to crack and employees emptying the machines sometimes suffered back strain from lifting the heavy bags. The pouring of coin into the counting machines was very loud and employees had to wear ear protection to prevent hearing damage."[12]

Today's machines are electronic. Caesars was the first Atlantic City casino to experiment with coin-free slots in 2001, but the trend consolidated when the new Borgata casino opened in July 2003 as a completely coin-free casino. The shift to completely cashless slots is due to the utilization of ticket-in/ticket-out (TITO) technology. Instead of coins, players are provided a magnetic card (also used as a loyalty card) that is loaded up with a cash balance like a debit card. The card allows a "slot data system" to extract information about gamblers and their play. Slot machine payouts are now made through a bar-coded ticket that can be redeemed for cash or inserted back into the machine to continue play. Changes in computer technology and software have spurred the growth of multi-casino progressive jackpots through slot machines linked across casinos, raising possible payouts, thus attracting more betting. For the older Atlantic City casinos that had to modernize their slot machines, including the electrical and mechanical infrastructure required to run them, the process took four to five years. [13]

Despite some initial trepidation, the technological changes were welcomed by the casino customer. No one is saddled with carrying around all that coin. The advances have also facilitated the employer's financial accounting and marketing plans. The results for casino employees are more mixed. The entry-level job of change person—walking the floor and providing change—has disappeared. (Several of our older participants had started out providing change on the casino floor.) Fewer slot technicians/slot mechanics are needed to fix the machines, since the most common breakdown involved coins getting stuck.

Slot attendants still cover the slot areas to ensure all machines are properly functioning and still handle jackpots. While smaller payouts can be redeemed by feeding a winning ticket into a machine on the floor or going to the cashier's window, a big win means the slot attendant has to spring into action. The job duties now principally involve providing customer service. The pay hovers near $8.00 per hour, with tips that you can keep yourself—but not nearly as much in tips as dealers earn: maybe $50–$75 per week, not $20–$25 per hour. According to Valerie, a slot technician, you walk your assigned section the whole time you are on the floor, an eight-hour shift, with three breaks. You have to attend to the lights on the machine, write up jackpots, and answer numerous questions from customers, who can make the job difficult. "How do you play this new machine?" "What's a hot machine?" "Where's the ladies room?" Attendants call in the slot supervisor only if there is a problem they cannot handle, as when Valerie was twice assaulted by different customers. Standing and roaming around your slot machine zone really takes a toll on your hips, legs, and feet, says Valerie. "I had to go out on medical [leave] a couple of times because of problems with my feet. And they had no mercy as you came back: Boom! You're in the busy section. They wouldn't give you a section that was quite simple to work."

Terrence was drawn to the Atlantic City area because of the new gaming industry and has been fixing casino slot machines since 1980. "I am a professional problem solver," he insists, "I'm not just a technician." He has fixed each generation of machine, from the early mechanical reels to today's sophisticated electronic ones. With his years of seniority, this tall, proud, jazz-loving, and erudite man earns $25 per hour, about $1,000 per week for full-time, year-round work. With his earnings, he supports an ex-wife and, when they were younger, two children. Terrence, as described in chapter 1, first learned his trade by attending slot technician school for sixteen weeks. He maintains his competencies through on-the-job training, avid reading, and tinkering with fixing things around the house. He says he has "manual dexterity" and is relaxed around technology. Normally confined to the slot areas, once or twice this mechanically gifted technician has been called to the casino floor to try to fix a roulette wheel. Terrence elaborates about one incident: "The little electric eye that reads where the ball goes, and it flashes on the screen. That malfunctioned last night, because we had a thunderstorm. And there's some kind of circuit that protects these electronic instruments, and that circuit just had to be reset. And they were confused about it. They asked me to do it. I was confused about it, so I very calmly looked into it, and familiarized myself with the technology, and decided to relax enough to let my brain take over, to theorize what could be done to get these things to work. And they were all malfunctioning. And the customers were still playing roulette while I was trying to get the thing done. And everybody asked me—people asked me, 'What's it like being a slot technician?' Well, imagine you have a party in your house, and something breaks in your house. Like the stereo breaks, and all of a sudden the sounds goes, everybody's partying, and you have to go—while they're drinking and having hors d'oeuvres and partying, dancing, you have to go behind there with a flashlight and a soldering iron, and fix this thing while people are dancing and all this confusion is around you. It's very difficult. I would much rather work in an isolated laboratory, but that's the make of the casino business."

Maintaining the old machines that took coins was a lot of work, a "tremendous amount of manpower," Terrence said. Today's space-age machines are more like large laptop computers. They eliminate the need for a hard count team, a cashier who sells coins, and many attendants who have to attend to problems with the machines. Management tried to reduce the slot machine workforce through attrition, but it wasn't fast enough, Terrence recalls. Eventually they began to lay people off by seniority, or by disciplinary records: "[T]hey said they were downsizing. And the only thing they could do was look at people who had blemishes on their work record. These were not severe infractions. In fact, one fellow was Day One employee. He had been out a couple of times on medical leave. I think they held that against him. Another guy had took—went out on leave to help his ailing mother . . . and came back when she died." He was fired. The general manager at the time had to execute a target goal of only one slot technician per 100 slot machines.

The overwhelming majority of casino workers work on the front lines, providing direct services to customers. Work in the service sector is different from work in agriculture or manufacturing. Services have three characteristics: (1) they are intangible, (2) production and consumption of a service happen simultaneously, and (3) customers participate in the production process. A farmer may never meet the customer who eats his or her broccoli and an auto worker will probably never know who purchases the cars that roll off the assembly line. But gamblers and dealers interact in the process of creating the experience that casinos are selling.

Working with customers is both rewarding and challenging. Interactive service workers constitute an emotional proletariat, according to sociologists Cameron Lynne Macdonald and Carmen Sirianni.[14] Unlike the quintessential proletarians who assemble objects, service workers' products are their customers' experiences. On the job, they attempt to evoke particular emotions in their customers, but must control their own emotions in order to do this. The skill required to do both while focusing on the detailed activities that create the service is often invisible, difficult to measure, and poorly compensated.[15] Yet the ability to do it well is a source of pride.

Dealing is performance, like acting or stand-up comedy. But rather than being on stage, dealers are right there in the pits. Gamblers are as diverse as the employees who cater to them. Dealers appreciate the funny ones, the generous ones, the ones who treat them with respect. They often have regular customers, knowing them by face if not by name. Patrice made friends with many of her regulars and would make birthday cards to send them. Many days on the job are marked by routine interactions with friendly customers out to have a good time.

These customers know their limits and stick to them. But drunk gamblers are bothersome. If a player is slouching at the blackjack table, he or she can be "flagged" by the dealer and a pit boss will come to evaluate whether the customer can continue to play. How often does this happen? About twenty times a week, says Laurel.

When gamblers are losing a lot of money, however, they can get nasty. The worst offenders throw things, like drinks—dangerous if they are served in real glassware. Or spit at you. Dealers have been called swear words such as bitch and mother-f*%# and the offensive c-word used to denigrate women. The f-bomb gets tossed around the casino a lot. When Donna dealt craps, she found it particularly difficult for women. "Women do not belong at the craps table," one customer snapped at her. Dealers have to swallow their own emotions and concentrate on transforming the emotional state of their cranky customers using humor, sympathy, or a firm setting of boundaries, depending on the situation.

Caroline told us she tries to push the nastiness aside because the pit bosses and shift managers know and recognize how good she is at her job. The recognition and respect from management really makes a difference. "How long have you been doing this?" one new shift manager asked Caroline. A long time was the answer, over thirty years. "I wish all the dealers were like you," he continued, and then he asked the favor. "Listen, you gotta go deal to this guy. We're going to give you a $100 bonus. He's gonna call you every dirty name in the book. Would you mind?"

This particular high roller was escorted up the steps to a private gaming area behind a curtain. He bet four or five hands at $30,000 per hand. Caroline started shuffling and said, "Hi, sweetheart." He replied, "Ha, sweetheart! I might like this." She looked him dead in the face and added, "Excuse me, sir, the last time you left I had to go home and take a cold shower," and his reply was, "I'm really gonna like this." The player screamed while Caroline smiled. Caroline's story continues: "So, I finish shuffling. I go to put the cards in and he goes, 'Put the cut card in," and I go, 'Whoa, baby, you don't just slam it in there; you got to stick it in where it feels right.' Like I said, I gave him a little bit of his own. But I made it fun. . . . I am an entertainer. . . . The next time I dealt to him, he lost $1.7 million, kissed my hands, and told the shift manager, 'I had a good time.'" Emil, also a high-limit dealer, occasionally tapped out to head to a VIP room upstairs, and said gamblers there bet "obscene" amounts of money, like $100,000 or $150,000 a hand. As a man, however, he did not endure the same kind of sexual innuendo that Caroline had to deflect.

Dealers have traditionally worn a conservative uniform and sensible shoes that help them withstand the many hours on their feet. But Atlantic City casinos are now hiring "entertainment dealers," primarily women. Graciela relayed that "corporate," meaning management, is going for "a certain type of look . . . physical attractiveness." These new dealers are younger, sexier, and are noticeable in their distinct uniforms. The skirts are very short. The required bustiers, reminiscent of a modern-day Victorian corset, show a lot of cleavage. They flatten and shape a woman's midsection while lifting up the breasts. Entertainment dealers are required to dance while they deal. They can be pulled into work for conventions and areas of the gaming floor set aside as a "party pit" or at one of the new table games brought into the casino bars. They are part of the increased sexualization of the casino industry in Atlantic City, marketing women's bodies to attract customers, discussed in detail in chapter 5.

To a person, the dealers said the security cameras were there to help them, to protect them against practices like past-posting—that is, posting a bet in roulette after the wheel stops. Some players will try to cheat the house if they think they can get away with it. When a dealer thinks someone is cheating, they can "call the camera" (security) because every game is being digitally recorded in the security room. That's where Sean comes in, working swing shift in a job title called "surveillance operator." Like an air traffic controller, he surveys monitors. His casino has roughly thirty of them covering just the gaming floor, and he can zoom in with any of them to investigate incidents, including potential cheating.

A dealer develops excellent peripheral vision while on the job and pays special attention to the "outside bets," the ones at the edges of the table. Dealers also become attuned to who the hustlers are. Hustlers hang around close to gamblers looking for winners. They suggest bets to you. They say, "Hey, your cards are getting good." They start rooting for you. They'll eventually deliver the come-on: "You're winning because I'm here. How about giving me twenty bucks?" This practice is not legal, but it happens regularly.

Even though his primary job description involves tinkering with machines, Terrence is not immune to the problems of abusive customers. His job also requires emotional labor. He is aware that many regulars are addicted to the same machine. When it malfunctions, they get mad. When they lose money, they get mad—sometimes to a point well past the line of decency.

One story is burned into Terrence's memory. One very drunk customer once said to him, "You know [Terrence], you're the biggest [N-word] I ever seen, man." Coolly but clearly, Terrence replied: "'Sir'—in front of all these people, the place was crowded as hell—I said, 'Sir, listen, you didn't have to use the N-word like that.'" It didn't end there. Terrence continued the story. "I was very humble at that point. He says, he goes, 'No, I'm serious man, you're the biggest f*#&in' [N-word] I ever seen. C'mere. Look at this guy! Oh Jesus. You know [Terrence], you know, if your cock is as big as the rest of your body, you'd be a great f*#&. I'm dying.' By then, I started laughing. That was the rudest thing ever happened to me. I started laughing, I laughed so hard, I, please God, I walked out of the room laughing, I ran down the bathroom, I thought I was going to throw up." His mature response to us was, "I'm not going to blow a job, a thousand-dollar-a-week job, over one asshole."

And yes, he has heard the tales and seen the evidence of gamblers refusing to budge from a machine if they have to go to the bathroom. We heard such stories repeatedly. He adds that he has a sense of responsibility because he roams around his assigned zone with the keys to the machines, with customers pestering him about how to rig the machines. "Customers," he says, "when they see you have the key to a slot machine, their imaginations run wild. And if I had a dollar for every time someone asked me to fix the machine for them, I'd be richer than Oprah!"

Each casino has to weigh how desperate for business they are against the dignity of their employees. But a great deal of misbehavior is tolerated. Graciela, a dual rate pit manager, said of casinos as workplaces: "Rules are gone. I mean, because you're listening to customers cursing all the time. . . . Take it in and let it go." Isiah agreed, adding about the skills needed on the job, "Just be able to handle stress . . . we have regular abuse and, you know, be quiet. Don't talk back to the customers."

Creating a life requires the income and benefits that lead to decent living standards, but also time, good health, and institutional supports for family and community. The ill-effects of shift work and smoking have always been a downside of the industry. Casino workers have little control over the hours they work. The rigid schedules of casino shifts and the point penalties for call outs make it more challenging to balance paid work with family/personal responsibilities, whether that means getting to the doctor, picking up children, or caring for a sick or elderly family member. Holly, a Borgata dealer, is positively remorseful about all the hours not spent with her son during his formative years. She built up her seniority to switch to the day shift so that she could have a more normal life, better integrated with other workers, family, and friends: "Swing shift—I would sleep all day and work all night. So I really had no time. And I lost a lot of time with my son, a lot of time that I regret. The casinos, I thought it was all glitz and glamour years ago, but I can't ever get back that time I lost." It also makes it hard to sustain marriages or partnership when the two adults are like "passing ships," working opposite shifts so that someone can be home with the kids. When is their "together time"?

In the scholarly literature, odd shifts in around-the-clock staffing are called "nonstandard" or "unsocial" hours.[16] A 2007 survey of 700 front-line casino workers in Atlantic City found that 2–3 percent "almost always" or "often" had (schedule) issues sufficient enough to interfere with their job. Another 15–20 percent were "sometimes" affected by these pressures.[17] In the survey, child care was the key issue for casino employees aged thirty to forty-nine years. In our interviews, we definitely heard repeatedly from workers, especially women, about the challenges of nonstandard working hours, in particular coping with child care and elder care. So did Dena Wittmann, as reported in her book chapter titled "A Day in the Night of a Casino Worker."[18] Wittmann's Mississippi casino workers with the least seniority started on the unpopular shifts and then moved to "better" shifts over time, shifts that helped to alleviate child care challenges. But they still had to work weekends.

Quality child care is not very affordable in the United States. According to a recent report by Child Care Aware of America, the annual cost of child care for infants, for example, can be as much as the cost of college tuition.[19] To help juggle child care, employees on the gaming floor have sought help from their mothers, grandmothers, brothers, friends, and neighbors. They have worked with teachers and school principals to involve their children in after-school programs, where they are available. Children have been passed off from one parent to another between shifts, or from school to babysitters or to grandma or friends. Laurel took a late shift when her children were young so that her mother could watch them, as her mother worked daytimes. "My mother was my right arm," she confessed. Graciela's experience was similar. She moved in with her mom for several years while her children were very young. For Lena, it was a family friend who enabled her to deal poker while her children were young. Isiah and his wife are a two-dealer family. They both work swing shift so that he can go to college during the day while his wife takes care of their five children and manages all their activities. When they were younger, Isiah's mother would help out with child care. Marlene's mother-in-law suffered a stroke and required elder care, which she shared with her husband. It's hard juggling everything, she says.

Casinos are one of the last bastions for smokers. New Jersey's Smoke-free Air Act banned smoking in most public places as of April 15, 2006. But cigar bars, similar tobacco-related businesses, and Atlantic City gaming floors were exempted. Still unhappy (and unhealthy) casino workers lobbied the City Council of Atlantic City to consider a local ban to close the "casino floor loophole." City government did approve a ban on 75 percent of the casino floor in April of 2007 and subsequently a total ban in October of 2008. The casino industry and the State of New Jersey worried about a negative economic impact of a total ban. As a result, it was rolled back to a 75/25 percent rule, a compromise that allowed casinos to keep both smoking and nonsmoking sections of the casino floors and improve their ventilation systems in doing so.[20] Anyone visiting or working in a casino in town calls the segregation of smokers ineffectual. Second-hand smoke remains a severe occupational health hazard for employees on the floor. One nonsmoking floor supervisor, Vince Rennich (his real name), reached a $4.5 million settlement with Tropicana in 2010 after suing his employer when he got lung cancer.

Our dealers complained often about smoke being blown in their faces, sometimes on purpose. Terrence has a hacking cough he can't get rid of because of the smoke. So does Donna; she says, "I never had a cough. I coughed constantly in that casino." Graciela developed asthma after only a few years on the job: "it's getting worse because [I] have to rely on more medication more frequently." When Ally, a dealer, goes to the doctor, he listens to her lungs and checks her lung X-ray. Then he asks: "Do you smoke?" She answers no, it's second-hand smoke from the casino. Isiah's unceasing dry, irritated, and red eyes are not soothed by any eye drops. Felicia recalls smoking and nonsmoking sections in the employee cafeteria: "In smoking, you look at the ceiling tiles, they are completely brown." We listened to grumbles about the smoke from self-identified smokers and nonsmokers alike.

If it's not exposure to smoke that contributes to a dealer's health problems, it's repetitive motion injuries (hands, wrist, elbow, shoulder) and/or back and foot pain from spending so much time on your feet. Numerous dealers described nerve damage and pain from carpal tunnel syndrome and related disorders in such detail that we winced. They had endured surgeries or were postponing them as long as they could. Playing poker is fun at home, but imagine shuffling deck after deck after deck of cards for five full-time shifts per week. Dealing craps, especially being on the stick, requires repeated bending over, twisting, and turning during a shift, which is really hard on the back, as in Jesse's case.

Jesse told us his back endured so much wear and tear and strain from dealing craps that one night it just gave out: it snapped in the middle of his shift—one or two discs in the lumbar spine. After being helped off the casino floor, he had back surgery. He alleged that the casinos are not complying with the Americans with Disabilities Act of 1990, or at least do not appear to be embracing it. Although Jesse dealt blackjack for years, after surgery he was ordered right back to the craps table. "I felt that they were in violation with me because they tried to do nothing," Jesse complained. "Nothing to appease my job. As a matter of fact, when I got back, the first job they put me on was dealing craps. I went upstairs and raised hell. I said, 'How you gonna put me, my first day back from back surgery, on a craps table?' He said 'Well, [Jesse], you're supposed to be 100 percent.' I said 'Whatchu mean? I got cut on; I'm not gonna be 100 percent . . . just take me outta craps.'" So they did.

The impressions and ailments related to us by the Atlantic City employees we interviewed have been borne out by scholarly articles in the field of public health. One relevant, large study of casino workers in

London, England, finds that 91 percent of them self-reported sensory irritation symptoms: red or irritated eyes; runny nose, sneezing, or nose irritation; sore or scratchy throat. A startlingly high percentage, 84 percent, reported respiratory symptoms: wheezing or whistling in the chest; shortness of breath; usually cough first thing in the morning; cough at all during the rest of the day or night; bringing up phlegm.[21] The authors compare their results to previous studies of workers highly exposed to second-hand smoke. There is consistency among the findings. Though most previous research has focused on bar and restaurant workers, an earlier study of casino workers in Victoria, Australia, shows comparable self-reported respiratory symptoms.[22]

In chapter 1, we proposed that *A good job is one that helps you create a life and reinforces a positive sense of identity.* Are casinos providing good jobs on the gaming floor, especially in today's economic climate?

Changes in corporate ownership and management have altered the atmosphere in Atlantic City casinos. The employees we spoke with live with the results. Speed-up and work redesign. Wages and salaries frozen for years. Cost cutting—everything from wages and benefits to the selection and quality of food in the employee cafeteria. The general consensus was that management used to treat people better. Several employees noted that the customers, too, were getting less. Dealers and slot machine personnel are walking on eggshells. Rising fear of being reprimanded increased insecurity. No one wants to be the next employee shown the door.

The largest cost cuts have come from reductions in staff and the trend toward part-time, temporary, and contingent employment. It is less costly to have lower-paid part-time dealers than more senior full-time dealers. When senior dealers retire or leave, they are not replaced. We heard over and over that getting a full-time job dealing in Atlantic City "is impossible." Because his hours at one casino were lowered, Isiah deals at two casinos to try to reach forty hours per week. Other part-time dealers cobble together shifts at more than one casino, too. A disciplinary point system is used to monitor attendance and performance, and modified if a top manager thinks it can be tweaked to cut costs. If you leave work without authorization, for example, you will be

discharged without warning, regardless of your yearly point total. We
were initially shocked to learn that employees garner points when they
use their official paid sick days—more points if you give notice at the
last minute. And it is not just staff cuts that have plagued the Atlantic
City casinos, it is employee benefits cuts. Ken griped, "They cut the
benefits, they cut basically anything that would be to your benefit, and
that's why the union came in for the dealers, because we were just tired
of it." Contributions to employee 401(k) plans were reduced, and in
some cases the employer portion of the contribution was eliminated
altogether. Further, eligibility for health insurance no longer coincides
with employment. You have to wait, says Graciela: "Now they make it
more difficult for people to get insurance." Full-time workers have to
wait thirty days. "You are lucky to even have health benefits at all" was a
common theme from our interviews.

Even smaller expenses were cut, such as holiday pay, two personal
days, and payments for unused sick time. These cuts affected veteran
slot technician Terrence:

> I had a perfect attendance record. So as a result of that, I had all
> these unused sick time [days]. Now, they had a policy where they
> said, if you had any hours over eighty, which is basically two weeks,
> you could get—they would buy that back from you at the end of the
> year, and you would get that check around, sometime around Christ-
> mas time. And it was a check for about over a thousand dollars.
> That's like a week's pay. Well, what happened was, one year, about
> this same time of year, Human Resources sent out a memo, says,
> effective immediately, we will no longer give out the Wellness
> Checks; they called them Wellness Checks. Well, in my opinion, I
> said, well that sucks. Because why couldn't they have just said, "ef-
> fective January 1"—[we] are no longer issuing Wellness Checks. And
> that really messed me up. . . . That was about three years ago. I was
> saying, I was telling people, I said, you know, it reminds me of—of
> the story of the Christmas Carol, where you know, they look—
> they're sitting having Christmas dinner, they look over to the fire-
> place, there was poor Tiny Tim's little crutch sitting by the empty
> stool. I said, "Those rotten sons of bitches. Took my money."

Then, since employees were not rewarded for perfect attendance,
they started using their paid time off (by calling out). So management
changed the PTO system, increasing penalties for some call outs. Ter-

rence hypothesizes that changes in casino management (and owner-ship) at the top led to consultants sitting with the human resources department to change policies to save money. Valerie, a slot attendant, recalls having two weeks of paid vacation in earlier days, "which is unheard of these days." And you cannot complain, adds Felicia, a twen-ty-year veteran slot attendant: "I'll never forget it. No matter how good you were, if you complained or tried to, 'You don't like it, quit,'" em-ployees were told.

Many employee cafeterias have gone downhill, too. With employers pinching pennies, the quality and the variety of food have fallen victim. Sometimes it is seemingly the little things that can make a difference in employee morale, especially for employees who cannot go out to eat and must remain on the casino property. For dealers and slot employ-ees trapped inside the casino for eight hours at a time, the employee cafeteria matters. It matters a lot. Emil's alarm clock goes off in the middle of the night so he can report for a 4:00 a.m. grave shift start. He says: "When we come in, it's like, there's like hard boiled eggs and oatmeal because it's a breakfast time. And it doesn't change until like noon. So, I mean you have cold cereal, hard boiled eggs, oatmeal, ba-con; they have a guy at the grill that can make omelets and stuff like that, but it's like, you want real food sometimes, you know, especially if you've been up. . . . I mean, at the point where they took out the hot sauce, the honey, the raisins, like little things they would cut back on the little things. A lot of people don't notice but I did. And the recent last five years, they really got chintzy with all their stuff, their food, everything. Like A1 sauce. I know it's expensive but they took that away. That was like the first thing to go. Even like their Tabasco sauce, gone."

Replacing full-time dealers who had benefits with part-time dealers with no benefits, and cutting out benefits, means that the New Jersey casino referendum promise of good jobs and good wages is a broken one. A job dealing or working in the slot machine section of one of the city's casinos is no longer an automatic ticket to a middle-class liveli-hood. Management was not spared, either, but was pared. Emil told us that "they fired loads, probably hundreds of them because of their salary." Full-time floorpersons or supervisors were replaced with dual rates.

Robin, a casino manager, has a unique perspective from multiple sides of the industry. She has worked her way up the chain of command, holding many of the job titles of the other employees we interviewed on the gaming side of casino operations. She remembers blackjack school and roulette training like it was yesterday. And she uses her management and supervisory training and skills on a daily basis, carrying out the efficiencies and cost-cutting dictates of even higher-ups. Robin reminds us that being on the other side of the labor-management relationship is hard too. She has had to "trim staff," that is, lay off people. She has had to evaluate what pits and games are open and closed and when to make really tough calls. As a human being, this role takes its toll, though in a different way from being on the receiving end of it.

A job dealing table games, poker, or tending slot machines at an Atlantic City casino was once a ticket to a middle-class life. It is no longer. Once it was easier for an entry-level dealer to move up into management, even into top management. No longer. Once a casino job was highly sought because it was fun and because employees were treated well by local managers who knew their workers by name and roamed the casino floor often. No longer. Employees are holding on as best they can while the workforce has dwindled and their take-home pay and benefits have shrunk. As we will see in chapter 6, some employees are trying to fight back by union organizing.

A good job is also one that affords the worker a sense of dignity and purpose. These intrinsic rewards are hard to find when you are subjected to obnoxious customers and working in an industry that often profits from addiction. Not surprisingly, the few studies that focus on subjective measures of job satisfaction among casino employees in places like Las Vegas and Macau indicate low employee morale, a chronic problem for the industry.[23] From encouraging each other in the cafeteria to volunteer work-sharing to save jobs, the frontline employees still working in Atlantic City gaming houses—especially the full-time workers who have committed decades of their lives to serving the gambling public—are hanging on for just one more hand, in hopes of better days ahead.

INEZ AND LILY'S STORY

Inez and Lily both have personal drive fueled by an immigrant commitment to the American dream. But they are at very different places in the earnings structure of the casino. Part of the discrepancy is due to differences in their education and language skills. Some is due to family responsibilities. Some, however, is simply due to the physical assets they were born with. Lily can make more money because she has the looks to work nights serving cocktails in a skintight outfit, while Inez works behind the scenes on day shifts in steamy kitchens and banquet halls.

Inez immigrated to Los Angeles, California, from El Salvador in the 1990s, joining her parents who had paved the way a few years earlier. A young mother, she left one young child with her family back home and traveled pregnant with her second. She soon relocated to northern New Jersey and began paid work in a factory. Factory life, Inez says succinctly, is a "very difficult job and you don't [earn] a lot of money." Worried about supporting one child in her home country and one in the United States, Inez and her boyfriend decided to look for better-paying jobs in the growing casinos of southern New Jersey.

The couple settled in Atlantic City. With very little knowledge of English, she began paid work in the busy kitchens of the Taj Mahal. Inez started reading newspapers to learn and practice English. She studied the names of dishes and utensils. She observed what her co-workers were doing in their jobs. She was a good student. Her efforts were rewarded with a promotion to steward.

A steward works behind the scenes preparing for banquets and special parties. The tables, the plates, the flatware, and the serving bowls, platters, and utensils need to be clean and set. Basically, Inez helps ensure spit and polish of the room. A steward needs everything perfect for the servers so the special event seems to flow effortlessly. It is a more difficult job than it looks. Banquets are fast-paced, with multiple courses, cups, cocktails, and cares. The kitchen is very, very hot, and noisy—"we are sweating everywhere," Inez declares. Her seniority garners her the top wage for her job classification (porter/steward) in the Local 54 union contract. This means Inez earns almost twice the federal minimum wage, about $14 per hour. Still, supporting what are now four children in a high cost of living state such as New Jersey is hard. Hers is not a tipped position but earns a straight hourly wage. In terms of pay, a steward or porter is comparable to a line server, a cafeteria attendant, a food runner, a restaurant host or hostess, and many jobs in housekeeping.

Besides punching in for the day shift, the first thing that Inez does at work is "go to the kitchen and check the board if we have any other events, because this can change at any moment and they can ask for a party one day before." Then she sets out to prepare for the day's booking. It might start out with a coffee and tea service for a group. There could be a business luncheon or two in the book. She even needs to do the setup for the evening during her shift. Because of the surprise factor, Inez tries to do as much as she can in advance. Clean dishes need to be ready. Are there enough cups and saucers? Are we short of dessert plates? The flatware/silverware and glasses need to be spotless. The tablecloths need to be laid out and the napkins need folding. She says it is an unending, revolving door of dishes coming out, dishes being cleared, dishes being cleaned, and dishes coming out again: "We do not stop." On New Year's Eve, she would be responsible for setting up for a group of 4,000–5,000 guests. Dishes—bread, salad, appetizer, entrée, desserts—that's at least 20,000–25,000 dishes alone!

Inez conveys she handles the tasks by breaking down the room. Break the room into sections. Break the event into parts. Except for preplanning, don't get ahead of yourself. Often there are multiple rooms to take care of, each with a different service requested. The maximum number she would have to prepare and restock is four or five rooms at once. Gradually, Inez's supervisor, a food and beverage manager or banquet manager, gave her more and more responsibility. "Okay," he would say, "we have a party for twenty-five people, make sure you do this and that" and she would.

Her attention to detail, organization, and advance planning reveals a bit of a Type-A personality. The right way to do her job, she maintains, is to "attend to it like it is your house. And in your house you want everything organized, everything in the place where it has to be." And her meticulousness: "Sometimes they bring me something very dark and I can polish and make it shine and I love that." Her coworkers and supervisors have grown accustomed to this over the years. Inez even has a sense of humor about it, and the ribbing that comes with her personality. She confesses: "I am a stickler when I do something, like I say 'Don't touch my stuff.' If I have my stuff clean I don't want nobody [to] come and touch and damage my job." Obviously, Inez has no problems with the white gloves that are required as part of her uniform. The whiter, the better.

When she steps back and surveys a room after setup, Inez says she feels a bit like a builder or a decorator, excited about the product of the teamwork. She contrasted that to when she is in the kitchen, just the regular day-to-day grind of dealing with the potatoes or cleaning the dishes: "Washing the dishes the whole day is boring to me," she said. The repetitive process of loading the dirty dishes into a large machine and then unloading the steaming, hot, clean dishes at the other end is less satisfying.

Inez feels lucky to work the day shift, 8:00 a.m. to 4:00 p.m. She uses one thirty-minute break in the middle of her shift to go to the cafeteria, about a five-minute walk, and eat a swift meal while practicing her English with coworkers. With a large event, though, she needs to report at 5:00 a.m. When this occurs, management will either change her shift times or pay her overtime (extend her shift). As specified in her union contract, management will ask workers to stay longer or, if the overtime is mandatory, provide a two-hour notice beforehand. But stewards and servers know that when they see a large banquet booked on the schedule posted every Friday, this can mean a ten-hour shift instead of an eight-hour shift.

What's good about her day shift is how Inez can better sync her own work schedule to her children's school schedules. Plus, the banquet staff rarely works weekends. In her years in the casino, she gave birth to two more children, plus the two she had when she started are both with her now. Her boyfriend was not in the picture long, so she has been raising four kids as a single mother. "We live poor," she says, giving an example. One day she would cook a chicken and her family would eat only soup. She would save the meat for the next day. She wishes she could be paid more, adding "years ago I make an account: how much money I need for my rent, how much money I need for everything. One day I was bored and waiting for one event and I think and I sit down and take a piece of paper and I write down. I was behind $150.00 what I really need." We learn some of her costs and calculations (as of a few years ago) and we infer others. At the time, she earned about $480 a week gross. Take-home pay after mandatory deductions (e.g., Social Security and taxes) would be at best 75 percent of gross or $360. Rent for her tiny apartment was a bargain at $400 a month ($100 per week). Child care cost more than rent, fairly expensive, but Inez got lucky. She found one woman who charged her $50 per week for each of the three younger children that needed care, so that's $150 a week. Bus fare to and from work ran about $20 per week. Take-home pay minus rent, child care, and transportation left her only $90 per week for everything else—food, utilities, clothing, health care . . . and things for the kids?! There was no money for short-term savings, no money for retirement, and no money to remit back home to family in El Salvador. No wonder she was short.

Inez put it into perspective for us: "So I work for the babysitting and then for travel. I didn't have money, I didn't pay my rent on time. I was waiting for the tax refund to come and give some money for the land-lord. He was a good guy, he let me live over there. Every Monday he was waiting for me for the fifty dollar I have to give him. Because at that moment they pay us on Sundays, so Monday morning I have the fifty dollar for him. The rent was $400 dollars so I give the fifty dollar for him every Monday and I, you know, don't have no money." Each week, having the landlord wait outside your door to collect rent that is owed because you cannot pay it at the beginning of every month is frighten-ing. She was one step away from eviction and dangerously close to needing to borrow money from a loan shark. Inez said she did every-thing she could to make it work because she knew in two years she was due for a $2-per-hour raise. Meanwhile, she felt the pain and embar-rassment of being a full-time worker and not making ends meet.

Trying to balance work and family can be equally daunting for a single mother. Inez agrees that it really does take a village to raise a family. She draws upon paid help, family, and kinship networks, and feels blessed by the kindness of schoolteachers. And she often feels the classic mother's guilt, as in when she told her oldest child he has to become responsible. "I say, you're not allowed to come home during the day. You have to stay in school [laughing]. You're not allowed to get sick. . . . You're not allowed to have a trouble with the school because I don't have the time to take you at the mid-shift at school." School opens at 7:30 a.m., so she drops off the kids, then hurries to her 8:00 a.m. shift. After the school day is a real challenge for her. Inez encourages her children to stay after school for projects, clubs, anything that would keep them there and safe.

On several occasions, she was tag-teaming child care with her brother-in-law, who also works at the Taj. He was getting on shift at 4:00 p.m. and she was coming off shift at 4:00 p.m. Allowing for the requirements of reporting early to punch in, there were close calls. Lots of running: her running toward the children in the drive-up circle outside the casino while he was running away toward an employee entrance—almost like handing off the baton in a sprint relay race. Once there was a small time gap of five minutes, so he let the kids into the casino. Children under twenty-one years of age are not allowed in casinos. Security saw them immediately. Inez was afraid she was going to lose her job. She had to plead with the security boss and promise that it would be the only time. Again, she felt remorse. "I take my kids and went to the car and I start crying, as I crazy and my kids are looking at me. . . . And I was crying for a while in the car and then I said, 'Sorry guys, it's not your fault, it's my fault.' I'm supposed to give you a better life, but I didn't have the opportunity to give. So it was funny, now I can see that it was funny but in the moment [I felt guilty.]"

While Inez makes less than $500 per week, Lily makes $200 per shift in tips alone. That's what makes her feel good, as she has a dollar target in mind to save for her future—a college education, marriage, and a house. Costumed beverage servers such as Lily employed at the Borgata casino are referred to as "Borgata Babes." She had to audition for the job in the designated costume: short miniskirt, constrictive black halter top designed to reveal cleavage, nude stockings, and very high heels. Her slim and fit appearance, along with her strong cheekbones, dark eyes, and attractive face, seem to be what society deems desirable. She is equal parts Asian and European, differentiating her "look" from other young women her age. For her job interview, Lily pranced around carrying a tray with a bucket of ice, a bottle of champagne, and glasses, and smiled a lot. She recalls that if you got past round one of the audition, you were provided with a rather large packet with details about liquors—where the rums are distilled, the different grades of tequila, the grains used in the vodkas along with their taste and finish, etc. And you left a sample of your hair for drug testing. You returned the next day for a written test. This is where her skills as a college student came in handy. Lily proudly announced that she studied hard for that test, which she passed, and passed muster with the managers. She started serving free cocktails on the casino floor. The casinos ply their gamblers with liquor, and the cocktail servers are part of the entertainment package.

Lily punches her time card at least ten to fifteen minutes before her shift. Management expects that the extra time is needed to arrive and get upstairs. She is then on the clock for an hour in the dressing room, doing her hair, applying makeup, and putting on a uniform. Everything needs to look perfect. No runs in her stockings or panty hose. No pins in her hair, as it needs to be long, blow-dried, and flowing. Earrings, but not too large and not too small—never larger than a quarter. She then squeezes herself into a black-and-white dress, ever so petite. Her uniform size is 00 (double zero), smaller than a zero. It is like a nineteenth-century corset, so tight around her rib cage that she can barely breathe, and constructed with the most advanced push-up bra on the market to make her bust larger than her natural "A" cup. For Christmas, the top is a pink bra with rhinestones and a Santa Claus hat with glitter.

The clock in the dressing room shows 9:00 p.m. The Borgata Babes, as the cocktail servers are called, are lined up, military style. The "girls"—there are only a couple of male servers and they don't work every shift—are reviewed up and down by their manager. "Those earrings are too large. Looks cheap. Change them." "I see a run in your stocking." Unacceptable. Lily and her coworkers head out to the casino floor. There they will spend their shift taking orders, delivering drinks, and fending off leering customers.

Lily loves to tie her long hair back, but on the floor, the women must wear the hair loose. Cameras, the eyes in the sky, are everywhere.

Employees can be summoned and sent off the floor if their appearance isn't perfect. In the middle of calling out, "Beverages, cocktails, coffee," in her station, Lily was pulled off the floor when her hair was in a bun. Her manager said "That's not glamorous, we're supposed to be glamorous here." She adds another example: "One time [the manager] . . . went up to security and saw a run in [a Babe's] stockings though one of the cameras. She called [the Babe] into the bar and said, 'You need to get new stockings. You have a run in your stockings.' Psychologically, that's just like—you feel like eyes are always on you." A new pair of stockings is not part of the uniform provided by the casino. The cost is borne by the employee (a nice pair is $6–$8), who must always have extras in her locker.

The Babes' appearances are continuously monitored. So is their weight. Babes cannot eat while on the floor. They have been disciplined for nibbling at the bar; even one olive is verboten. Lily shared a rumor that circulated among cocktail waitresses, that Borgata president Bob Boughner had said, "I don't want my waitresses looking like the rest of the fat cows in Atlantic City."

Lily understood her job as a sex object. She had even taken some women's studies classes at a local college. But she took the job because she needed income quickly. One night, she had a row with her religiously conservative parents and by the next morning she left to set up a new home with her boyfriend. Borgata Babes earn generous tips, over and above a base wage of around $5 per hour. The pay is excellent for a young high school graduate trying to pay for college and buy a home. Borgata Babes who were chosen for the casino's annual Babe calendar could make extra money, $150. That's pocket change compared to the casino's revenue earned from a popular $10 calendar that flew off the shelves.

To survive, she endured a "truly degrading" job, as she calls it. "There was a time when I really felt like—I had always done very well in school, I always thought good about myself when I was in school, that I was capable of doing things. Working there, I came to a point where I just felt like I couldn't go back. I felt so bad about myself. I felt like that was the only thing I was capable of doing. It's so strange coming from me because I always felt capable. It does something to you that, you know, like Kafka's *Metamorphosis*, you start to see yourself become. . . . It's just like that. You criticize it and then you become it. And that's the worst part. The looks—it's constant sexual harassment, constant, constant—by employees, by everyone. You walk into the room and all the employees just look and stare you up and down. You bend over to get something and you turn around and you see three pit bosses just checking you out. It's so disgusting after a while. It just feels disgusting. Not only that, but to be told—for example one of my managers wanted me to stand up, and said, 'Come on, this is not brain surgery. It's just cocktail waitressing.' They just don't look at you like a human being. As much as they hate to be looked at themselves—because they have bosses too—they look at you the same way. You're a number. This is all you're capable of doing. They won't even talk to you like real human beings." The undermining of her own sense of herself was what bothered her the most.

There is no bargaining about your hours. Her shifts are seven hours long, with five and one-half hours spent on the floor. There is no complaining about being "mandatoried," that is, assigned mandatory overtime, even if you need to get home to a sick child. There is little sensitivity to an early out if you feel sick on your shift. If you go to see the casino nurse for any reason, you will be drug tested. Lily remembers, "I went into the bathroom and I heard her [a coworker] in the next stall crying—it was some kind of stomach problem. I said, '[Gina], are you okay?' She said, 'I'm in pain.' The way she said it, it brings tears to my eyes right now when I say it now. You just want to scream. You want to say, 'My God, we are human beings. We are people.' But you are made to feel threatened that there are 'ten million girls' who want to replace you."

Because paid work is so enmeshed with peoples' identities, it is not surprising that being a Borgata Babe follows you into your home life and your dreams at night. According to Lily, it's obsessive: "I never leave that place. And that's why I really want to quit. It's not a job you leave when you go home. When you feel that's all you can do. When you feel degraded the whole day it follows you home. You feel like you're low the entire day. You feel you belong to the Borgata. It's not that you go to work. It's 'you go home.' You know what I'm saying? It's a reversal. You feel like the casino's doing you a favor by allowing you to go home. That's what you feel like. It's so strange when you think that I'm only there for five and a half hours, working for five and a half hours. It follows me on my days off. It's things that people say or people do, or the way customers need things—it follows you home."

Who has the better job? The worker who earns more money but experiences a constant assault on her dignity as she is continuously sexualized? Or the worker who takes pride in the small details of her job but is ground down by worries about paying the bills and caring for her children? Hard to say. They are just two single women trying to keep themselves afloat in a society that doesn't seem to value their hidden skills.

5

THE SQUEEZE ON SERVICE

Many of the frontline service jobs in the casinos have no direct connection with gambling. Working in a casino hotel or restaurant involves many of the same duties as working in regular hotels and restaurants. You check in the guests, make the beds, set and clear the tables, recite menus, take orders, serve the food, mix drinks, and schmooze the customers. With one big difference. Your customers are probably losing money. Most of them expect it and handle it gracefully. Many of them are happy with the comps that you help provide—free drinks, free meals, free shows, free rooms. But not everyone.

Nora, a customer loyalty representative, was hired right after college in a frontline service position at the Borgata. She earned about $11 per hour standing behind the tall customer service desk for an entire shift. The busiest days were when the casino was running special promotions, like giving out prizes, occasionally dearer ones such as Vespa scooters and cars. Attracted to the position because of an interest in marketing, she soon learned that she faced a dead-end career ladder. She was stuck at the desk, signing up new customers, checking points, and explaining promotions and the rewards structure. It was hard to stay on her feet all day. "It was tiring. I mean your legs definitely get sore and cramped but yeah, you have to stand." Sometimes reps would take their shoes off under the desk, but would quickly put them back on again when the supervisor was near. Because they were gambling away their money, customers expected things in return. "Some of them were very nice and some of them were, you know, awful; they would throw their [loyalty] cards at you if they didn't agree with it and you just basically had to stay behind your desk and apologize and stand your own and you couldn't move and you just had to deal with it." She decided to move on, getting a job in a medical office.

Heather, a married suburban mother with a no-nonsense demeanor, has worked in a casual restaurant in one of the Trump properties for over twenty years. Her work record is spotless, and she enjoys many of her regular customers. When she came back from sick leave, some of them hugged her saying "We missed you!" and "You can't leave again!" They ask her about her kids. One customer, though, accused her of ignoring him for fifteen minutes, even though the time stamp on his check disproved it. He told her supervisor, "Well, yeah, I lost all this Goddamned money! I don't want this bitch waiting on me." Heather refused to put up with the name-calling and asked her supervisor to let someone else serve him. But he got increasingly unruly and they had to call security to remove him.

Walter, a studious-looking waiter who works swing shift in a family-style restaurant, views such customers as a challenge. His job, as he sees it, is to try to make them feel better. Walter told us, "People that lose a lot of money, when they leave me, they are happy and that's no small talent." Still, he finds the chronic gamblers who reappear at his station during swing shift depressing: "I recognize when people have a gambling problem. I mean, this is the third day that I've fed you this week and you're here with a thirty-dollar comp. . . . I look at your clothes and I size you up and I know what you're talking about and I kind of know a little bit about you now. And I'm going, 'Why are you here?' And so I've been able to, um, effectively intervene with people that are going down a dangerous path. I mean, I see people start with the thirty-, fifty-dollar comps and then a couple months later it's twenty, then it's ten, then it's five and I realize that they've cashed out their house. And that they ruined their kids' education. But all this time I've been a 'family member,' feeding them every day or every couple days. And I've been able to yell at people and tell them to go home. 'I fed you yesterday! I went home and went to bed and came back to work today and you're still here, you haven't left. You've gambled all night!' And I can call someone on that because I'm a family member now; I'm their waiter. And I've been able to, you know, get them to leave. Maybe not long term . . . but I made them leave one time and I feel good about that. . . . He's giving me a big tip for a meal that he's being comped and he's a good—he put stuff in my wallet. He's a good customer but I don't really need his $5. I need him to go home."

Guest room attendants (housekeepers), though, see some of gambling's worst effects in the relatively private spaces of individual hotel rooms. Manuela told us that the customers who were not regular gamblers were the most troubled: "When they get used to come every week, the player know[s] that they gonna sometime win and sometime lose. The only thing that they say is, 'I'm sorry; I don't have tip for you because I lost everything this week.' But when the people are not used to gambling and they come with expectation that they are going to make money and they lost everything. . . . I got this Cuban guy—he lost everything, even his house. And I found him on the sixteenth floor trying to jump [in the indoor atrium]. . . . He was in his underwear. . . . He wanted to jump. If we didn't get there, maybe he jump."

Manuela has over two decades of experience cleaning rooms in the casinos to support her family. So she had seen other sad stories where she did not arrive in time. Succinctly put, "But we always find people in the room"—meaning dead bodies. The deaths are usually not suicides, she said, just elderly people who drank more than their bodies could withstand. One patron, shortly before our interview, was dead in the room for three days because he had put up a "DND" or Do Not Disturb sign on his door. Usually, it wouldn't take so long because "when we see that one room is closed and nobody is coming out of it the whole day, we call the supervisor and say that in that room I did not see any action." In this case, however, no one noticed until the smell started seeping from the under the door. Finding bodies, people having sex, or evidence of drug use happens often enough to affect how Manuela feels about her work. She claimed that "The worst, I think the worst job in the casino is housekeeping because every time that you open one of those rooms you do not know what you are going to find."

Of course, on the whole, the day-to-day experiences of these non-gaming frontline service workers in the casinos are less dramatic. The employees we spoke with appreciate their jobs, their coworkers, and many of their customers. But like their colleagues in the gaming pits and tending the slot machines, their work lives have been impacted by changes in the industry—and not for the better. The corporate strategies to attract new demographics and to trim budgets discussed in previous chapters have reshaped what they do and how they do it. Most importantly, their relationships with management, their feelings about how they are treated, and their job security have diminished. Since many service workers are union members (unlike the dealers), they rely more and more on seniority rules to protect them from efforts to replace them with cheaper labor. The dynamics of these changes play out differently for various types of jobs; we can only cover a few representative positions here. We look at cocktail servers, food service workers, and guest room attendants. To set the context, however, we start with the question of who works in these various jobs.

While dealer jobs are relatively integrated, frontline service jobs in casino hotels and restaurants tend to be stratified by race, ethnicity, nationality, and gender. These employment patterns did not originate in the casinos; they have a long history in the service sector. Many service jobs are rooted in the kinds of tasks that women traditionally did as unpaid household labor. Gradually, this housework has been commodified, that is, it has become something the middle class pays others to do instead of doing it themselves. From the late nineteenth century to the early twentieth century, U.S. middle-class households started to emulate the practice of the wealthy in paying for servants and other domestic workers. The location did not change, but who did the work evolved. Who was available varied regionally as waves of immigrants settled in different locations, but the general pattern was that women of European descent left domestic service and the work became associated with African American women, Latinas, and other minority women.[1]

In the late twentieth century, the next phase of commodification took place. Paid domestic labor left the home and became the basis for the expansion of service sector businesses like fast food, child care, nursing homes, and home cleaning services. Because this work was thought of as "women's work," new opportunities arose for women in the labor force. Middle-class mothers increased their labor force participation and attachment. At the same time, these busy working mothers expanded the market for the services that employ women. But the historical legacy of domestic service continued to shape employment patterns, according to sociologist Evelyn Nakano Glenn. White women (and sometimes men) tend to be favored in the frontline jobs. In contrast, Glenn found that "Racial-ethnic women are employed to do the heavy, dirty, 'back-room' chores of cooking and serving food in restaurants and cafeterias [and] cleaning rooms in hotels and office buildings."[2]

Despite progress in occupational integration, these patterns have largely continued into the twenty-first century. In a 2013 book, *Behind the Kitchen Door*, Restaurant Opportunities Center United founder Saru Jayaraman observed: "Again and again, I saw the pattern. Even when the front of the house was a little more diverse, the workers in the back were almost always darker than the workers in the front." Of course, the higher-status, managerial and professional positions in kitchens, such as chefs and butchers, are often the terrain of white men. Later she added, "People are segregated in the restaurant industry by position within the restaurant (server, busser, dishwasher), segment of restaurant industry (fine-dining, family-style, or fast-food), and location (poor, middle-class, or upper-class neighborhood)."[3] African American men have the most difficulty breaking into frontline service jobs, according to a study by Philip Moss and Chris Tilly.[4] Beyond individual bias, they may face institutional barriers like policies requiring workers to be clean-shaven. Since African American men with curly hair are far more likely to have a condition called pseudofolliculitis barbae that makes it difficult to shave, such policies have been considered discriminatory in their impact.[5]

Similarly, hotels, as a "home away from home," mirror traditional gender roles in how work is allocated, according to Amel Adib and Yvonne Guerrier. Men are concentrated in management, craft, and semi-skilled positions, but women serve the guests. Ethnic minority and immigrant women wind up with the dirty work, while lighter-skinned women are in jobs where they need to be "friendly, helpful and sexually attractive."[6] Adib and Guerrier found that workers know which hotel job categories are considered appropriate and inappropriate for people like them, and what this means in terms of the expectations for their behavior and persona on the job.

We do not have formal data on the employment patterns in the casinos, but our interviews indicate that the findings of previous researchers hold true. The reasons for the stratification of casino employment are complicated, involving the preferences of individual workers, language skills, the influence of cultural norms, and employer hiring practices. The work of serving cocktails is gendered female. Evidence supplied by the Borgata in a lawsuit, for example, indicated that between February 2005 and December 2010, 646 females and 46 males were employed as cocktail servers called Borgata Babes.[7] Bartenders and bar porters are disproportionately male in the casinos, but women do mix drinks too. Guest room attendants are largely female immigrants.

Food service, both in the front and in the back of the house, follows familiar complex hierarchies of gender, race, and ethnicity. African Americans sometimes have difficulty breaking into positions that directly serve customers. Especially men. Jesse, an African American man, said it took years to move from backroom and security jobs into a dealer position. He wore a beard, and said that most of the black men he knew did as well. But the first casino he worked at had rules about being clean-shaven. Another had a policy that permitted only certain mustache and beard styles and supplied employees with sketches of beard styles that were and were not permitted. Jesse reported to us that the image of the banned Fu Manchu beard, which he associated with African American men, also depicted a man with thicker lips. He viewed the rules as discriminatory, sending a message about who would be hired.

As the casinos have increasingly brought in new ethnic groups and diversified their workforce, who works where has evolved. But there are still hierarchies. Isiah, a dark-skinned Latino, started in the kitchen as a runner (bringing food to the buffets) before his English improved enough to transition to becoming a dealer. Chefs and cooks are white or occasionally African American, he said, but everyone else in the kitchen is "Spanish" or from India. Keith, who is white, had worked with very few African Americans in the high-end restaurants where he spent most of his career. But he had witnessed some changes as other minority groups moved from the back to the front of the house: "Latinos in the kitchen, in all capacities. Another broad stroke, I'd say Pakistanis, Indians are coming on the floor [working as servers]. . . . And of course before then, it was the Asians: Filipinos and Chinese; they are still, but that's changing."

In contrast with the extensive literature on occupational segregation by gender, race, and ethnicity, we know much less about the occupational profiles of lesbian, gay, bisexual, and transgendered workers.

There is a paucity of data, and studies thus far have focused on demonstrating the existence of wage penalties and employment discrimination rather than occupational distribution.[8] One early study did find some occupational differences between lesbians and heterosexual women and between gay and heterosexual men. The authors hypothesized that some lesbians and gay men may gravitate toward occupations with higher levels of tolerance, but their results were inconclusive.[9] A more recent study indicated that both lesbians and gay men are more likely to work in gender-atypical occupations than their heterosexual counterparts.[10]

In our study, we interviewed four self-identified lesbians and had informal conversations with several gay men in the industry (who were not in frontline jobs). One of the women, a former pit boss, said that she felt attitudes in the industry changing. When she first started in the industry in 1979, she wasn't "as open." She would run into coworkers at local gay bars but to the rest of her colleagues her personal life was a mystery. She remembered being asked by one supervisor to wear more dresses, and was able to deflect the request by saying she was uncomfortable with the shape of her legs. Still, the industry was more accepting than other places she had worked. Based on our conversations, lesbians and gay men in the industry have created informal social networks that intersected work and community to support each other. One story we heard involved the early days of the AIDS crisis and going to a supervisor to quietly explain why one relatively closeted gay man was seriously ill. One couple we interviewed, both in the industry, were highly closeted. Still, those we spoke with agree, the industry, like the larger culture, is becoming more openly accepting.

Gambling, smoking, and drinking—the three vices seem to go hand in hand. There are plenty of places to drink at a casino. There are bars and cocktail lounges, some with live music, that could be mistaken for any chic urban watering hole. Casino restaurants serve drinks and offer patrons stools where they can chat with the bartenders and grab a bite to eat. Increasingly, the casinos offer high-end nightclubs with celebrity deejays providing dance music, bottle service instead of individual drinks, and a youthful crowd dropping lots of money. But for those gamblers glued to the slot machines or looking for a hot streak at the tables, the casinos offer free drinks brought right to where they sit or stand, by cocktail servers who receive tips for their labors. In fact, cocktail servers who work on the casino floor need to be licensed by the state, as do any other employees directly involved in gaming.

We interviewed three cocktail waitresses at different stages in their careers. Ruth, who worked the gaming floors handing out drinks for decades, retired when her fifty-something-year-old body could no longer do the job she loved. Lily, a twenty-something Borgata Babe, worked her way up from the floor to bottle service at a club called mur.mur. But she quit because she found the environment and treatment of employees toxic. Zoe has been plying free drinks to gamblers since Day One. She is matter-of-fact about the work, but is volunteering more with her union out of frustration with changes at the Caesars-owned properties.

Zoe prefers working on the casino floor to working in a cocktail lounge: "Number one, you were not responsible for any checks, any money. It was just free drinks. The more drinks that you could pump out, the more [tips] you made so you were responsible for only your, only what you wanted to make that day yourself. You didn't have to wait around for someone to come into your lounge. . . . The casino floor was where you wanted to be." That sentiment was true for Ruth as well. She described the job as "like being in business for yourself." Ruth enjoyed the hustle and proudly claimed, "I worked no harder if the boss was on the floor, or in the building, out of the building, I could have cared less. I was there to pick up every dollar that was out there. I needed no supervision." The younger server, Lily, saw things differently. After a few years of serving drinks to gamblers on the casino floor, Lily had the opportunity to transfer to a swanky, new Borgata nightclub—one of the first to introduce bottle service. Customers would routinely spend $1,000–$5,000 per night, so the tips were four or five times higher. In order to get a table, a group had to purchase a minimum number of bottles, more bottles on a crowded Saturday night than a slower evening.

Cocktail service is a job that perfectly illustrates the concept of "doing gender." Feminist scholars argue that our gender identities are not anchored in our biology. They are social constructions produced through our daily activities, as we behave in ways that conform (or don't conform) with social norms and that differentiate us (or don't) from the opposite gender. Gender, in this view, is partly a performance.[11] Cocktail servers and their customers routinely perform gender. For example, when we asked about the qualities it takes to do her job well, college graduate Zoe told us, "The funny part about it is. . . . One of my favorite sayings, when people . . . get real complicated on their order or they ask all sorts of technical stuff, and I always kind of look at them and say 'Look, you know,' and I say it in a cute way, 'I applied for this job in a bikini. Don't make it too hard.'" And then she proceeded to share the many invisible interpersonal skills needed to get more tips, to avoid conflicts with handsy customers, and to diplomatically cut off customers who've had too much to drink.

As noted in chapter 3, however, newer or revamped casinos accentuating upscale demographics are increasingly hiring younger cocktail servers, altering uniforms to be more revealing, and marketing the sexuality of their employees. Appearances are monitored closely. When Ruth was hired in 1979, she interviewed in a business suit. Her uniforms changed every few years, and she thought that "One worse than the next. . . . They could have designed the coolest uniforms that could have relatively flattered anyone. No. Over the years, you could imagine in twenty-six years I saw a lot of uniforms. We never had, like today, the sleazy type uniforms."

In contrast to when Ruth was hired, Lily had a very different interview experience in the contemporary era. She reached out to us for a follow-up interview because she wanted to describe what she went through to land a promotion to bottle service. The audition and socialization process was more extensive than the earlier interview and exam she had completed for the casino gaming floor position. This new job orientation was probably unique, since it took place when the club was first opening. It illuminates, however, the changing corporate culture that is increasingly sexualizing employees in cocktail service and other jobs. In this case, she felt sexually harassed by a manager who was about to become her boss.

Several women, including Lily, accompanied managers in a limousine for a long night on the town in New York City. They visited four or five posh nightclubs to get a sense of what Borgata was trying to replicate in Atlantic City. Lily recalled: "By the time we got done with the second one (it might have been the third one), one of our managers was completely drunk. And I was dancing with one of my girlfriends who was gonna be working at the club. He came up behind me, and started dancing with me. And he said, very quickly, he said, 'Oh, you're definitely getting the best shift.'" Even though the job really didn't have different shifts, his behavior stung. She was disappointed in herself for not increasing the physical distance between them and responding more forcefully. "It's such an awkward position. Because you want to say to yourself, if that happened—which I always thought—I would definitely just say, you know, come right out and you know, be very forward about it, and you know, really confront, confront the person. And I found myself having that kind of nervous laugh about it. And then later, you're like, 'God, why didn't I just, like, yell at him, and just say something?'" On the ride home, the same manager tried to put his head in her lap and his hand up her leg. This time she told him it was "not okay." She knew she could report him, but she said that "economic and social factors" stopped her. So he became one of her bosses, continuing to make suggestive comments periodically.

Sexual harassment from both managers and customers occurs no matter how a woman dresses and it affects employee morale. A study in the *Journal of Gambling Studies* found that casino employees who reported being sexually harassed were less satisfied with their jobs, less committed to the organization, and more likely to quit, as Lily did; she is now in graduate school.[12] Of course, higher turnover rates do not always trouble employers if they prefer to cycle in a younger, fresher crop of employees at the bottom of the wage scale. Other studies support the idea that employees in sexualized jobs are more likely to view harassment as part of the job and are therefore less likely to view it as a problem. For them, their work role is a sex role.[13] For example, Zoe has no problems calling security and rolling the security film if a customer is out of line. But she also sees dealing with sexual harassment as part of the job: "I knew going in, like I said, I interviewed in a bikini, so I knew that, going in twenty-eight years ago that that would be part of it. So, I'm not overly sensitive about that. I have seen people that are." Ruth felt her uniform helped her separate her role at work from her real identity: "Somehow you can put this on and you can be a different person. You can step into the role; like an actress. . . . It helps you get into the mode of, you know, this is not me."

Ruth also insisted that inappropriate behavior was rare: "How many thousands of people must I have waited on over the years? Most people . . . and I would say most of the girls would say the same thing, they were nice." She could only remember calling security once: "One night, I did have a guy, I'm walking down the aisle and he grabbed my ass. I nearly died. But you don't take it as offensively as today's age. It never occurred to me to file some kind of charge against him, nor would it even today. He grabbed my ass, he obviously had too much to drink. . . . I cursed him out. I embarrassed him. . . . I might have told a security guard, 'Get this jerk outta here.' But one time in twenty-six years? I mean, this could happen in an office for God's sake. I'm sure it happens more frequently in an office."[14]

Lily, in contrast with Ruth, found that the culture and managerial policies at the bottle club made harassment by customers common-place, even though an employer can be held legally liable if a provoca-tive uniform or other policies are viewed as inviting harassment.[15] In her words, "It's just considered part of the atmosphere, part of what is expected in the job." All-male tables would often treat their club experi-ence like a proverbial bachelor party. She described herself at work: "Here I am, I'm like half-naked, and I'm dolled up, and I'm here to serve you. And the outfits, you see how short they are. I have to bend over to pour drinks. I have to bend in front of them. . . . They see me like that. And they look and treat me like they see me, which is like a piece of meat." Her job was to say, "Here's your menu; just let me know what you would like." She said a common response was, "Are you on the menu?" Touching the servers was formally against club rules. So Lily would report this behavior—grabbing her butt or brushing her breasts—at least once or twice a week. Then one of the managers told her that she was the server who had the most people kicked out of the club. It seemed more like a warning than an innocent comment. More like, "Just loosen up."

Management also encouraged servers to dance on the dance floor. Professional dancers were paid to get up on a platform to dance. But one box was always left empty for a server. Another box was left empty for customers—but specifically women or girls. If a male customer got up there, Lily reported, he would be asked to get down. The length of time a server was instructed to dance on the box depended on who the customer was. Spending more money meant more time watching your server dance for you. The dance requirement might have been a clever tactic to forestall discrimination complaints. A loophole in Title VII of the Civil Rights Act of 1964, which bars employment discrimination against protected classes, allows the sex of the employee to be a *bona fide occupational qualification* (BFOQ) only in narrow circumstances. Entertainers are one permissible category, so sexualization of various casino jobs is sometimes accompanied by adding the word "entertainment" to their job title.

Lawsuits based on various practices related to appearance have been lodged by cocktail servers against Borgata, Resorts, and Golden Nugget, though none have been successful so far.[16] In the case brought by Borgata Babes, they contested the policy that they could gain no more than 7 percent of their body weight. Among their allegations, some of the servers asserted that managers encouraged them to take laxatives to lose weight. Superior Court Judge Nelson Johnson, author of *Boardwalk Empire*, issued a summary judgment letting the policy stand, insisting that "Plaintiffs cannot shed the label babe; they embraced it when they went to work for Borgata." He also noted that the audition for the job implied that they were part entertainers.[17]

The Borgata, however, is not the only venue that has hypersexualized their servers. Harrah's was accused by about forty employees of creating a "culture of accepted sexual harassment" at the Pool, a nightclub surrounding the swimming pool where the cocktail servers wear swimsuits. One manager in particular was accused in thirteen different lawsuits of pressuring female employees to drink on duty and then making verbal and physical advances. Two male employees claimed they suffered retaliation when they tried to report the harassment, and managers in human resources were sued for covering up the problems. The outcomes of the cases are still undetermined.[18] But they speak to a disturbing pattern.

Not every casino is following the extreme model of sexualization that Borgata and Harrah's have adopted, and observers argue that sex is a much more dominant narrative in Las Vegas. But the practice is becoming more commonplace and changing what was a secure, unionized career into the kind of short-term job that burns out employees quickly. During Ruth's career, she and her coworkers aged in place. As she observed, "We may have started young, but we all ended up old there." If the casinos no longer want older women serving cocktails, Zoe argued, they could pay the servers enough to be able to retire or help them transition to other jobs, instead of firing them or pressuring them to quit. But, as one legal scholar analyzing casino employment practices has observed, "When a job has a sexual component, people assume that there are few other qualifications needed for the job."[19] Such assumptions tend to depress wage rates and block career mobility.

Zoe is the only one of the three still on the job, but will not be there much longer. Her workplace, Showboat, has experimented with the iApp system where "cocktail ambassadors" take drink orders electronically or customers place their orders on touch screens. Her job now involves only delivering the next tray of drinks, as described in chapter 1. Her work is timed so there is no leeway to chat with customers, eroding both job satisfaction and tips. Some of her coworkers and her union have tried to petition the Division of Gaming Enforcement (DGE) to rule against the practice. One aspect of the job that was both challenging and a source of pride for Zoe and others was the legal requirement to monitor how much customers have consumed and to cut off drunks. Local 54 is arguing that the new system prevents cocktail servers from performing this function. But Caesars argues that the system reduces their staff requirements and consequently costs.[20] The DGE determined that the union had to take up the issue through the collective bargaining process and refused to intervene.

For Zoe, the job is no longer fun. And it's hard to explain that to her old customers. Zoe lamented, "I still have people that come, long-term people that will come and look for me. I can't serve them any longer and I can't talk to them anymore because I'm being timed." She used to "know their whole families" and was "invited to their weddings" but that's been taken away. She told us she was looking forward to retiring or moving on to something else in a few years. But she knows that her pension, fully vested after ten years as negotiated by her union, is substantially less than those of the bartenders (mostly male) who mix the drinks for her. The cocktail servers have worked 32.5 hours per week for decades, while the bartenders have a normal 40-hour work week. Pension contributions are based on the number of hours worked, so "a bartender that works forty hours and has worked the same amount of years that I might have worked is probably, his pension is going to be higher than my pension."

She was trying to hold on for a few more years until her husband retires and their kids have left the nest. Until, that is, Caesars announced its intention to close Showboat. Now she will be forced out sooner than planned. She isn't ready for retirement, so she is looking outside the industry—as are thousands of other employees about to lose their jobs. In fact, she is contemplating working for her international union, to go, as she told us, wherever the fight is.

Casinos typically offer at least as many dining options as bars. Some gamblers want minimal interruption for nutrition and look for a quick bite from a food court, noodle bar, or café. A middle-income gambler might play just enough to get one or two free comps to an all-you-can-eat buffet and feel satiated by the transaction. High rollers, on the other hand, can be given hard-to-get tables at expensive enclaves. Destination dining establishments bearing the names of celebrity chefs draw in patrons who hustle past the smoke and the dinging slot machines just for a good meal. The working conditions across these establishments can vary as much as the food. Most of the workers are covered by the Local 54 contracts, but some private restaurants are permitted to hire nonunion labor, a compromise following a 2004 strike. Overall, however, servers and the employees who support them from behind the scenes report that their jobs are becoming harder and harder. Cutbacks in staff mean a speed-up for servers, with less time to interact with customers and consequently fewer tips.

The food servers we interviewed, all white, had each worked in the casinos for more than fifteen years. Both of the waiters with experience in fine dining, Peter (a married father) and Keith (divorced), were male. Keith's chic restaurant for high rollers had closed, and when we spoke he was juggling multiple jobs at two different casinos, both facing possible closure. Walter, who is single, had worked in a coffee shop for years. Heather, married with children, had seen her casual restaurant transition through various names and identities, and kept her seniority through the changes. We also interviewed one Latina, Inez, a single mother who worked in the back of the house, washing dishes and prepping for banquets. They are all union members, though they varied in their level of activism. All of them indicated pride in their ability to provide good service and frustration with institutional changes that make it harder to meet the standards they set for themselves.

Food servers try to find self-respect in their jobs. Sometimes the working conditions or attitudes of their supervisors make this difficult.

Walter, for example, revealed that "I look after my own work; I control my work, I understand my work; I'm proud of my work. . . . But a lot of my coworkers suffer from low self-esteem because they are only food servers." He wishes management recognized the professionalism of their staff: "I have a college professor from Mexico in mathematics as a dishwasher. . . . I have people that are highly literate in Spanish and are teachers. . . . There's this whole 'You're just the help' kind of thing going on." Inez, not surprisingly, made similar comments, observing that supervisors assume that if you do not speak English you must not be smart. Snap judgments are made: "If they see something dirty in my t-shirt . . . they can see me in a different way. They don't realize how much work I do to make this happen." She added, "So you know, sometimes we feel like they think we are the lowers, like people who don't have anything. They don't know who we are." But, in her mind, "My money is same as your money. I can buy anything with twenty dollar as you."

The employees keenly felt the loss when they could no longer provide the level of service they previously provided due to changes in corporate priorities. Good service takes time. Keith and Peter both worked their way up to the position of captain at high-end restaurants in the days when a team of servers catered to the high rollers who were comped meals in the most exclusive restaurants on their properties. Keith reminisced, "You could not walk through that restaurant door unless you had played $100,000." He took pride in the work: "Initially, it was elegant, beautiful, difficult but rewarding. It was interacting with people and making a good living. All of those things. And interacting with your coworkers, management, feeling value, all of these things that you would expect to fulfill your, you know, your sense of person. Now, here we are, production, we are, that's what we are. How can you produce more? That's really what it is."

Keith never carried a tray in the old days. They either wheeled the food out on a cart or carried individual plates by hand. The experience was elevated, and there was less wear and tear on servers' backs and knees. Now he is serving burgers and carrying heavy trays. Despite being fit, he feels the change physically. And he misses the autonomy that the teams had to cater to the needs of their customers. These days the supervision is much more direct and the managers show employees less respect: "Now, I have to say that I see managers curse at employees and get away with it. I mean, when I say curse, I mean, just screaming at them, f-bombing them, just, it's so different." Peter agrees. He thinks it was actually more efficient to have more servers because you needed fewer supervisors. But management's attitude has changed: "They think it's too many people taking care of one table, which I think, sometimes, you need more eyes on a table. You don't need a manager behind you, you know, just chirping in your ear, bringing you down. You need people lifting you up all day long."

Even working in a coffee shop, Walter saw a difference. In the earlier days, he said, the casinos were more service-oriented. Today, it's "Turn and burn. Turn the table over and get 'em in and get 'em out." At the same time the pace has been increasing, his stations have gotten larger. Now he covers six tables instead of four. So he has to prioritize, based on who is likely to tip well: "If you have six tables, you can't be giving them all good service, and you're picking who you're not giving good service to. As much as my boss likes to pretend that I can do the work [that I did with four tables], I can't. So, I'm saying, 'Well, you're done!' And I'm concentrating on the other four or the other three or the other five." Walter enjoys educating his customers about food, telling us: "I have a very big rap about getting people to try new things. . . . I'll teach them about coffee or chocolate or different kinds of olive oil. . . . Some of my coworkers think I'm wasting my time from turning and burning, but I think in the long run that's what I want to do." It is harder and harder to find time for these small satisfactions.

Increasing station size is just one impact among many of staff reductions. Heather now has to ring up her own checks. And if patrons walk out without paying, management tries to dock it from her pay. Walter claims, "It's not doing the same work I was doing twenty years ago. It's doing more work. There used to be a lot of help. There were traditionally bus people to help food servers. And that, there has been a reduction in the number of bus people that are available. So where I used to maybe share a bus person with another food server, maybe that bus person might have four food servers to help out. . . . I think those are the primary reasons for what I would call job speed-up." Keith says there are more expectations for servers to stock supplies and clean. In the back of the house, Inez has seen a lot of firings. It is harder to get forty hours of work per week, and overtime is a thing of the past. At the end of a long day loading and unloading dishes, lifting, and carrying, she feels like "not any part of my body is working."

Food servers and kitchen workers in the casinos have union jobs so their base pay and benefits are generally higher than comparable workers outside the industry. But the servers still rely on tips to pay the bills. Walter proudly admits, "I'm considered a tip hustler; I can get money out of a stone." But under his sped-up working conditions, it's getting harder: "As I've been getting older, I've been getting slower so I can't get by on sheer speed, what other servers do. I have to get it with finesse and that turns three-dollar tips into four-dollar tips and one-time customers into regular customers. There is no relationship between the bigger the check is, the more your tips. There is a relationship between the better your interaction with the customer is, the bigger your tip is."

Heather's response to the changes has been to distance herself from her work. She feels that management "kinda just forgot about the employees." Her base salary was up to over $8 per hour, so she had to be on her guard: "We always feel they're always out to get the Day One people who could be replaced with cheaper newcomers." So, she confided, "I kinda changed my attitude over the years. I don't really want to take anything in this job too seriously. It is six hours a day of my life and that's it. I have a whole world outside of this place." Peter is still a bundle of energy and enthusiasm for his work. But after trying a stint in management and experiencing a callous response to a family crisis, he needs to put work behind him at the end of his shift and concentrate on his family and community. Keith thinks things have degraded to the point of "an open struggle between management and workers." He is "fed up with it" and hoping to move on soon. With both his employers on the verge of closing, he may not have a choice. Inez worries about how much longer she can do her job. She does not have the savings to think about retiring, at least not here in the United States. But her work is "hard and heavy" and she cannot see herself still doing the job ten years from now. She thinks she may have to transfer to something that pays less or go back to her country of origin.

Part of the skill set of hotel guest room attendants (GRAs) is that all the work they do is meant to stay relatively invisible. Ideally the GRA slips in and out while the guest is gone for the day. Guests tend to notice the tasks that were overlooked, not the work done well. Much of the communication is nonverbal. Guest and worker may smile briefly as they pass in the hall. A guest might leave a note of appreciation with the tip or ask her for some extra supplies. Depending on hotel policy, the GRA might leave a note or a chocolate on the pillow. Social invisibility surrounds cleaning staff in many settings, from domestic servants to janitorial services. And immigrants are often hired for cleaning and other jobs where social invisibility is expected.[21] It is also not surprising that GRAs tend to be female since women are viewed as naturally adept at cleaning domestic spaces.

Their jobs are both familiar and unfamiliar to guests. Most people who stay at hotels know something about how to make a bed or clean a bathroom. But most of us haven't considered how the GRA's workload is allocated or monitored. What does she do if a DND sign on the door prevents her from keeping on schedule? How does her employer distribute the work when one room is "dirty vacant" and the next is only a "makeup" (guest staying over)? Who keeps track of her progress and where she is at any given moment?

Both of the guest room attendants whom we met were immigrants who used to be teachers in their country of origin. Most of their co-workers, they reported, are Latina, Indian, or Bangladeshi. Both of them followed their husbands to the United States and found their way to Atlantic City in search of a better life financially. Manuela's sister already had a job at Harrah's when Manuela decided to leave her husband and move out of the Bronx. For ten years, she balanced two housekeeping jobs; now that her kids are grown, she just has one. Aparna did not know what housekeeping was when her husband took her to the personnel office. But she was glad that her job offers a nine-to-five schedule, rare in the industry. Both GRAs were trained by coworkers when they first started.

These two proud women are employed by two different casinos. Aparna's employer, Tropicana, has maintained the typical work process that assigns most housekeepers to specific floors and rooms. Energetic and optimistic, Aparna has a fairly positive attitude about her job. Manuela's employer is experimenting with a system apparently designed by "efficiency experts." She feels like "just a number" to her employer, whose new system has made doing her job well even harder. The changes have made her more militant about helping her union stand up to the employer.

Even though they are socially invisible to many of their customers, they have the same kinds of stories of bonding with regulars that we heard from dealers, food servers, and others in frontline service jobs. Regular gamblers come back to their favorite casinos. Some of them, especially those who are superstitious, like to stay on their favorite floors. Those who do will get to know the guest room attendants. And, as for so many service employees, ongoing relationships with customers give the job meaning. Aparna is proud when one of her customers asks for her floor, and insists that the tips are not what motivates her: "We're not doing the job because of the tip. Because of the guest. Because we want to do them a nice service." Having them come back is a sign that she has done her job well.

Aparna and her coworkers must complete 14 "credits" per shift. In a simple example, that would be 14 rooms, with some being rooms where the guests have checked out (called a "dirty vacant") and others mid-stay rooms (called "makeups"). But rooms are different sizes. A bigger room counts as 1.5 credits and suites can be 2 or 3 credits. If a guest has a DND sign outside the door, the guest room attendant loses the credit and is assigned an additional makeup room, if there is one. If a room is "too messy," she reports it and gets assistance or gets credit for the extra work. So there is some flexibility in the system to make adjustments. Overtime can be mandatory. Her progress through her section is monitored by using the phone in the room when she enters to dial into a computer and enter her code. If a guest takes items like extra shampoo off of her cart, it means an extra trip back to the supply closet.

Manuela works at a Caesars-owned property—the same company that introduced the iApp system to make cocktail service more efficient. There is a new system for cleaning rooms that has squeezed much of the enjoyment out of her work as well: the TIDY program. First, the program increased the number of credits she must complete to 16; she used to do 14 like Aparna. The big change in the system, though, is called looping. A computer keeps track of her credits and sends her to different floors and different parts of the building to meet her quota, combining dirty vacants with makeups. She can no longer take extra care on one aspect of the job one day, and focus on another aspect of the same room the next day. She can't double back and fix something because she is several floors away. And she is much less likely to have regular customers. In the old days, "We used to get our guest's last name. So when you was coming into that room, I want to pull your last name and make you feel like home. I know you, we used to take our time to clean those rooms."

And cleaning the rooms is more complicated than it used to be. In a competitive casino economy, the hotels are in an arms race to increase amenities for the guests. Manuela wants recognition for the added work involved in each room: "There was no refrigerator in that room. No six pillows like now. Now we have six pillows on each bed, a refrigerator. . . . We have a coffee maker. We have more to do. It is time for the company to recognize what we do." From Manuela's perspective, the focus on a younger customer demographic is not a step in the right direction. Their hard partying also makes her job more difficult. But, she pointed out next, she and her coworkers have not received a raise in ten years. She is stuck at $14.42 per hour, which is better than the salary for the new hires. Once again, we heard that management is targeting workers with seniority, presumably hoping to hire new employees for a lower starting wage or to not replace them at all.

She is acutely aware from her union that Caesars Entertainment is owned by the "hedge fund." And that the company is saddled with debt and struggling. It saddens her that properties that once were rated five stars are becoming run down. She goes through the list—Bally's, Harrah's, Showboat, and Caesars—and claims "They are dirty. The guests are not happy. They don't make no money and they treat all their employees very bad." Borgata was a good employer in her mind, as was Atlantic Club before it closed. But too many of the other houses are cutting back on benefits. The city, she said, has changed since when she arrived in the early 1990s: "When I move here, there was a place where you can find a lot of work. The pay was good. . . . I think it was growing, Atlantic City was in progress. Everything has changed in that twenty years. It's not the same town that was before. . . . It's going back to like it was, Atlantic City was before. It was ugly. The pay was no good. . . . Workers here, they don't care about us no more. They only care about making the profit."

Managerial strategies to rebrand the casinos and cost cutting by owners perceived as detached from day-to-day operations are reshaping the work experiences of frontline service employees, affecting their perceptions of job quality. There are similar themes in many of their stories, just as there were among the dealers and gaming supervisors depicted in chapter 4. Tangible returns from work—wages and benefits—are no longer what they once were. Belonging to a union garners some protections that unorganized workers lack, as described in more detail in the next chapter. Given the highly stratified nature of these varied jobs and the workers in them, however, there are some unique perspectives from people in different occupations. And casino owners have chosen to respond to the pressures of competition in ways that have distinctive impacts on specific jobs. While some cocktail servers, for example, are increasingly sexualized as part of the rebranding, the four Caesars properties are focused on cost cutting via the iApp system. These managerial strategies are choices, and each has its own pluses and minuses.

If, as we contend, a good job is one that helps you create a life, then pay and benefits are critical. The pay in these jobs varied. Inez and Manuela struggle to support their children as single mothers in jobs that pay more than they would in a nonunion environment, but were still relatively low-wage. Lily could save up enough money during a short stint serving cocktails to pay for college and buy a house with her boyfriend. While she hated the demeaning aspects of her job, it paid well. Their union helps negotiate and administer their benefits, including health care and pensions. Heather said that the benefits were the main reason she continued to work. Several employees emphasized their defined benefit pension plan as important, and something they were having to fight with their employers to maintain. Other workers emphasized the importance of their jobs in providing for their families. The problem, they all agreed, is that full-time jobs with decent wages and fully paid benefits are fast disappearing. And for the jobs where tips matter, the drop in patrons due to market saturation has affected take-home pay.

Career ladders in many frontline service occupations are short and less specific than the promotion ladder for dealers. Cocktail servers do not see much opportunity for upward mobility. Other employees expressed reluctance to take advantage of limited advancement opportunities when they were presented because they would forfeit the security of union representation. In union positions, seniority rather than favoritism determined such working conditions as how shifts were allocated. The grievance procedure protects them from arbitrary dismissal. And when a short career ladder means small financial rewards for moving up a rung but limited chances beyond the next step, staying put seems safer. This was why Aparna turned down the opportunity to become a supervisor. Several waiters we spoke with had started out in the kitchen or as bussers. In the old system, you could advance from server to captain before becoming a maître d' (or maître d'hotel) as Peter did. These days, however, the hosts and hostesses that greet guests are usually in a deskilled position that greets and seats but is not actually managing the staff.

But building a life is about more than material provisioning. It requires time away from the job and supportive institutions, including employers who treat their workers as human beings with complex lives. The phrase "just a number" kept coming up. Every employee has a number that indicates his or her rank in terms of seniority, and more frequently it seems that this is their only identity to upper management. These complaints were particularly vocalized by Caesars employees and workers at other properties emphasizing efficiency and cost reductions. In contrast, the Borgata, which markets itself as upscale, generally gets good grades from workers (other than Lily) for its treatment of them. Even the food is better in their cafeteria, we were told. In fact, Borgata has tried to skim off the cream by stealing the best employees in addition to well-heeled customers.

As with the dealers, the 24/7 nature of the industry takes its toll on work-life balance for employees in many of these jobs. Some workers, like Aparna, deliberately avoided becoming dealers so that they could work nine-to-five. In fact, one of the attractions of the GRA positions was the regularity of the work schedule. This was true of employees in other back-of-the-house jobs. Dario, an inventory control clerk, wanted a job where he could spend time with his children so he decided to stay off the casino floor.

Food and beverages, though, are available at all hours. Walter complained, "It has a tax on other parts of my life, like, I have no social life. Nights and weekends, I always work, and holidays." He continued by telling a story: "One year, I don't know what happened, but it was like

7:00 and they had too many servers. And it was New Year's Eve, and they said 'Do you want to go home?' And I walked outside and it was 7:00 and I had no idea what to do on New Year's Eve at 7:00. I had never made plans for New Year's Eve in my whole life! I was always at work." Peter tried the traditional male fast track into management but discovered it didn't pay off the way he thought it would. Now, as a waiter, he still works nights and weekends, but usually clocks out at a decent hour. His restaurant shifted everyone, even senior workers, to shorter hours, but as long as he works more than thirty-two hours per week he has access to benefits. Heather worked breakfast and lunch, even though the morning shift paid less, to have a better schedule for her family. Her life was organized with military precision to take care of her family, function on the job, and pursue a college degree.

Having health insurance matters, but when you have illnesses and injuries, you still need an employer who permits you to deal with personal issues. Heather's son had a serious illness, and she was able to take a leave of absence without too much difficulty. The experiences of other workers varied. Having seniority helped. Both Ruth and Zoe have problems with their feet, after years of carrying heavy trays in high heels during their six-hour shifts on the floor. If a cocktail server provides medical documentation, she can get dispensation to wear flat shoes instead of heels. But the long-term wear and tear on the body of many of these jobs is intense due to so much standing, walking, bending, lifting, and carrying. Even something as simple as making one bed after another, year in and year out, can cause back and wrist injuries. Every long-term server and housekeeper had some kind of nagging injury.

Exposure to chemicals also impacts workers' health and well-being. Both Aparna and Manuela supply their own gloves. In fact, Manuela said her leadership role at work started when a coworker asked to borrow her gloves to clean up vomit. Manuela told the supervisor if they didn't start supplying gloves, she would contact OSHA. So now gloves are supplied, but she still finds the ones she buys herself sturdier. If asked, the GRAs can get masks. And if they develop a reaction to a particular chemical, they are supplied something different. Walter has filed OSHA complaints. Restaurant kitchens, he observed, are dangerous places. One OSHA complaint had to do with storage and handling of industrial equipment like slicers, mixers, revolving ovens, and blenders. The other came about because he noticed that the outside cleaning service wore extensive protection while using chemicals to clean the kitchens. But the regular staff was expected to keep working in their regular clothes walking in and out of the space being cleaned. He investigated and found that the combination of chemicals being used was dangerous. Standing up for health concerns—for himself and his co-workers—worked. After so many years, he claimed, "Now I know everything about OSHA regulations."

Cigarette smoke is particularly harmful during pregnancy. A number of female employees in jobs where they are exposed to smoke shared that they had dropped out when they became pregnant. Permitting smoking at the workplace thus induces labor force intermittency, costly to women in the long run when they give up seniority, wages, pension accruals, and experience that leads to career mobility.

A good job also reinforces a positive sense of identity. The gender, race, and ethnic hierarchies that are common in the service sector are particularly apparent in these casino jobs. Workers construct their work identities actively, not passively, in the face of these status hierarchies, looking for meaning in doing their jobs well or from other family and community activities. While cocktail servers have jobs that ask them to perform gender in ways that can be demeaning, the women in these jobs look for ways to maintain their dignity. And immigrant women who are often socially invisible on the job find ways to make themselves heard.

In all of these jobs, workers tried to take pride in providing good service. While manufacturing workers traditionally derived their sense of identity from creating useful products (according to historians),[22] in service work the product is experience. Building relationships with customers is critical because service work is interactive. Good relationships with coworkers and managers also facilitate good service. When these relationships get frayed in the name of efficiency, the employees feel the brunt of it but the quality of service—the product that casinos are offering—suffers as well.

APARNA'S STORY

Aparna is an educated immigrant in what we often consider a low-level job. Many people never pay much attention to the housekeeper who cleans their hotel rooms or brings them an extra towel or a roll of toilet paper. She is often invisible, except to some regular customers who know her by name and request a room on her hall. An upbeat woman who always says "You have to love your job to do your job," Aparna found to her surprise that housekeeping made sense as a career, especially the stable hours and job security that comes with being a union member. In fact, she has found an outlet for her hidden talents as a union representative for her coworkers: helper, listener, fact-finder, and problem-solver. As long as you don't call her a maid: "I don't like that word," she tells us.

Aparna is from India, the oldest child from a large family—"very poor and very happy," in her words. As part of her early education, she developed skills in sewing and jewelry making. This experience with detailed work may be one reason she wears glasses today on her round face and her hands, seen when she expresses herself with gestures, look both rugged and delicate at the same time. She always planned to work. "I grew up as an independent woman," she insists with pride. She went to college in India to try to advance herself. Meanwhile, her future husband, Prajit, returned to India from the United States to find a wife; a relative recommended him to her father. "And I got a phone call that today you're gonna go see the guy, and I said, 'Dad, are you joking? I'm here, I have my exam in, like, one and half months and I'm here home studying, and you think I have to go and see the boy?'" But she was devoted to her father, so she went to Mumbai by train to meet Prajit. They decided to marry only an hour after meeting. Aparna remembers with a laugh: "I said yes because he was so good-looking guy!" But she first insisted that she be allowed to remain home to earn her college degree. Once she finished college, she took English classes to prepare for her new life. Aparna then joined her husband in the United States. The newlywed couple lived with his parents, in a household totaling thirteen people.

Aparna started out by helping with Prajit's family's business, a small store. She continued her English classes and her self-assigned home-work: She would read one English book, then one book in her own language, one English, one other, and so on, alternating between the two. When helping customers in the store, Prajit encouraged her to complete whole sentences, not just answer "yes" or "no." She also stud-ied the New Jersey driver's manual in English so she could pass the written test and get her license. Aparna felt that if she could drive, she would again be independent, and then it would be the right time to plan for children. When the business was sold a few years later, Prajit started a new job as a slot attendant in an Atlantic City casino. By this time, they had themselves and two children to support.

On a whim while vacationing, the entrepreneurial couple bought a sandwich shop and a home in Florida. She stayed for ten years, he for six. They tried living apart, Aparna with the children and a second business in Florida and Prajit back in the Atlantic City casinos. After four summers of growing kids coming to the Jersey shore to see their father, they sat down and did some family budget calculations; they decided it was better to reunite under one roof, in Atlantic City. So Aparna and the children moved back. Soon after, Aparna started her first job at Tropicana as a casino hotel housekeeper. "First job." That's what she thought: it would just be her first job. She still is a housekeep-er—a guest room attendant—twelve years later.

She was trained for the job by a coworker. It took five days, learning different floors and different towers of the hotel. Aparna found many of her coworkers were also newer immigrants from India and Bangladesh as well as Latinas from Puerto Rico and Central and South America. There was camaraderie among the staff. And she became exceptionally good at her job. Aparna would approach each day with her own mantra,

"I'm going to be something today, I'm going to learn more, I'm going to be helpful to someone."

At Tropicana, guest room attendants are usually assigned to the same area each day, and they get to know the regular customers. As she goes from room to room, she calls a phone number to indicate where she is in her routine. Supervisors also make the rounds once before lunch and again after lunch to check on how things are going. People think the job is easier than it is, according to Aparna. "Housekeeping [is] so much hard work." You work with a lot of chemicals to do the cleaning and "people get allergic to it," she adds. Changing twenty-eight beds a day (fourteen rooms, two beds per room) causes much wear and tear on the back, the knees, and the wrists. The bathroom is slippery. One coworker fell while rehanging a shower curtain. A back injury kept her out for six months.

One of the reasons Aparna never followed through on an original ambition to become a dealer is that she works regular 9:00 a.m. to 5:00 p.m. hours. The regular schedule is a real plus because of child care. But you can expect to work either Saturday, Sunday, or both days. She tells us that she earns about $12 per hour plus tips, but the amount of the tips varies widely among individual customers. She hasn't noticed any patterns about who tips well and who doesn't. Her care about her guests shows. She has amassed regular customers over the years and they can be generous. At reservation or check-in time, they request Aparna's floor or section. One of her regulars, who used to visit weekly with her husband, continued to come and stay in the same room after he passed away. She called Aparna to wish her a happy birthday one year. And when the woman stopped coming, Aparna tracked her down in a nursing home and called her periodically because the former guest didn't have any family left of her own.

She survived a difficult period of mass layoffs with ownership changes at Trop from 2006–2008. The local press reported on the turbulence in great, gory detail, some facts proven, others alleged: ignored or deferred maintenance, dirty and dusty hotel rooms and public areas, overflowing toilets, cockroaches, bedbugs, unsanitary eating facilities, piles of garbage, and the like. City health inspection reports showed disproportionate areas rated "unsatisfactory" or "conditionally satisfactory," relative to the Trop's casino floor space. Casino patrons complained. Employee labor unions, led by Local 54, criticized and challenged management. Tropicana was called "a dump." The problem was cutbacks in staffing to save money. From 2006–2007, the new owner, Columbia Sussex Corporation, cut 900 jobs (about 20–25 percent of its workforce), including security officers—though those latter cuts would have been worse had the Casino Control Commission not stepped in due to safety concerns. Tropicana's casino license was under review during this turmoil. In a drawn-out two-year saga, the Casino Control Commission fined the casino $750,000, denied a license to Columbia Sussex, and placed the Trop under a trustee. Columbia Sussex kept fighting and appealing in state courts. Eventually, the way was cleared for a bankruptcy auction. In 2009, the Tropicana was sold to a group of creditors led by billionaire investor Carl Icahn. Aparna recalls working overtime during this period, taking on extra work because nonunion employees in other departments were losing their jobs. Morale was low across the board.

Things have improved since that time, but she still wishes for more respect and appreciation from management. Attendants are disciplined ("written up") for various guest complaints. Guests tend to complain about purported stealing. This is quite common, actually. It's easy to blame the housekeeper. As a guest room attendant, it's difficult to defend yourself from these charges. Aparna provides an example about a guest losing her earrings. Suppose her earrings are bothering her. They might be diamonds, or gold. The guest puts them on the bed and forgets about them. The earrings get caught in creases when someone sits on the bed. Then later, the attendant comes in to change the sheets, not noticing the earrings. When the hotel guest looks on the bed after the sheets have been changed and doesn't see them, the employee is charged, and gets a write-up.

That's just for a pair of accidently misplaced earrings. Sometimes an accusation comes from gamblers—including drunken gamblers—who lost their money, or mislaid or sold their jewelry, or perhaps they just want a free room. Security personnel have to be called when a hotel guest claims that $1,000 or $10,000 was taken from a bag in their room. She groans, "They always think the casino guest is 100 percent right. That's not true. A guest is never 100 percent right," Aparna asserts, adding, "What about employees? Employees don't have a heart? They're never right?" That's why employees are continuously written up. And fired.

One time Aparna was in the security office for almost three hours! She was charged with stealing a purse. Or leaving a guest room door ajar so that someone else could slip in and steal the purse. To this day, you can hear the stress in her voice as she tells the story, her voice rising an octave and the words rushing out as she explains how the mystery unfolded. Aparna entered a woman guest's room to clean it. The guest was in the bathroom talking on the phone. Aparna said, "I'm sorry, I'll come later." The guest insisted, "No, no, no, I'm just going to be five minutes." The guest left while Aparna was cleaning, taking her purse and fidgeting with it as she left. Aparna quickly finished cleaning the room and went on to a new room on another hall.

Meanwhile, two other housekeepers started cleaning the room next door on the same hall, a "dirty vacant" (meaning the guests had checked out). The original guest came back and absent-mindedly put her purse down in the room with the open door that was being cleaned; then she went back down to the casino floor. When the guest eventually went back to her own room and didn't see her purse, she freaked out and called security. As Aparna was grilled by security, she stood her ground: "I don't have any purse! I don't know nothing. The last thing I know is—how I'm going to steal the purse because I was cleaning a different room? . . . I say 'You think I'm going to lose this kind of job? For, like, a few dollars? Why?'" They went over and over the timing from the logs of her calls from each room and reviewed elevator security cameras to watch the guest come and go. After sweating like a suspect under interrogation, she went home not knowing if she would get fired.

During the night, a new guest checked into the room where the purse had accidently been left. The new guest saw a purse on the dresser, assumed the room was occupied, and called the front desk to ask for a different room. Much confusion ensued as the front desk insisted the room was unoccupied. Security eventually sorted out the mystery, and the purse was returned to its owner. But no one thought to call Aparna and tell her she'd been cleared, not even when she arrived at work the next day. She only learned that the mystery had been solved by overhearing other workers discussing the incident. "And I went and talked to my manager. I said 'At least I was expecting only one phone call from you. One phone call from you.'"

Over the years, Aparna became increasingly concerned for employees getting written up for this, written up for that, then fired from their job. She would fight to get their jobs back. Her fight for worker rights and against unfairness, disparate treatment—sometimes discrimination, she says—is what drew her to union leadership. She was actively sought out by a Local 54 vice president. He took to visiting the housekeeping department during lunch break. He spoke with Aparna, then he asked her if she would become a shop steward for her department. She thought about it but wasn't sure. Turned out that he became a regular visitor for about three months, repeating "I'm still here, waiting for your answer." She eventually said yes. She likes helping her coworkers, especially preventing many of them from getting fired for unsubstantiated accusations. And she monitors the points (accumulated for absences, lateness, and other policy infractions) in their files, which are supposed to expire after a year. Unfortunately, she could not prevent the firing of a longtime friend and coworker after her final write-up. Every employee isn't perfect, she says, but "when any employee comes to you with any problem, you're going to believe it first." Then she does her research, because her job as a union rep is to "find out what is true."

This hard-working woman strives to improve the experiences of the roughly 300 customers and coworkers whose lives she touches every day. The quality of her interactions with people matters the most for her. That includes her family. While making her way in the United States, she has helped out her younger siblings, her mother, and her father back in India. After all, it was her father that made the match with Prajit, something that she agrees was meant to be. But her husband was laid off from his longtime casino job as his employer saw business decline. He has been turned down for employment at several casinos in town. "They want younger" people, Aparna says, and Prajit is nearly sixty years old. Until he can find work, he stays with his adult daughter's family quite a bit and helps care for his grandchildren. Her college-educated son is working at a casino restaurant in Atlantic City, still seeking that first professional job in the business world. Aparna's income is even more essential for the family at home and in India. After almost two decades on the job, she says she will continue in this job until her body gives out.

6

COLLECTIVE VOICE IN TURBULENT TIMES

Keith, a former member of a union contract committee for servers, bartenders, and other hotel service employees at a casino hotel, has sat at the bargaining table across from management in awe of the labor leaders fighting on his behalf: "I am just so impressed at their ability to negotiate and to see, to out-maneuver, you know, when they are being attacked," he exclaimed. And, as the previous chapters have shown, Atlantic City's casino workers perceive their job security, their living standards, and their well-being at work as under attack. In this context, labor unions provide the resources, expertise, and solidarity that elevate workers from relatively powerless individuals to a collective body speaking with a single voice. Fortunately for some of the workers we met, unions have a long history in Atlantic City's hospitality sector. New Jersey is a U.S. state with one of the highest percentages of union members (called "union density")—teachers, police officers, firefighters, communications and office personnel, transit workers, truckers, and people in the building and construction trades. So Atlantic City's hotel and restaurant workers were unionized long before the casinos came to town. In contrast, the gaming jobs on the casino floor were unorganized—at least until recently.

As the local properties have been merged into companies with casino, hotel, and restaurant holdings around the country and even around the world, the new owners have imported previously successful restaurant brands. Many of these operate in less densely unionized locales.

These celebrity chefs and name-brand eateries are not always accustomed to formal contracts, grievance procedures, and work rules. The right to keep their union and the right to keep their jobs have been of paramount importance.

Two key issues for casino restaurant employees have been: Who gets hired when an outside company or celebrity chef opens a restaurant in a union casino? And who gets hired, or hired back, when a casino shuts down a restaurant and reopens it under a new name? Or if the casino itself is sold to a new owner? One vivid memory for Keith is the protection of union jobs when a restaurant reopens. Suppose a traditional Chinese restaurant shuts down and is replaced by one with a modern Asian fusion theme? Those restaurants—what are termed "outlets"—must recall former union workers and preserve their seniority. Indeed, the right to retain his job as casinos swapped one type of cuisine or décor for another was an important element of decent work for Keith and his fellow workers who are members of Local 54.

For Keith, this was a major victory: "The last one, last meeting that they [ownership] were selling, technically selling the building. They are going to have to sell [casino name], so therefore they would have to make it most appealing to the prospective buyer in terms of contract legacy. So they are trying to really pare down everything. I mean it was absurd what they offered. They always offer something pretty unbelievable but this is particularly like yeah, no, there's another word for this. But so, what the union negotiated was the right of return, which is pretty amazing. So two years' right of return . . . so the right of return says you have, whatever happens with that space, that physical space, whether it's maintained, whatever, you have all your seniority. You have all your rights that you have gathered. Two years!!! I just went 'Yes!' That was pretty huge."

As noted by a reporter for the *Press of Atlantic City*, "down on the gaming floor there is a hole in the labor movement. While blackjack players are served cold beers and hot coffees by cocktail waitresses sporting union pins, they are being dealt cards by at-will employees."[1] Until 2007, dealers and other employees associated with the casino games were not unionized. Enter the United Auto Workers (UAW), one of the largest unions in the United States. After steadfast organizing, a wave of union representation elections occurred in the spring and summer of 2007. Dealers in the gaming pits at four of Atlantic City's casinos voted in favor of representation by the UAW.[2] Slot technicians followed with majorities in two gaming houses. Some of the organizing campaigns also included related frontline occupations working in areas such as keno (a lottery-type drawing), horse racing simulcasts (the only sports betting currently permitted in Atlantic City), and slot machine repairs. Cashiers, who sell and redeem chips, were also in some of the units.

Numerous past efforts to unionize Atlantic City's gaming employees had failed. What changed? The casino's twin promises of urban economic development and good jobs had faltered. Informed by our interviews, we found that deteriorating working conditions have contributed to a shift in employees' attitudes toward their jobs, their employers, and consequently unions. The swell of mergers and acquisitions distanced management from employees. Cost-driven policies to speed up work, reductions in the availability of full-time work, technological changes in the industry, and an increasingly punitive work environment created a backlash among the workforce. One advantage that the UAW had was direct experience representing dealers at three casinos in the Detroit area—the first successful drive to unionize dealers in the United States. Unions—even the Detroit-based UAW—became industry "insiders," in part because casino management are increasingly viewed as "outsiders."

Around the same time, successful efforts to win union representation for dealers occurred 2,500 miles west in Las Vegas, Nevada. In 2007, dealers at Caesars Palace and Wynn Las Vegas voted in favor of joining the Transport Workers Union (TWU), AFL-CIO. These election victories brought gaming into the union stable in the form of TWU Local 721, joining their much larger union locals in air, rail, and transit. During the same year, workers at Foxwoods Resort Casino in Connecticut signed cards requesting representation by the UAW; one year later the Mashantucket Pequot Gaming Enterprise and the UAW agreed to negotiate under tribal law. Clearly, the historical moment for starting to unionize casino dealers had arrived.

The timing should not be surprising. Labor unions emerged out of social movements of people seeking control over their lives amid the ups and downs of business cycles and economic restructuring. Job protection and job security are fundamental nonpecuniary benefits secured by being a member of a labor union. Such nonpecuniary compensation must also be accounted for when evaluating the economic impact of gaming, according to economists familiar with the industry.[3] Both the long-established hotel and restaurant union, Local 54 of UNITE HERE, and the newer contracts covering casino dealers in United Auto Workers Region 9 have secured measurable gains and held back further erosions of job quality for workers in the New Jersey gaming industry.

Labor unions have been significant in the building and growth of our nation, beginning with the alliance of skilled tradesmen in major cities along the Atlantic seaboard such as New York, Philadelphia, Boston, and Baltimore. As skilled tradesmen became wage workers, these alliances evolved into labor unions during a period of labor union militancy that accompanied nineteenth-century industrialization. These early craft unions, along with the industrial unions in steel, automobile, and rubber manufacturing that were formed in the 1930s and the service and public sector unions that expanded in the 1960s and 1970s, had major influences on wages and working conditions. Many large employers, especially in oligopolistic industries where profit margins were less tight than for smaller firms, accommodated themselves to collective bargaining. Formalized seniority rules, grievance policies, and temporary layoff procedures actually brought stability to labor-management relations. However, after decades of membership growth, unions in the late twentieth century faced challenges. Roughly one out of three workers belonged to a labor union in 1953, at labor's peak. According to the Bureau of Labor Statistics annual news release on union members, the percentage of wage and salary workers who are members of a union fell below 20 percent for the first time in 1983 (18.8 percent) and dwindled to 11.3 percent in 2013.

When the Professional Air Traffic Controllers Association (PATCO) went out on strike in 1981, few would have anticipated that it would be a landmark event. The conservative and independent-minded union of white-collar professionals had supported the candidacy of Republican Ronald Reagan in the 1980 presidential election. These well-paid workers asked the Federal Aviation Administration (FAA), their employer, for a pay increase; but they also had serious concerns about their long hours of work staring at airport monitor screens. The FAA required a forty-hour work week plus overtime, while Canadian and European air traffic controllers worked much shorter hours. PATCO argued that the long hours without enough breaks for the human eyes were a health hazard for the workers and a safety hazard for the airline passengers. President Reagan's Secretary of Transportation fired all 11,300 federal air traffic controllers who refused to cross the picket line and return to work. Relying upon a little-noticed Supreme Court decision from 1938, the FAA was allowed to "permanently replace" the striking workers. While the workers were technically eligible for new positions that opened once the strike ended, because of downsizing the layoffs were, in effect, permanent.[4]

The PATCO battle became the model and symbol for a new era in U.S. labor relations—an era of renewed management hostility to unions. Private-sector employers began to use the PATCO precedent to permanently replace striking workers. Soon the threat of replacement poured cold water on union militancy. Globalization of the world economy also meant that the United States was no longer as dominant in manufacturing. Companies began to shift operations overseas to countries without strong laws protecting workers' rights to organize. Union avoidance became standard practice in industries as diverse as health care and construction.

Unions became strained, as resources diminished with membership. Strategic divisions emerged between those who emphasized the need to organize new workers in private-sector service industries and those who concentrated energy on protecting the eroding position of manufacturing workers. A new generation of labor leaders has worked to invigorate organizing strategies to both acquire new union members and to forge bonds with community-based organizations and other initiatives to rebuild union strength, strength not measured by the percentage of union members alone. The U.S. labor movement is now led by twin federations, the AFL-CIO and Change-to-Win.[5] These two labor federations work alongside each other to improve the conditions for working families in the United States.

The pros and cons of labor unions have long been debated. One of the strongest defenses of the economic role of unions in the United States is the classic 1984 study by Richard Freeman and James Medoff, *What Do Unions Do?* Written as the backlash against unions was taking root, Freeman and Medoff contrasted two faces of unions. The monopoly view of unions depicts them as obstructions to the efficient functioning of market forces. Union work rules,[6] according to this argument, depress productivity, dampen employment, and redistribute wages from unorganized to organized workers. In textbook market theory, any party who is unhappy with the terms of a proposed transaction has one way to express themselves: exiting the market. We don't buy products we don't like. We close unsuccessful businesses. Freeman and Medoff note: "By leaving less desirable for more desirable jobs, or by refusing bad jobs, individuals penalize the bad employer and reward the good, leading to an overall improvement in the efficiency of the economic system."[7]

Union proponents, instead, emphasize the unequal bargaining power that exists when individual employees interact with large corporate employers. They argue—and Freeman and Medoff document—that higher union wages have positive spillover effects for nonunion workers, by forcing employers to compete for the best workers or raise wages to discourage unionization. These spillover effects reduce income inequality. Higher wages in unionized sectors can actually increase productivity by inducing management in mature industries to innovate. Most importantly, however, Freeman and Medoff introduced the idea that union representation and collective bargaining offer workers the opportunity for "voice." Collective voice is a meaningful alternative to exit. Voice enables employers to respond to the festering problems that reduce productivity, including favoritism, perceptions of arbitrary treatment, excess inequality, and other conditions that depress employee morale. Using this framework for their empirical study, Freeman and Medoff concluded that "On balance, unionization appears to improve rather than to harm the social and economic system."[8]

Thirty years later, in his book *What Unions No Longer Do*, sociologist Jake Rosenfeld argues that the decline in union membership and thus labor clout has meant setbacks in what unions once did for the macro economy. Median wages have stagnated. Income inequality has grown. Labor-supported legislation—from making union elections easier through simple "card-check" to immigration reform to minimum wage increases to work-family balance—has had difficulty moving through the U.S. Congress and being signed by a U.S. president.[9] The influence labor once held in local, state, and national political races has also faded. Unions have fought hard to hold onto gains within strong union states and industrial-business clusters while attempting to newly organize workers in others, occupations like janitors; fast food workers and servers at Starbucks; retail workers at Walmart, Target, Ikea, H&M, and Rite-Aid; and gaming employees such as dealers.

The campaign to unionize Atlantic City's dealers on the gaming floor is part of the new wave of organizing. And we will get to that. But the largest union in town represents approximately 40 percent of the workers in Atlantic City's casinos, about 13,000 of them. These cocktail servers, bartenders, restaurant servers, buffet servers, hotel bellmen, janitors, hotel maids, and kitchen staff are represented by Local 54 of UNITE HERE. UNITE HERE resulted from a merger of the Union of Needletrades, Industrial, and Textile Employees and the Hotel Employees and Restaurant Employees International Union in 2004. HERE dates to 1899. UNITE is itself a combination of the International Ladies' Garment Workers' Union (ILGWU), founded in 1900, and the Amalgamated Clothing and Textile Workers Union (ACTWU), founded in 1914. UNITE HERE is the largest union of gaming workers in the world, representing about 100,000 casino employees in the United States and Canada (out of 270,000 members overall).[10]

Atlantic City's Local 54 of UNITE HERE is led by union president Robert (Bob) McDevitt, a middle-aged white redhead with a fiery personality—one who will not shy away from a battle. When he was nineteen years old, he started in the industry as "barboy" from 1981 to 1983 at the Playboy casino. After relocating to Philadelphia for four years, he returned to Atlantic City as a part-time banquet server at Showboat in 1987. A year later, he was successful at landing a full-time job as a banquet server at the Claridge. By that time, at the age of twenty-six, he recalls wanting a full-time, unionized position because he was no longer a young kid and had to think about benefits: "I work hard. I got a kid to feed, ya know. I'll do whatever I have to do."

And work hard he did. McDevitt continued his part-time job at the Showboat while working full-time at the Claridge, "probably the best environment I ever worked in" because he had a great boss. She practiced a "culture of cooperation" at the workplace, unlike a lot of catering managers and directors who "can be real assholes." Casinos have what McDevitt refers to as different kinds of hierarchy, and job classifications help set people apart from one another. But the banquet workplace at the Claridge under a supportive manager was different: "We would go into the back room and we all ate together—the cooks, the waiters, the bartenders, the dishwashers." He added: "I mean, we never had a grievance. . . . If I could take that environment and bring that to the rest of the industry . . . it's really dependent upon the management." What made that banquet bartender job a "great job" was the good money he earned, respect, and good management. He only took on a job at Taj Mahal as a banquet bartender because the hours and pay were better, continuing to work part-time at Showboat, now as a room service waiter. He cut his teeth on union activity by serving on the negotiations/contract committee in 1994. In 1996, motivated to run for office after what he felt was a very bad contract, McDevitt was elected as Local 54 union president. He has been at the helm of Local 54 since he was thirty-four years of age, and has served multiple successive terms as union president. He led Local 54 through two difficult strikes against the casino houses in 1999 and 2004.

Local 54 has elevated the wages and working conditions of Atlantic City's hotel and restaurant workers so that they could join the middle class. *Boardwalk of Dreams* author Bryant Simon reflects on the role of Local 54 in the age of gaming, specifically, at the end of the twentieth century: "Like the new Las Vegas, the new Atlantic City economy is a bit like the old Detroit. Backed by the strong arms of Local 54 of the Hotel Employees and Restaurant Employees International Union (HEREIU), casino workers make a decent living. With two people on the job, families can buy a new 2,000-square-foot house and a piece of the American Dream."[11] McDevitt is proud that the union has created "living wage" jobs for members, jobs that make more money than he does as union president. Good bartenders and cocktail servers with the right shifts earn $60,000–$70,000 per year. A gourmet food server can make $100,000 per year. Senior guest room attendants are paid $15–$16 per hour, with full benefits. As a comparison, the New Jersey hourly minimum wage was $6.15 in 2006, $7.15 in 2007, and $7.25 in 2009. In a state-wide ballot question, New Jersey voters approved a constitutional amendment in the November 2013 election to increase the minimum wage to $8.25 in January 2014, and thereafter index it to inflation. But the minimum wage for tipped employees remains $2.13 per hour. (If their tips do not bring them up to the minimum, employers must pay the difference.)

Local 54 engages with Atlantic City political leaders and regulatory authorities on issues that could affect their members. Politics is another site where unions can express voice in order to effect change. The union has weighed in with the Casino Control Commission on applications for new casino owner licenses. The union has commented on the city's transportation planning and redevelopment. It has supported other unions in their drives for initial organization, contract renegotiations, and strikes.

For instance, in October and November of 2007, Local 54 stood firmly in opposition to the Tropicana Casino getting its gaming license renewed. Local 54 and other local unions were concerned that cutbacks in 15 percent of its workforce to cut costs were endangering public safety. McDevitt told the *Press of Atlantic City* that management had left too few workers to keep the bathrooms clean or maintain security. Aparna, a housekeeper at Tropicana at the time, confided that the layoffs during that time period contributed to the public spaces in the casino looking "messy." She and her coworkers took pictures of garbage collecting in stairwells.

These were not the "first-class operations" intended when New Jersey voters passed the gambling referendum. The International Union of Operating Engineers Local 68 agreed that unprecedented staffing cuts had become a safety risk. Unions were joined in their efforts by the National Environmental Health Association. After holding a convention at the Tropicana in June of 2007, the environmental health specialists group wrote a fifteen-page letter to the Casino Control Commission specifying the unhealthy conditions, asserting the place "looked like a dump." At the New Jersey Casino Control relicensing hearings in November of 2008, customers of the Tropicana complained of bedbugs, roaches, dust, overflowing toilets, and smelly rooms. The New Jersey Casino Control Commission agreed. Then-Tropicana owner, Columbia Sussex Corporation (headquartered in Kentucky), was denied a new license. The casino was placed into stewardship and emerged from bankruptcy reorganization two years later. The level of service returned to normal once the casino changed hands again.

Walter, a food server, is a former shop steward with Local 54. Manuela and Aparna, guest room attendants, are also shop stewards in casino hotels. They are proud to fight for their coworkers and solve problems. Walter comes from a union family and got involved with the union soon after being hired. He claims,

> My proudest accomplishment at work had nothing to do with serving food. It all had to do with the union stuff and being a shop steward. It all has to do with getting other workers to fight the boss and in a situation with the casino we're fighting a boss, we're almost power-less. Even the presence of a big union, even in the presence of a union on a big strike, individual workers and small groups of workers are really powerless against their rather arbitrary and rather mean and poorly trained supervisors and restaurant managers. And in hun-dreds of small examples in small ways I've been able to get workers to fight back and win things and stand their ground and maybe even stand their ground, lose, but still grow from it. And that's by far the only reason I still do it. Because after ten years [serving food], some-times when I go home at night, I have to go in the bathtub and lie in the bathtub. It's no longer easy.

Originally Aparna hoped to move from housekeeping to dealing, but dealers had not yet won union recognition rights: "You know what, I don't want to change my job, because, one thing, housekeeping's a secure job because it's a union business." She was recruited to become a shop steward because they didn't have a steward of Indian descent. Reflecting on her role, she observed, "So, [being a steward] kinda make me feel good. I didn't know so many people got so many problems through management." Two years later, Aparna was offered a supervi-sory position. Her position in union leadership was a factor: "Because they knew we were doing good job, me and my co-shop steward. We were like top of the head, we were doing good job. So he said, 'Leave your key here, we're going to transfer [you to a] supervisor.'" She told him she had to think about the offer and pondered it for a few days. In her words, she was "thinking, thinking, thinking. Then end of the day, I called my coworker [and told her] 'It's your life. I cannot say, but think it over what your heart says.' . . . And then I went home and I said, you know what? If I become supervisor, within three months, winter is coming and I'm the first one to get lay-off." Her story continued, "So, I went, you know, to office and I say, 'You know what? I love what I am, I love my job. I love helping my coworkers, so I decided I'm not going to be transferred to supervisor.'" The fact that the bump in pay was marginal at best affected her decision as well.

Manuela was recruited for the contract committee after becoming active during the Local 54 strike of 2004. The way that the union leadership identified her as a potential activist was by asking other employees. Manuela said her coworkers were asked, "When you have a problem, who do you go to? Who is the person that goes with you to the office?" Manuela's name kept coming up because "every time somebody come to me, . . . I say 'Let's go. Let's go talk to somebody.' That is the way that I get started." One of her chief responsibilities is explaining the union contract provisions to the many employees who do not speak English as a first language.

> Every time that I sit down with somebody from the back of the house that doesn't speak English that is how I explain to them in my language. Because there are a lot of immigrants, like people, Hispanic people, came here [and] we are so hungry for money. We don't have time to learn the language because we have to deal with the payment of our rent, our family, and if we are working in those places and we don't know any of our rights, we don't know how we get paid things. I feel very happy because I have helped a lot of them to understand.

Inez also serves on her local union contract committee. She says she would not have a pension without her union. It's not much, but it is something more than millions of workers have. Inez's union work is fun, though she must do it on her break time, not during her shift. "You know it's fun in two ways," she explains. "People don't know anything and people want help. But they don't know how to get it. And they don't know how hard we work for that. . . . And people don't know, and people don't know where they can go if they need something, so it directs people to go the way they need to go. And some people don't know they have a pension; some people don't know the insurance is paid for. So when I give this information to the people, I see that they feel good and I feel good too."

Another employee, who recently took a leave of absence from her job to work with the local, says that organizing is now a continuous activity, not just something done the first time a union is voted in. Effective tactics go beyond the traditional grievance procedures that monitor contract compliance: "My job is to try to organize [the employees in one casino owned by Caesars] to stand up and take on management . . . instead of the old system of file a grievance. That's not going to solve the problem. . . . It doesn't work. Corporations don't honor those. They just—it's a senseless paper. You get a lot more results with people standing up for their rights and barging into an office and saying, 'No, you are not going to do this.'"

Like their counterparts in Atlantic City, union activists also take pride in their work in Las Vegas and Reno casino hotels, as found in interviews conducted by social workers Susan Chandler and Jill Jones.[12] Not only did their committed women activists highlight their efforts to achieve better wages and benefits, but they also improved job security and input into a work environment that fostered family and community well-being. The union difference is clear, the authors of the qualitative study argue: "Margaret, a Reno cocktail waitress, said it this way, 'When you go from . . . a nonunion house to a union house, the difference is night and day.' Union, according to the women, means higher wages, better benefits, job security; dignity on the job, a reduction in discriminatory practices, the creation of a leadership cadre within the casino, and better service for the customers."[13]

During the 2008 financial crisis and the ensuing economic downturn, Manuela, Inez, and other Local 54 contract committee members have worked to preserve their gains through new contracts. Members won smaller pay raises, but maintained their pension and most health benefits. Some planned increases were deferred in an amended contract, for example at Borgata, to match newer contracts at other casinos in town. Neither casinos nor labor was immune to the aftermath of the Great Recession. Local 54's membership declined alongside casino employment, and the union tightened its own belt with expenses such as officer salaries. When Revel opened in the summer of 2012, Local 54 set its aim to organize the new megaresort's hotel and restaurant workers. The struggle took two years, as summarized in the next chapter.

In the early days of gaming in Atlantic City at Resorts casino, there was a quasi-formal organization that served as an informal grievance procedure for dealers. It was called a dealers' council. If a dealer was having a problem and was called up by management, the dealers' council would be informed first, and would set out to investigate the problem. Say that Resorts wanted to fire you. A member of the dealers' council would call you up and then look into the problem before swift, unilateral action was taken. One dealer we interviewed, Caroline, thought this process worked so well and so fairly that she is trying to bring it back at another nonunion casino where she works: "I'm trying to get it back. I'm talking to [named manager] now and telling him how good this was." Caroline provided an example about a dealer threatened with being fired when her daughter was sick. Caroline recalled that "She [manager] would say, 'Bring us documentation.' . . . And we would check her record from the time she was hired. There was a time for six months when [she] was calling out. Well, then, we'd go to management and we'd fight for her and say 'Listen, her daughter's better now. She had this time. We want to give her a shot.'" To Caroline it was the "greatest thing in the world."

The dealers' council at Resorts provided a mechanism for voice, especially over day-to-day disputes. It is not, however, a substitute for collective bargaining. The dealers' council does not give employees a say over wages, benefits, and working conditions. Empirical research has found that union representation also leads to greater job satisfaction and lower employee turnover.

The opportunity for real union representation emerged just before the onset of the Great Recession, infusing new life into a pivotal social movement. In the winter of 2007, the UAW began with card signing at Caesars and Trump Plaza. By February, enough pledge cards were signed to comfortably petition the National Labor Relations Board for a union election. The March 17 vote at Caesars was overwhelmingly in favor of unionization, 572–128 (over 80 percent in favor). This vote was followed by eight more elections (including two more for different groups of Caesars employees). Five more groups of employees voted in favor of union representation and three elections were losses.[14] The UAW election outcomes, both victories and losses, are arrayed by employee group, election date, and vote tally in table 6.1. After the initial wave of organizing campaigns, the process stalled. Five casinos—Harrah's, Resorts, Showboat, Borgata, and the Trump Taj Mahal—have still not held elections. One worker we spoke with who was employed at what was then Trump Marina, where the union election was lost, felt that the UAW had made a mistake by trying to organize too many gaming houses at once. A solid contract in one house first, according to this observer, would have provided the impetus for further unionization drives.

Casino management fought strongly against the organizing drives. Management's tactics are carefully orchestrated, and typically overseen or run by professional consulting firms expressly hired for their expertise in labor relations. An important academic study finds that over three-quarters of employers hire consultants when confronted by union organizing campaigns.[15] Organized labor has learned much about these anti-unionization campaigns from former, self-described "union buster" Martin Jay Levitt. Levitt shared his secrets from more than 250 campaigns in the United States in *Confessions of a Union Buster*.[16] The techniques he employed over a twenty-year career and wrote about in 1993 have been refined over time. Key methods used by management in fighting a union drive include hiring outside consultants to manage the campaign, to help insulate management from the direct line of fire

Table 6.1. UAW Election Outcomes in Atlantic City Casinos, 2007

Casino Name	Employee Group(s)	Election Date	Votes (For–Against)
Victories			
Caesars	Dealers, cashiers, keno and simulcast employees	March 17, 2007	572–128
Trump Plaza	Dealers	March 31, 2007	324–149
Bally's	Dealers	June 2, 2007	628–255
Caesars	Slot technicians	August 23, 2007	20–11
Tropicana	Dealers	August 25, 2007	626–157
	Slot technicians	October 22, 2007	19–2
Losses			
Trump Marina	Dealers, dual-rate dealers, race book writers	May 11, 2007	175–183
Atlantic City Hilton	Dealers	May 26, 2007	268–316
Caesars	Cashiers, pit clerks and part-time slot technicians	September 1, 2007	42–77

Source: Figart and Mutari (2008)

and thus retain any bonds forged between middle managers and their workers; "captive audience meetings," where workers are ordered to attend meetings to hear presentations by consultants and managers with information or misinformation designed to frighten workers about unions; and litigation or any other tactic to delay a union election, such as challenging a category of workers who may be eligible to vote in the election or insisting that a category of low-level managers be included in the class of voters.

The targeted Atlantic City casinos employed a variety of tools from this anti-unionization campaign toolkit. They held captive audience meetings. They fought for dual rate dealers to be included in the unit. They challenged election results.

The Trump Marina employee was called to required meetings run by a hired consultant. Even years later, she was nervous speaking about these meetings, which is why we are not giving her pseudonym: "Well, we had meeting after meeting with people, anti-union people, to come into the casino and tell us what unions were like and what the unions could do." Consultants have a typical script, for example: Do you know how much you will be paying in union dues? Why do you want to pay union dues? Why do you want some outside organization to come between you and your supervisor? Isiah, a dealer with experience in several casinos, was working at Bally's during that organizing campaign. Isiah acknowledged, "Yeah, they wanted to talk to us about the union, like try to discourage us from following the union. And one of the management [guys] came and asked me, I mean, one of the big bosses came and asked me what I thought about the guy [consultant] because he wanted information, my opinion. But luckily, I didn't give him any." He continued: "I heard stories that some of the people were trying, like people could be deported—the people for the union—or you could lose your green card." Laurel added that in another casino, "the union got wind that they went around to all the Asian people and the foreigners and told them, 'If you vote for the union you're gonna get your green card taken away.'" Even Asian pit bosses were used to put pressure on Asian dealers to vote against the union. Threats like this can be a scary, effective ploy in a labor market that draws new immigrants.

As it turned out, the fading job quality faced by workers resulted in more favorable votes for the UAW, with six election victories, compared to three losses. Shifting managerial strategies. Multinational corporate ownership. Replacing full-time dealers with part-time dealers, and other methods of cost cutting. Overall deteriorating working conditions. Such changes ignited tensions between labor leaders who adhere to a high-road model of casino operation and some of the new corporate managers who are viewed as importing a low-road strategy from other jurisdictions. Since New Jersey is a strongly pro-union state with a relatively progressive political culture, these changes generated a backlash among employees, contributing to the success of the unionization drive.

It is not surprising, then, that one of the successful campaigns was at Tropicana, the company that laid off 900 workers, approximately one-fourth of their workforce. Several local managers with experience in Atlantic City objected to the cuts and were fired, indicating a clash between the local corporate culture and the new management. The Tropicana battle, being waged at the same time as the UAW's unionization drive, indicated a fissure between "outside" management and "local" workers. The successful ouster of Columbia Sussex demonstrated clout, as local political leaders and regulators felt political pressure to side with labor's cause.

Two of the other houses where the drives were successful, Bally's and Caesars, were both owned by Harrah's Entertainment (now renamed Caesars Entertainment), a target of many employee complaints for its cost-cutting practices and work restructuring. The union drive occurred at this largest player in the market, shortly after the leveraged buyout by private equity firms. Burdened by debt after the acquisition, the new operators were determined to wring more profits out of the properties.

The UAW already represented gaming workers in Detroit, which helped them overcome their outsider status. In contrast, corporate decision makers were the new outsiders. Several workers expressed nostalgia for hands-on managers in the early days of the casinos. Caesars dealer Laurel indicated that she had seen a change in the corporate culture created by an increasingly distant management. Management, she contended, realized its errors once the UAW instituted card-signing: "Our other presidents that we had . . . walked around saying 'Hi' to the dealers . . . made you feel like you were . . . you know what I mean? That you were something. . . . Now, [name of current president] . . . we've seen him walk around the casino one time, never said hello to anybody, and then tried to be our best friend at the [captive audience] meeting: 'I'm really sorry I screwed up with the benefits. I'm really going to try to change it.'" She was emphatic that middle management in her casino had continued to treat employees with respect despite the unionization drive, but noted that this was not the case at other casinos.

Ken, who has worked in the casino pits since 1979 and viewed many of his coworkers as family, articulated: "That's why the union has come in to Atlantic City, because it came from, we came from, basically, working at . . . a mom-and-pop operation to a large-scale corporation, and [a] corporation is just so faceless that they just, when it becomes large business, they just cut the corners to the point like, 'What can we do, and who will sacrifice?'"

Another key issue that tilted in favor of the union drives, confirmed by our interviews, is the casino smoking ban. In 2006, New Jersey passed a state-wide smoking ban in public spaces that exempted the casino floors. Workers resented the differential treatment won by casino lobbyists. Local 54 President McDevitt observed to the local newspaper, "I think for a long time benefits have been an issue for the dealers—that's not exactly a secret in Atlantic City—but I think that their fight against smoking on the casino floor was really the tipping point in the realization that they could organize themselves . . . and they resented the casino's position regarding smoking on the floor."[17]

While the Atlantic City case should not be read as a road map for how to unionize dealers and other service workers, it can be read for insights about some specific conditions under which service sector organizing may be successful. It certainly helped that dealers organized in a location where other unions were already well institutionalized, in a city with a longstanding commitment to the industry. The maturation and consolidation of casino gaming contributed to a shift in managerial strategies that generated resentment among the dealers. Deteriorating working conditions and the feeling that they were no longer treated with dignity as valued assets for the organization sparked resentment. For those employees who appreciated many aspects of their casino jobs—from the pay to the interactions with well-behaved customers—the answer to deteriorating working conditions is voice rather than exit.

Once a union has secured an election victory, other anti-union schemes can be deployed such as challenging the outcome of a union election or fairness in the election process, stalling at the bargaining table, or trying to get a new union decertified by getting petition signatures for a new election (as in union election, take two). These are three tactics used by casino management to delay the deal for a first union contract. It took nine months before contract negotiations began at Caesars in late 2007 and about four months before they started at Tropicana in January of 2008. The big issues were wages, job security, medical benefits, and pensions.

Trump Plaza and Bally's took their oppositional stance to unions one step further; they refused to sit down and bargain with the UAW. The elections at these two properties were aggressively contested by management. Trump Plaza appealed the NLRB decision to certify the union. So did Bally's. An appeal process takes months, effectively slowing down the collective bargaining process. In May of 2008, the NLRB did uphold the Trump election victory. Once management will not negotiate with a certified labor union, the union has the right to file an "unfair labor practice" (ULP) complaint. A ULP complaint eats up plenty of time. The UAW took this step against Bally's. Meanwhile, Trump Plaza exhausted their last appeal to the federal courts.

The years 2008 and half of 2009—eighteen months—yielded no progress at the bargaining table. Scheduling and attending bargaining sessions neither means nor guarantees genuine progress. A series of unproductive meetings where management merely "shows up" so as not to be accused of "bargaining in bad faith" is termed *surface bargaining*. UAW Region 9 leader and bargaining team member Joe Ashton shared his views about sitting at the bargaining table: "At Caesar's Atlantic City, the company liked to brag that it has had more than 50 meetings with the UAW bargaining team. That's true, but very little has been accomplished because the company won't budge from its initial proposals."[18] His short guest editorial in the *Press of Atlantic City* continued, "Why is Harrah's [parent company of Caesars] willing to reach a deal with housekeeping and hotel staff, but not casino dealers?"[19]

Timing for negotiations could not have been worse for the UAW or better for management. The U.S. economy was in the midst of a financial crisis and the Great Recession, the worst economic downturn since the Great Depression. Economic downturns put bargaining power in the hands of management. In general, bargaining power means the ability to induce the other side to make concessions that it would not otherwise make. For example, in economic downturns, it is easier to replace workers, so management holds the line on wages and benefits. On the other hand, strong growth periods favor workers since they can vote with their feet and seek better compensation elsewhere and labor unions can point to other negotiated contracts with more generous compensation packages.

The UAW lost their patience with management; the battle for a first contract got nasty and it got public during the peak of the 2009 summer tourist season: "Clashing billboards by the United Auto Workers union and Harrah's Entertainment line major thoroughfares leading into the resort. The two sides also have turned to television, radio and newspaper advertisements to slam one another over unsuccessful contract negotiations for dealers at two Harrah's-owned casinos [Caesars and Bally's]."[20] As Atlantic County residents and researchers, we watched keenly for weeks the dueling billboards promoting dueling websites, dueling newspaper and television ads, and dueling letters to the editor. The UAW organized summer rallies downtown on the Boardwalk and Pacific Avenue, picketing outside of Caesars and Bally's, shouting slogans such as "The Dealers Make, the House Takes," "We Want a Contract," "No Contract, No Peace," and "Hey, Hey, Ho, Ho [Harrah's CEO] Gary Loveman's got to go." Members from other New Jersey unions, as well as unions in neighboring New York and Pennsylvania, joined in the rallies that continued through the summer. In mid-July 2009, at the height of the protests and media blitz, dealers at Caesars and Bally's took a vote and authorized a strike, if necessary, as a step to try to force negotiations. Interviewed by a reporter, Debby, a Caesars dealer for twelve years, said striking is "a weapon," but members would prefer to work out a fair contract. "They (Harrah's) need to know what they're doing is wrong."[21]

Dealers had been worried about job security before the recession; the recession only boosted their fears. Concerned about cuts and moves to replace senior full-time dealers with part-timers, Walter M., a dealer at Trump Plaza for seventeen years, indicated that having a contract would mean job security for people like him: "The more seniority you have in the casinos, the closer you are to the door. They have to pay benefits for you and a better salary. They're using the economy as an excuse."[22] Harrah's Eastern Division President J. Carlos Tolosa fired off his own letter to the editor in defense: "For two years, we have nego-

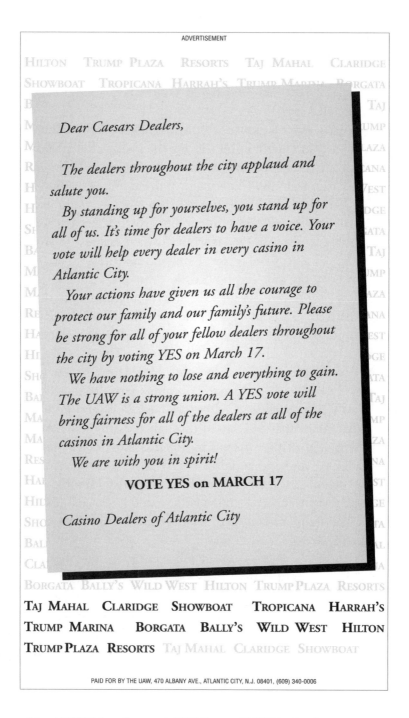

Figure 6.1.   UAW Advertisement, 2007 *Source:* UAW Region 9

tiated with the UAW in good faith. We have attempted to educate the UAW about the differences between our hospitality business and automotive manufacturing. We have asked for a reasonable proposal that allows us to remain economically competitive. And, due to the recession and downturn in the gaming industry, we have taken difficult steps, such as changes to benefits, to reduce layoffs and keep as many of our employees working as we can. How has the UAW responded? With attempts to disrupt our business."[23]

After the adrenaline spikes during the summertime rallies, discouraged dealers displayed even more discontent. By the fall of 2009, at least 30 percent of Trump Plaza dealers signed a petition to drop the UAW as their bargaining agent, that is, decertify the union.[24] Overtly or covertly encouraging a petition of signatures to hold a decertification election to kick the union out is another ploy shared in *Confessions of a Union Buster*.[25] A petition sent to the NLRB for review causes yet further delays, as the board must then rule whether to hold a decertification election. UAW officials claimed that the signatories were merely the same dealers who voted against the union in the first place (the vote was 324–149, with 31.5 percent voting against). The NLRB dismissed the decertification petition, pending the outcome of the final appeal of the original March 31, 2007, election in federal court.

Negotiations with Tropicana's dealers and slot technicians, who also voted in favor of the UAW in 2007, were also stalled. The UAW appealed to Tropicana's new ownership and new management in August 2009 to jump-start the bargaining process. Talks formally began between the UAW and management in January 2008 and about sixty meetings were held between then and August of 2009. According to the *Press of Atlantic City*, Jeff Binz, an international representative for the UAW, grew tired of repeated meetings in which attorneys for Tropicana would not even agree to contractual language that was already company policy. He said, "They were just putting up this wall. It was a stall tactic."[26] Nearly three years to the date of the election, after productive negotiations, a deal—called a *tentative agreement*—was struck and a new contract was soon ratified in a membership vote. Tropicana's full-time dealers at the top of the wage scale at $8.75 per hour would be eligible for as much as an 18 percent raise over the term of the five-year agreement. One labor scholar put it this way:

To reach any sort of agreement now would be a "huge step forward" for the UAW, said Philip Harvey, a Rutgers University professor of economics and law who studies unions.

"If there's any union in the country that understands what can happen when an industry identified with a particular city goes into decline, it's the UAW," Harvey said, referring to Detroit's shrinking auto industry. "I would expect them to be very responsible and pro-active in developing a relationship with (the gaming) industry." With the city's 11 casinos losing revenue to out-of-state competition, Harvey added, the union and Tropicana must have a shared mindset: survival. That may include the union having to make concessions with a first contract.[27]

Finally, UAW Local 8888 in Atlantic City, New Jersey, had attained symbolic and tangible legitimacy. The new contract at the Tropicana was important in turning the tide toward reaching inaugural agreements at nearby gambling houses. Three months later, in mid-November of 2010, the second agreement for gaming floor workers was reached at Caesars. Within a week, Bally's, another Caesars property, came to terms with the UAW and dealers were set to ratify a new contract, the third in the city. Five-year contracts in these three casinos means that over 2,000 dealers were covered by the first-ever collective bargaining agreements for dealers in Atlantic City's gaming pits.

After two years of operating within the context of the collective bargaining contracts that expire in 2015, it appeared that the UAW and the unionized casino houses worked collaboratively and the bitterness of the campaigns were put in the past. UAW's local regional director spoke of a "partnership" with management at Bally's, Caesars, and Tropicana while Tropicana's CEO and President, Tony Rodio, once a UAW critic, added "They have been wonderful . . . a good business partner."[28] The UAW still hopes to win elections and negotiate contracts with all of the remaining gaming properties. When the Trump Marina was sold and rebranded as the Golden Nugget, the UAW began anew with its campaign. The saga at Trump Plaza continued for several more years. The federal appeals court ruled in favor of management in May 2012, overturning the NLRB certification of the 2007 election. The UAW was still boxed out by the time Trump Plaza's owners announced their decision to close the property in the fall of 2014. The

UAW, in addition to Local 54, began a quiet campaign at Revel, but made no headway before the 2014 closing date.[29]

In good economic times, unions representing gaming, hotel, and restaurant workers in the casino industry have been able to secure higher wages and benefits as well as input into better working conditions. Their earnings are far more than in the nonunion food service industry, where workers are struggling to feed a family and fighting for increases in the minimum wage. As McDevitt said, "It's not Walmart. . . . You know, twenty miles out of here, you can't get a job for more than $8 an hour."

In Las Vegas, the story has been similar. University of Nevada–Las Vegas economist Jeffrey Waddoups conducted a novel, side-by-side city-pair study of unionized frontline casino hotel workers in Las Vegas and nonunionized workers in Reno, Nevada. Union membership resulted in a substantial wage premium, according to Waddoups: "[T]he typical worker in Las Vegas working as, for example, a baggage porter, kitchen helper, or guest room attendant (maid) among other highly unionized occupations, earns an average of 40 percent more in hourly wages than his or her counterparts in the identical occupations in Reno."[30] Further, by lifting the wages of less skilled workers at the bottom, the increased bargaining power of Las Vegas unions has reduced overall wage inequality.[31]

Unions matter even more, perhaps, in difficult economic times when hard-fought gains can be consolidated and union contracts may help prevent an erosion of benefits. That doesn't mean there are not concessions at the bargaining table, or that those concessions are necessarily welcomed by union members. For instance, food server and longtime union activist Walter is critical of some of the concessions that the union has made, starting with the 1994 contract. That contract, from his perspective, "was devastating to the industry and to the workers of Local 54." New hires took a longer time to get to the top wage rate than older hires; this introduced, in his opinion, a two-tiered wage structure. There was a wave of efforts to reform the leadership of Local 54 following this unfortunate contract and in the wake of investigations into financial irregularities, according to Walter. Soon after, McDevitt ran for union president as a reformer. But while a later 2005 strike under the new leadership resulted in some victories, especially over health care benefits, the constant pressure for concessions makes bargaining gains, like those Keith described in the opening of the chapter, even more notable.

So maybe wage increases are delayed, or at percent levels lower than the rate of inflation. Or it takes more time to move from the entry-level or new hire rate to the top rate. The title of a 2013 annual research volume of the interdisciplinary Labor and Employment Relations Association is fitting for describing the difficulties negotiating during the financial crisis and Great Recession and its aftermath: *Collective Bargaining Under Duress*. The book's chapter on hotels and casinos by Jeffrey Waddoups and Vincent Eade finds that between 2005 and 2011, union workers continued to earn more than nonunion workers, with generous benefits packages for casino workers in larger jurisdictions such as Las Vegas and Atlantic City, like health care insurance and pension plans.[32] The protections and security that come with union membership are sustained in good times and bad.

The first edition of *Why Unions Matter* by Michael Yates was published in 1998. In the preface to the 2009 second edition, the author recalls: "I showed with clear and decisive data that union members enjoyed significant advantages over nonunion workers: higher wages, more and better benefits, better access to many kinds of leaves of absence, a democratic voice in their workplaces, and a better understanding of their political and legal rights."[33] Yates argues that this is still true. And employee voice matters even more today because workers are vulnerable in an increasingly global, high-technology, cost-cutting, corporate-friendly, and union-unfriendly slow-growth economy.

PETER'S STORY

Peter had his heart broken twice while working in the casino industry. First he lost his daughter to a sudden, rare illness. Second, after working his way up from server to team captain and then to assistant manager at a casino restaurant, he was fired for taking time after attending what would have been his daughter's eighth grade school graduation; he wanted to share the experience with his daughter's best friends. Fired. No warning letter. No discipline. Just fired after more than a decade of service. Now he uses his organizational and people skills as a high-end waiter in a celebrity chef restaurant at the Borgata and on behalf of his labor union, Local 54.

The gregarious Peter, with dark curly hair, dark eyes, and a big, easy smile, has worked in restaurants since he was a teenager. He has been a dishwasher, a busboy, a cook, a cocktail server, a waiter, a maître d', and an assistant manager—thirty years' experience across a number of Atlantic City casinos. To gain experience, he put in his time assembling fruit platters, running the omelet station, and serving cocktails in a lounge and show room. It was working the omelet station where his personality started to shine: "Then, every once in a while, since I was like the funny guy, and I was talking to everybody, they actually brought me out to their omelet station. So, now here I am out on the floor as a cook at the omelet station, having a blast, talking to people, having a great time. So, it was fun and I got that feeling back, you know. It's a feeling that you get and you just know it when you're there. It's sort of like when you see a puppy and you're, like, I'm gonna get that puppy!"

When an opening arose to become a food server in a nice steak-house, he went for an interview with the boss. After handling all the basic questions about the business and passing an on-the-spot quiz, Peter's answer to a final question tells much about his personality and ambition. When asked "Where do you see yourself in five years?" Peter says his reply was: "Well, there's no rush, but I do see myself standing behind your podium, and I'll be the boss. I'll be one of the best bosses in Atlantic City. And, again, no rush for you to leave because you've got five years to look for another job." Peter got that server job. At this high-end restaurant, the staff worked in teams: a captain, two servers, and a busboy would all be assigned to a station. He asked to be put on the weaker team, to the surprise of his boss, and help to lift them up. Which he did. Two years later, he would be promoted to server team captain and be voted in as union shop steward. He was popular, with many requests for his tables, as a server and as a captain. His base salary was low, but his tips were high. He and his wife earned enough to support four children.

Both management and the staff wanted him to be promoted to as-sistant maître d'. By then, he had been there for five years. Everyone had confidence in his leadership skills. Peter knew the promotion would take him out of the bargaining unit. It was risky. "I'm in management's hands at this point. And it's kind of a volatile situation. Because you don't know after being in the union for so many years, if they didn't like you, you're out the door," he divulged. The staff encouraged him. They thought he would be a good boss. And so he was—one of the best bosses in Atlantic City.

The protection of a union grievance procedure was one thing Peter gave up to become a manager. The other thing was tips. He took a pay cut to move up. But he had to if he wanted to be another rung higher, closer to the restaurant manager job title. And it made sense to him because he could now really take care of everyone on the floor. It worked out. When the maître d' resigned, Peter was immediately thought of for that post. The boss gave it to him, but kept him at the same assistant's salary for a six-month probationary period. Peter was thriving: "I took care of my guests and they took care of me. . . . I oversaw the room. . . . I would touch every single table." He would tell a joke, engage customers in stories, and ensure people were having a wonderful time. He studied his reservation sheets. He prepared tables for his regulars; he had their wine on the table when they walked through the door. Peter took great care of his patrons at that same steakhouse for over a decade. It was all good, until it wasn't.

Anne, Peter's daughter, became ill one Thanksgiving. She passed away three months later. "A rough time for me," Peter laments. He poured his grief into fund-raising to support research into Anne's form of cancer—and into work for another year, until the following spring when the date approached for what would have been his daughter's graduation from eighth grade. All of her friends begged him to attend graduation, to see their gowns, to watch them strut across the stage, to celebrate their absent friend. It was emotionally difficult, to say the least, but Peter did attend that eighth grade graduation. He called out of work for a week in order to recover. Then came a slap on the other cheek, he said, "[T]he following week I get a letter saying thank you for your voluntary resignation. You have a good day. From [employer]." Peter adds, "It was pretty hard to take after you give literally half your life to an organization."

Peter went in for a meeting with management. They apologized and offered him his job back. His grief had turned to anger. He was having none of that: "And I said you know what you can do with the job? I said if you would do that to me—my daughter passes away and you give me a cookie basket that's like, maybe, $10, for the passing of my daughter. And then you go and fire me the week of her graduation?! I said, so, when you change the regime that you have in here, maybe, I'll think about coming back." He walked out. A restaurant worker with Peter's skills, ambition, and personality would not be out of work for long. His wife checked for openings online. Sure enough, he was soon called in for an interview.

The Borgata was expanding and Peter interviewed for a server position in one of the newly opened celebrity chef restaurants. They knew him. They knew his reputation. They had employees who used to work for Peter, and listed Peter as a reference. An old boss walked by as he was finishing up the interview and came over to chat. Later that day, Peter received the job offer over the phone. They even offered him a position in management, right then, on the spot. Yeah, he thought, been there, done that, and how did that end up? The restaurant kept insisting that Peter was overqualified, but Peter kept insisting that "I just need to be a server." He now had other priorities. He wanted to work his hours and go home to his family. He wanted to be more involved in fundraising, and in his community.

Peter now works the dinner service at one of the best casino restaurants in the city. But it is different from the old days. The service is less formal than he is used to. Captains, he says, are a thing of the past. Now the team is just "one server, one busser." This showman talks about the spiel which is as natural to him as drawing a breath, describing the food that is way beyond steak on a plate: "It's a prime piece of meat cooked over a mesquite wood grill, sliced, cut into strips over Armagnac peppercorn sauce, served with roasted potatoes." Peter provides an example of how one evening could be profitable for him, when a guy comes in and orders a bottle of Quintessa for $400. That's a pricey red wine from Napa Valley, California. He adds, "Boom, there's an $80 tip." High-end servers, according to the norms of his workplace, share part of their tips with busboys, bartenders, food runners, the coffee person, and, if services are used, the sommelier.

With Peter's seniority and membership once again in Local 54, he seems quite happy. It's steady work, and as much job security as you can have in the casino economy. At the restaurant, Peter is required to work weekends. But that's okay with him because the tips are greater. And he works the night shift, hours that garner the highest earnings as a waiter. Like many servers in restaurants, his regular paycheck is zero, meaning $0.00. As Peter explains his paychecks, "A lot of them are zeroed out." The hourly wage is below federal minimum wage, offset by the mandatory deductions for Social Security, Medicare, unemployment, disability, and in New Jersey—one of the few states to have such a benefit—paid family and medical leave. He lives on his tips, which can amount to $750 or so per week.

Peter is thriving because he has managed to find balance among a job that he likes and is good at, family, and community. The fundraising work he does in the wake of his daughter's death has been rewarding, and it takes up more and more of his free time. He relishes the time he spends with his other children and grandchildren. And, ever the man who can't sit still (he shares that he sleeps only four hours a night), he is contemplating getting involved in local politics. He sees his future as serving in the casino and serving the public. While we were interviewing him, his cell phone kept ringing, with calls from friends, fellow union members, and supporters encouraging him to toss his hat into the ring for public office. This charmer is a talker, and a listener. He just gets people. He practices forgiveness and doesn't hold grudges. Difficult customers? He has a system for that. "It rolls off [me] because I look at it almost like a Rubik's cube or Sudoku [puzzle], where you're gonna find the solution." By the time they are done with their meal, it is like "Wow, what a great time. We had a blast, thank you." As he says, "I shoot for the stars, Why you gonna shoot for a cloud that's right in your face?"

7

PUBLIC INVESTMENT OR SOCIALIZED RISK?

Government is intimately and intricately involved in the casino gaming industry. When she worked for the New Jersey Casino Control Commission, Bernice spent years on the gaming floors alongside the casino employees. In her crisp navy blue jacket with a triangular patch denoting her as a CCC gaming inspector, she was easily identifiable to casino patrons. Visibility was part of her job, one of the important elements in assuring customers that the games were legitimate. Her keen eyes had to watch everything as she circulated the floor. Who is working where? Are the customers having any problems? Where is trouble likely to break out? During her ten-hour shift, she had to focus on everything.

She would keep meticulous records in a logbook, noting infractions and problems that arose during her shift. Underage patrons who snuck onto the floor and tricked a harried cocktail server into giving them drinks? Call security and write it in the log. A dealer whose key employee license had expired or a compulsive gambler who had put himself or herself on the exclusion list? Walk them off the floor and write it in the log. Accusations of cheating? Escort the accused from the table, consult with surveillance officers and floor managers to review the video, resolve the controversy, and write it in the log. Keep tabs on whether the requisite number of security guards are on the floor. Someone's missing? Talk to the desk sergeant. Still missing on the second swing around the floor? Write them up in the log.

The other important tool for her job was the keys. In Bernice's words, "Keys was very important. The keys open everything on the casino floors: all the slot machines, all the doors, anything that had to do with anything with money—period! Because that's what it was. We oversaw the money." For example, it was Bernice's responsibility to let the dealers into the secure room where they picked up their decks of cards at the start of their shifts. And, when she wasn't walking the floor, it was usually because she was in the count room. Money is picked up from the tables every day; slots less often now that they are coinless. Then, they went to the count room: "Once we're in and then the doors lock, nobody can come in. We got money on the table, it doesn't even matter—it could be the supervisor—he wasn't allowed in there. So then they dump the money, they count the change, they count the bills. . . . They do all their verifications. The lowest might have been maybe three million [dollars]; the highest fifteen million or more." The daily tabulations of gaming win in each property, once overseen by CCC inspectors like Bernice, were how the state monitored the take in order to calculate its share. And it prevented money laundering for organized crime. Her work was part of the tight regulatory system that New Jersey had pioneered since the 1970s.

Casino management and their advocates had long clamored for looser regulations in New Jersey, citing the less regulated environments in other states. Regulations, they said, added to costs and costs ate into profits.[1] Starting in the 1990s, these calls for deregulation led to incremental changes. Where once the CCC was involved in managerial decisions such as hours of operation, which games could be offered, how decks were shuffled, and even approving advertisements, its role was gradually curtailed. Then, in the middle of a summer tourist season in 2006, the state legislature and then-Governor Jon Corzine (a Democrat) failed to reach a budget agreement, shutting down the state government. Among the nonessential state employees who could not report to work were the CCC inspectors like Bernice. Without them on the gaming floors, gambling was not allowed, and so the slot machines, roulette wheels, craps tables, blackjack, poker, and other games stopped for three days following the busy Fourth of July holiday. Gamblers headed home. The local economy reeled. The state was embarrassed. And the casinos' workers and management were united in their furor.

In the aftermath, legislation was introduced that would enable the casinos to self-regulate for up to a week in the event of another budget impasse. Corzine finally got the measure passed in 2008. But this was only the first step. Those seeking to deregulate the industry found a new ally in a former federal prosecutor and self-proclaimed "tough guy" Chris Christie, who took the reins of state government on January 19, 2010. The Republican governor needed no rookie year. He quickly established a seven-person Advisory Commission on New Jersey Gaming, Sports and Entertainment. Its recommended amendments to the Casino Control Act, which passed with bipartisan support in early 2011, transferred most of the Casino Control Commission's functions to the Division of Gaming Enforcement in the Office of the Attorney General. The DGE became the primary regulator, and the CCC was limited to issuing gaming licenses. Among other reforms, the legislation eliminated the requirement that gaming inspectors be continuously present on the casino floor.

This is how Bernice and over 100 other gaming inspectors came to lose their jobs. According to the CCC's website, their staff was reduced from 260 to less than sixty with ninety days' notice; only fifty-six of the displaced workers were rehired by the DGE.[2] Since the casinos paid Bernice's salary while the state covered her benefits, most of the savings went to the casinos. Minimum staffing levels for security officers, surveillance personnel, and pit bosses were also abolished, facilitating some of the cutbacks discussed in chapter 4. Changes in internal control systems no longer had to be approved by regulators. Bernice questioned the changes: "What happened was that the casinos wanted to take over their own properties. . . . How can you come in and just rewrite bylaws that have protected the industry and employees?"

Yet at the same time that Governor Christie was championing deregulation and tighter state budgets, he was also continuing public involvement in the industry in other ways. Both northern and southern New Jersey interests wanted to turn around the economic engine that was Atlantic City. Governor Christie executed a power grab that increased state rather than local control over the industry and Atlantic City, as well as a massive, $261 million bailout for the floundering Revel project, both described in this chapter. The Revel subsidy was listed as one of ten "megadeals" in New Jersey tracked by the national advocacy organization Good Jobs First. Like many of these handouts provided by state governments, the Revel project did not lead to the quantity or quality of jobs promised in advance.[3]

In fact, Christie has presided over what the Trenton-based research institute, New Jersey Policy Perspective, has termed "a surge in subsidies."[4] Such active involvement in support of the private sector should not be surprising. When competition intensifies and profits diminish as an industry becomes saturated, businesses frequently look to government. Despite the rhetoric of conservative politicians and the economists whose work they cite, government involvement in markets is ongoing. It just takes different forms depending upon who is in charge.

Public policy makers are as much a part of casino gaming as Bernice and her fellow regulators were part of the casino's day-to-day operations. The market for gambling is a state creation. The industry could only develop and flourish by chipping away at longstanding prohibitions against legalized gambling. Back when the New Jersey Casino Control Act was enacted in 1977, gambling—whether legal in Las Vegas or illegal everywhere else—was associated with organized crime. New Jersey's highly regulated model of casino gaming helped legitimate the industry nationally, making it safe for Wall Street and the rest of the country. Regulating casinos was thus integral to the normalization of gambling. Planning was as important as entrepreneurship in the expansion of casino gaming. To this day, state governments promote as well as regulate the industry, sometimes combining both functions within the same agencies—a troubling practice.

Casinos, like many other businesses, also benefit from public involvement through infrastructure development. Many of the Casino Reinvestment Development Authority (CRDA) expenditures benefit the casinos directly, by underwriting construction projects, or indirectly, by attracting tourists with more non-gaming amenities. Recent economic development investments listed on CRDA's website include a Visitor's Welcome Center, Boardwalk revitalization, and shopping complexes such as the Walk urban outlet mall and the Pier Shops at Caesars (an upscale mall built on a former amusement pier that is filled with national retailers and designers, as well as restaurants and a food court).[5] Direct assistance to the casinos by CRDA includes new hotel towers to draw conventions and expanded non-gaming facilities in the casinos themselves. Such projects dovetail with the product differentiation strategy designed to remake Atlantic City.

Development subsidies are another means of encouraging local economic development. Development subsidies are defined by the advocacy group Good Jobs First as "cash, tax breaks, and in-kind benefits given to companies to offset the costs of opening or expanding a new facility."[6] The often well-intentioned objective of development subsidies is job creation, paid for through tax expenditures (forfeited tax revenues). Revel is not the only casino to benefit. Following the fanfare over the Revel development subsidies, both Resorts ($5,055,556) and Harrah's ($24,128,000) were quietly awarded Economic Redevelopment and Growth grants in 2012, according to the New Jersey Economic Development Authority website.

Government nurtured the industry to meet particular public purposes—not simply to generate profits for shareholders. In exchange for these various forms of public support, the casinos are supposed to benefit the community by providing good jobs, bringing customers for local businesses, and using local vendors. But, as documented by Good Jobs First, development subsidies, including those provided to the casinos, are rarely transparent, lack binding requirements or "clawback provisions" if rosy job creation projections are not met, and are seldom subjected to rigorous cost/benefit analysis. They redirect funds away from public goods and usually go to large businesses with lobbying power rather than small, local businesses.

In addition, the casinos provide tax revenue to the state and local governments. The appeal is that such taxes are supposed to draw revenue from outsiders rather than state residents. For this reason, many of the first states to legalize gambling positioned casinos near their borders or in tourist havens like Atlantic City. The taxes are also portrayed as voluntary because they impact those who choose to gamble.[7] New Jersey assesses an 8 percent gross gaming revenue (GGR) tax, paid every Monday. The state also assesses casinos 1.25 percent of GGR to be directly invested in CRDA-sanctioned projects or to be deposited with CRDA to purchase CRDA-sponsored bonds.[8] These rates are far lower than most states with commercial casinos. Remember the "pay luxury tax" square between Boardwalk and Park Place, in the Monopoly board game? New Jersey casinos must also charge a luxury tax of 9 percent on show admissions and hotel rooms and 3 percent on alcoholic drinks, on top of the 7 percent state sales tax. However, the state caps the combined rate at 13 percent, cutting their sales tax accordingly. For example, a concert ticket in Atlantic City would be subject to the 9 percent luxury tax, so the state sales tax would be reduced to 4 percent to meet the cap. There are also hotel room occupancy fees (1 percent), hotel parking fees ($3 per day, mostly to CRDA), and a tourism promotion fee ($2 per day for casinos, but $3 per day on comped rooms). In 2013, the casinos and their patrons provided the State of New Jersey with over $200 million in gaming taxes, another $100 million in sales and luxury taxes, and about $54 million from the various fees.[9] The city and county governments primarily derive revenue from property taxes, but the assessments on casino properties have been declining.

While the casino industry has a distinctive relationship with government, most businesses benefit from public investments, are subject to regulations, and provide tax revenue, jobs, and other social benefits. Debates among economic analysts are frequently portrayed as dueling ideologies between those who believe that free markets allocate resources efficiently and those who think that the imperfections of real-world markets require some limited government intervention. *Intervention* is a telling word. It implies that private-sector market mechanisms can and do operate independently of political and social structures—that government is an external force that we can choose whether to unleash. Political economists frequently point out that this depiction is nonsense. Drawing upon the work of Karl Polanyi, political economists assert that markets are, in fact, generally produced by and through government action.[10]

Many businesses, in fact, rather than championing free markets, look to government to shield them from the harsh realities of competition or to assist them in externalizing their costs of production. For example, patents and copyright protection give people or companies property rights over their innovations, limiting the ability of others to produce similar products. Businesses are protected by police and firefighters, hire employees often educated by public or charter schools, utilize public roads to transport goods and customers, and rely on the courts to enforce contracts. Government programs that clean up pollution from factories or that augment low incomes of the working poor can be said to *socialize* the costs of production. Saying that such policies constitute government involvement in markets does not make them wrong. Instead, we need to recognize that such "rent-seeking behavior"[11] is part of the normal course of doing business for many firms, especially large corporations. Equally endemic to markets are the demands on government by workers to protect them from economic instability with a social safety net and boost their bargaining power via low unemployment rates, collective bargaining rights, and other means. Despite the rhetoric of free markets, "every facet of the economy is shaped by policies that could easily be altered," according to Dean Baker of the Center for Economic and Policy Research.[12]

In his book *The Predator State*, James K. Galbraith takes the argument a bit further. He argues that principled small-government conservatives did once exist. In recent years, however, they have been largely supplanted by those who espouse a laissez-faire ideology but are, in fact, engaged in predation. Predation, in his words, is "the systematic abuse of public institutions for private profit or, equivalently, the systematic undermining of public protections for the benefit of private clients."[13] He contrasts predation with the productive relationship between the public and private sectors in the mid-twentieth century when his father, John Kenneth Galbraith, was an advisor to President John F. Kennedy. James Galbraith attributes the evolution to an institutional shift away from corporations run by their managers to an economy of holding companies owned by private equity and other investors focused on short time horizons. Firms have become commodities to be bought and sold for quick profits rather than just sites for the production of commodities. The new financial capitalists, he asserts, are more interested in capturing the state to line their own pockets than in limiting its scope.

Whether we view socialization of costs as a mainstay of market economies or predation as indicative of a new phase, political economists point out that we need to distinguish public policy initiatives that advance the broad public interest of a variety of stakeholders from those that primarily benefit just a handful of "vested interests" (a term popularized by institutional economist Thorstein Veblen). The relationship between the privately held casino industry and public sector governance is, therefore, complex. At times the investment of public funds appears to be mutually beneficial, to advance the public interest. We can understand why politicians in Atlantic County and throughout the state have scrambled for ways to prop up the industry. Other motives, however, can complicate the picture. Corruption is, of course, always a concern, and has a long history in both the state and the city. But a cozy relationship between political and business leaders can also inadvertently distort policy makers' perception about whether and when business interests and the public interest are in harmony. For this reason, it is critical that economic development strategies are transparent and accountable.

Further, as state and local governments have seen their coffers diminish—especially during the Great Recession and anemic recovery—generating revenue from casino gaming has become more of a priority. In some cases, this has meant greater complicity with cost-cutting strategies as desperate measures to keep the casinos' doors open and tax revenues flowing. Deregulation has assisted with the process.[14] Unfortunately, as we have seen, cost-cutting measures displace the goal of creating good jobs. Economic development, as we have noted, requires incomes that circulate through the local economy. Our concern is that specific aspects of the 2011 overhaul of New Jersey casino gaming, outlined in this chapter, have either intentionally or unintentionally undermined the goal of generating sustainable livelihoods for casino employees and their families.

The complexity of private versus public interests in the casino gaming industry is not unique to New Jersey. For example, New York governor Andrew Cuomo cited both jobs and tax revenues in 2013 as he sought to expand gambling in his state from racinos and tribal casinos to full-fledged casino resorts. According to a *New York Times* reporter, Cuomo advocated casinos in upstate New York as a "bold move to bring jobs and tourism to economically depressed regions." Yet at the same time: "Mr. Cuomo has already used the prospect of expanded gambling to find more revenue for the state, brokering three recent deals with Native American tribes to settle longstanding contract disputes and other issues. The deals, most recently with the Seneca Nation, will bring the state hundreds of millions of dollars in revenue-sharing from the tribes in exchange for geographic exclusivity."[15]

On the other hand, cities and states expecting big payoffs may be as disappointed as any novice gambler. A set of empirical studies by Douglas Walker, summarized in his book *Casinonomics*, found, to his surprise, that casinos had no positive impact (and possibly even a negative effect) on state revenues. In order to capture potential substitution effects (the fact that money spent on gambling could have been spent on other taxable activities if casinos were not available), Walker focused on total state revenue (minus federal contributions) in all fifty states from 1985 to 2000; he measured the impact of the volume of gambling on revenue, controlling for other relevant factors. The model, as he notes, lumps together states whose gaming industries are at very different stages of development and that have drastically different tax rate structures on gaming activities, so his findings are not definitive. Walker concludes, "Our results show that casinos may be ineffective or counterproductive in the long run in terms of tax revenue generation. . . . Legalized gambling may not always be the 'golden egg' that it is sometimes promoted to be."[16] This is particularly true as casino gaming proliferates; the goal of taxing tourists in lieu of one's own citizens is more and more elusive when people gamble close to home.[17]

Recently, casinos seem to be appropriating resources from public coffers. For example, Atlantic City borrowed a reported $250 million over a three-year period in order to refund property taxes to some of the casinos after losing assessment appeals in court. The assessments on casino properties are based on how much income they generate; as their revenues have plunged, the rates set back in 2006 are much higher than current conditions would warrant. Most of the casinos have filed appeals and have been granted refunds and/or credits against future taxes, lowering the city's tax base by over one-third. Closure of the Atlantic Club intensified the problem. The casino abatements have devastated the city's fiscal position, leading to a bond rating downgrade. They have also drastically increased residents' and small business taxes, and rippled outward to raise county tax rates in surrounding communities.[18] And this does not include the tax expenditures for the Revel project by the state.

Once again, it seems that Atlantic City's experiences foreshadow trends elsewhere. Just down the interstate in Delaware, for example, Governor Jack Markell was announcing an $8 million "temporary" bailout of that state's three casinos. The justification for the bailout was the financial squeeze felt from high taxes and increased competition.[19]

Only two weeks after assuming office in 2010, Governor Christie issued Executive Order No. 11, appointing a seven-person Advisory

Commission on New Jersey Gaming, Sports and Entertainment. It kept no minutes or records of its meetings, prompting some groups to accuse the commission of meeting in secret and violating the state's open-records act. By late July, the commission had issued a short, twenty-nine-page report, calling for a complete overhaul of New Jersey casino gaming, horse racing, and relevant entertainment. Governor Christie accepted their recommendations the following day. These included the restructuring of the regulatory agencies and elimination of regulations described above, along with a five-year moratorium on racinos or casinos elsewhere in the state, meaning that there would be no slot machines or video lottery terminals (VLTs) at the two state-owned racetracks: the Meadowlands and Monmouth Park. This was a win for southern New Jersey over northern New Jersey. The stated objective was to bring Atlantic City back to economic health as a tourist destination first, before entering the convenience gambling market in the northern part of the state.

The win came at a price, the erosion of local control. The transfer of regulatory power from the relatively independent Atlantic City–based Casino Control Commission to the Division of Gaming Enforcement was part of the picture. When it was established, no more than three of the five members of the CCC could be from a single political party; it was to be "in, not of, the Department of Treasury." Praising New Jersey's approach several years before it was dismantled, Atlantic City attorney Nick Casiello Jr. argued that this design was "to ensure the greatest possible independence from political influence." In contrast, he observed, "since the Office of the Attorney General reports to the Governor, the Division is not as structurally isolated from influence as the Commission."[20] The number of commissioners was whittled down to three through attrition in 2010, and remains at this smaller size commensurate with its diminished duties.

A self-described senior policy advisor from the office of Governor Christie's chief of staff assumed command of the DGE. In a 2012 interview, Director David Rebuck outlined his vision for the agency as looking out for the industry's interests, saying, "But, the big picture is— and it's what I always ask the industry: What do you need to compete and succeed in this new environment? It's my goal to know what that is and to help them get that done in a way that ensures integrity and public oversight."[21] His attitude reflects the conflation of two responsibilities: regulation and promotion. DGE career staff members, meanwhile, are diligently assuming their new assignments and attempting to be responsible guardians of the public trust. The casinos do not always get their way; Trump Plaza was rebuffed by the DGE when the casino requested permission to completely close its table games for part of the overnight shift on weekdays.

A far more sweeping and controversial recommendation called for placing Atlantic City's casino and entertainment district under state authority. The proposal essentially took part of the city away from Atlantic City's elected leaders. Governor Christie did not mince his words in his official announcement: "Atlantic City has had a historically corrupt, ineffective government."[22] He added that he wanted a clean and safe tourism district. The governor called for all public hearings, consultations, and legislative debates to be completed within a year, proclaiming a deadline of July 1, 2011.

The movers and shakers influencing the direction of Atlantic City and the New Jersey economy had concluded that bigger and better casinos were necessary but not sufficient for a turnaround. Despite the growth of tourist amenities, the city itself continued to have a tarnished reputation. People perceived crime as a problem, regardless of what a careful reading of crime statistics actually showed.[23] People blamed the images of urban poverty in surrounding neighborhoods for discouraging visitors. One way to read these complaints and the ultimate response is that a racially diverse city with a local government largely in the hands of African American political leaders was incompatible with the upscale image that Atlantic City sought to project. In the words that open the master plan eventually developed to implement the governor's vision, the tourism district was "intended to create a vision for changing perceptions of Atlantic City."[24] While insisting that they wanted to work with the governor, many—though certainly not all—local city officials remained skeptics. In fact, there was considerable unease between then-Atlantic City Mayor Lorenzo Langford and Governor Christie throughout much of the reform planning. At one point during the turbulent year of negotiations, the mayor alleged that the governor promised a partnership with the city and then broke his promise. Mayor Langford even threatened to sue the state over its Atlantic City plans.[25]

The first sketch of a conceptual map for the newly proposed state district was published in the *Press of Atlantic City* on July 22, 2010, coinciding with Governor Christie's announcement. It included non-contiguous sections of the city around the casino hotels such as the shopping and restaurant area known as the Walk and parts of the city's marina. Leaders took care not to use the word "takeover" and instead referred to the Atlantic City restructuring as a "private-public" partnership. The semantics—word choice and word order—are important. Democrats such as Senate President Stephen Sweeney, who initially opposed a "state-controlled" district, eventually warmed to the idea when phrased as a partnership.[26] The governor and legislature just disagreed on exactly which public entities should be in partnership with which private partners. But the phrase also sidestepped the important question of why the state has the right to override local democratic governance institutions. As one local resident complained, "The people in this city have less and less to say about our city and what happens in it. We don't have the ability to say anything anymore."[27]

The bill to create a state-run tourism district (S-11) passed with even more support than the bill (S-12) to ease state regulation of gaming. Governor Christie signed the landmark legislation package on February 1, 2011, at the construction site of the Revel, hoping to spur financing of the casino and economic development in the casino's South Inlet neighborhood. While technically contiguous due to the designation of particular streets and the Boardwalk as part of the district, the shape of the final map of the tourism district is more convoluted than a gerrymandered political district.

The legislation technically transferred control over this oddly shaped district to the Casino Reinvestment Development Authority. Democrats, especially local State Senator Jim Whelan, forced Christie to acquiesce to giving administrative authority to the preexisting agency rather than creating a new public-private venture. Christie did, however, manage to force out the executive director of CRDA and install some new appointees.[28] CRDA was granted broad powers: "jurisdiction to impose land-use regulations, implement development and design guidelines and implement initiatives that promote cleanliness, commercial development and safety, undertake redevelopment projects, and institute public safety improvements in coordination with security and law enforcement personnel. CRDA also has jurisdiction over the rules and regulations affecting the control and direction of traffic within the

Tourism District, has approval authority of road projects, and has the right to exercise eminent domain."[29]

In short, governance of a large swath of the city is now in the hands of an entity whose seventeen-member board of directors includes fourteen seats appointed by the New Jersey governor, plus the state treasurer, the state attorney general, and lastly, the Atlantic City mayor. Two of the gubernatorial appointees are designated for representatives of the casinos. In our interview with Zoe, the fifty-something cocktail server whose parents optimistically worked on the 1978 initiative, she voiced the concerns of many locals: "I'm fearful of that because [of] who's running our state now. It's worrisome for me." A union activist at a Caesars-owned property, she made an analogy between the state government and the private equity interests running her workplace: "They [TPG and Apollo Management] wanted to make money for themselves to suck it out to take it somewhere else to the next capital gains that they could make. Is the state going to do the same thing? Are they going to take everything they can get out of Atlantic City and move it up to where most of the wealthier Jerseyites are? I don't know. I'm fearful of that. I don't have faith." By blaming local government for Atlantic City's problems, attention was being diverted from the impact of the national macro economy, the way social problems like crime were exacerbated by gambling and tourism, as well as longstanding structural problems such as eroding tax bases facing many local governments.

Atlantic City has always been a divided city, but now it is official. The state cherry-picked the areas it wants to control, essentially ignoring the poorest residential communities in the city. The geographic and fiscal division evokes images of racial segregation. The casinos, casino hotels, and other major tourist attractions are in a district run by an administrative entity of the state. The rest of the city, largely poor and African American, remains in the hands of the municipal government and the mayor. That Governor Christie, who appointed the advisory commission to develop the plan, is white and then-Mayor Langford is black increases the appearance that this takeover has similar racial politics to other recent cases where state leaders have usurped power from local governments in largely African American cities to further economic interests.

One prominent case study that has attracted more national media attention is the story of Benton Harbor, Michigan.[30] The corporate home of Whirlpool Corporation, Benton Harbor is a once-prosperous and racially mixed city on the eastern shore of Lake Michigan, abandoned by most everyone except a core of African American citizens. The last Whirlpool plant in Benton Harbor closed in 1987, though a corporate headquarters remains. The state takeover was executed under a 2011 (Michigan) Emergency Manager Law. State-appointed Emergency Manager Joseph Harris is, in the words of a *New York Times* reporter who wrote a profile of the controversy, "[b]lissfully free of the checks and balances of democratic government." The use of an emergency manager was coupled with a scheme that corporate, state, and some community leaders promised would revitalize the local economy: a luxury golf resort surrounded by hotels, shops, and new housing. Part of the land came from what had long been a public park. Some of the financing drew upon public funds channeled through nonprofits in a public-private partnership. But "Harbor Shores" has not drawn the wealthy Chicagoans and other upscale customers it was supposed to bring, and the development process stalled. Benton Harbor is viewed by progressives like MSNBC analyst Rachel Maddow as a harbinger for national trends. It certainly seems to have been forged in the same fire as the tourism district scheme for Atlantic City.

A 2013 study by the Pew Charitable Trusts identifies nineteen states that have laws permitting states to intervene in financially distressed local governments.[31] The report is generally favorable about the need for state governments to assist older cities whose economic and fiscal base has weakened. However, Pew is concerned about the ad hoc nature of the grounds and process for state involvement. The range of interventions pursued by various states can be mild or aggressive, including such measures as debt restructuring, renegotiating labor contracts, raising taxes and fees, providing emergency financing and technical assistance, or, in a few states (including Michigan), dissolving or consolidating the local government entirely. The report briefly acknowledges that local governments often resist such financial oversight, but asserts that fears about "the usurpation of democracy" can be allayed by engaging "stakeholders." The unspoken assumption is that the state or its appointed representatives are somehow better able to make the hard choices. In response to the Atlantic City takeover, however, historian David Schwartz, director of the University of Nevada–Las Vegas Center for Gaming Research (he was born and raised in Atlantic

City) observed, "You're taking away control from the local government. But it's possible that the state won't be more efficient than local government."[32] For this reason, citizens should be wary of aggressive intervention measures such as those in Atlantic City and Benton Harbor.

In a dramatic election upset in November 2013, white Republican Don Guardian beat incumbent mayor Langford. As a socially liberal and openly gay Republican who campaigned heavily in immigrant and African American communities, Guardian was able to draw votes and support from diverse constituencies who usually vote Democratic. Guardian was, at the time of his election, executive director of a former nonprofit called the Atlantic City Special Improvement District that worked with local businesses on beautification projects; CRDA had absorbed the Special Improvement District as part of the tourism district plan. Guardian's victory in the mayoral race was helped by the perception that he would be better able to work with the state authorities and casinos. Interviewed by the local press on the third anniversary of the takeover, State Senate President Stephen Sweeney suggested that Guardian's election may have forestalled the state from further increasing its oversight of city governance.[33] And better relations with the state matter: The new mayor immediately sought state aid to help offset the fiscal disaster wrought by the declining tax base and abatements to casinos.

Whose interests were served by the takeover in Atlantic City and at what cost is still an open question. It is early to assess the concrete impact of the takeover, especially since the transition faced numerous initial delays. As a first step in taking control of the district, CRDA was responsible for producing a master plan. After issuing a Request for Proposals (RFP), the work of preparing this plan was outsourced to a team that included Jones Lang LaSalle, a global real estate services firm; the Jerde Partnership, an architecture and urban planning firm; Birdsall Services Group, public engineers; and Hill Wallack, a Princeton-based law firm. The master plan that they produced articulates three phases of development, essentially reviving and expanding the same concept of a destination resort for more than gambling that was sidetracked by the Great Recession. As in Benton Harbor, the grandiose plans seem to be a boon for real estate developers and the construction trades.

Some of the practical results of CRDA's administration of the tourism district have been increased funds for policing and increased frequency of street cleaning—echoing Christie's emphasis on a clean and safe place for tourists. A 2012 CRDA annual report proudly discusses its efforts to create a walkable city, including facelifts for the facades of buildings and landscaping.[34] Major building projects have been undertaken or are in the works. Meaningful changes have been slow, however, and come nowhere near offsetting the decline in living standards for casino employees wrought by cost-cutting measures and casino closures.

The master plan publically declares a vision of a "total and diversified city for all seasons, for all ages, and all social classes." There is evidence, however, that the poor are not truly welcome in the tourism district. Reading the CRDA annual report more carefully, one can find a nebulous reference to the need for "specific attention to the City's density of social service issues" and "relocation efforts."[35] These refer to an initiative to move critical nonprofit social services such as the Atlantic City Rescue Mission, a soup kitchen, and an addiction recovery center out of the walkable district. The Christian-based rescue mission is the largest shelter in the state, and serves as a magnet for homeless from surrounding towns and counties. In addition to beds, the mission serves around 700 meals per day, offers a medical clinic and mental health services, and provides work-readiness programs. Some locals complain that social service agencies in surrounding communities practice "Greyhound therapy," meaning they give patrons bus tickets to Atlantic City. Officials, including the governor, are on record as saying that providing these services is incompatible with revitalization of the tourism district. CRDA has even pressured the mission and other local charities to require the homeless to undergo a centralized registration process in an Atlantic County office building before being allowed access to any of their charitable services. When the president of the mission resisted turning away people on their doorstep, the mission's Board of Trustees ousted him.[36]

Under the heading "Removing Blight," the 2012 annual report lists thirty-seven sites identified for demolition and twenty-nine buildings demolished. CRDA has been taken to court over the use of eminent domain to usurp property and to condemn two public housing developments. In their place, CRDA is envisioning mixed use projects (housing and retail complexes), including one in the neighborhood surrounding Revel.[37] The Boraie project's rental units were predicted to lease for at least $1,000 per month, save for 20 percent of the units mandated as affordable housing.[38] The undermining of local democratic control over the form that economic development will take in Atlantic City's future seems to have led to displacing the poor and lower-income residents who have called the city by the sea home—the classic dynamic of gentrification.

Governor Christie signed the two laws overhauling the casino industry and creating the tourism district in Revel's yet-unfinished shell. On the same day, the state Economic Development Authority (EDA) provided the spark that led to the much-anticipated opening of the new casino in the summer of 2012.

The idea that Revel would somehow be a "game-changer" or "save" Atlantic City persisted during the years leading up to completion of the project. Revel's signature was more than its anticipated size, originally projected at 4,000 rooms and 7,000 parking spaces.[39] Revel was designed to amplify industry trends by marketing itself as a luxury resort that happened to have gambling rather than as a casino. The word "casino" was prominently absent from the property's name. Every one of the deluxe rooms would have an ocean view. Keith, who works two casino jobs, one of them at Revel, told us that he admires the vision: "The concept was to bring back to Atlantic City the upper crust, the millionaires, focus on non-gaming." As discussed in chapter 3, targeting upscale consumers was the strategy that drove the Borgata's success and is well suited to an era of spiraling income inequality. It is also an appealing counter-move against those who decry casinos for preying on low-income customers.

Wall Street financial giant Morgan Stanley initially acquired the site adjacent to Showboat in 2006 and plans were quickly developed to construct a megaresort and develop the surrounding area. However, once the U.S. financial bubble burst a year later in 2007, the project encountered major obstacles in securing financing from private or public sources. Morgan Stanley, reeling from the escalating financial crisis, dropped out of the project and wrote off around $1 billion in losses. Revel Entertainment Group CEO Kevin DeSanctis scrambled to keep the project alive for years, even as construction completely halted in 2010. State legislators exerted considerable political pressure, although some local political actors—including Bob McDevitt, the president of the largest casino workers union—expressed concerns that Revel would simply crowd out existing casinos rather than create new jobs.[40]

Despite these objections, the Christie administration came to the rescue. An Economic Redevelopment and Growth grant from the EDA allocated $261 million in tax breaks over twenty years in order to help Revel Entertainment Group secure financing for the project. A substantial portion of the funds was to be designated toward economic development projects intended to gentrify the South Inlet neighborhood around the resort. The tax breaks would only take effect once the resort opened its doors for business. Tax breaks in hand, financing was secured and construction resumed.[41] Creating jobs was a reason for the tax breaks, including a promise to hire some city residents; but shortly before it opened, Revel announced that almost 40 percent of its workforce would be part-timers.[42]

And so the resort opened with great fanfare during the summer of 2012. Beyoncé (Knowles) performed the first four shows in the new concert venue, including one attended by First Lady Michelle Obama with her daughters, Sasha and Malia Obama. Other celebrities mingled with throngs of visitors and curious locals. What they found was a glistening package. As described by one blogger:

> Revel is trying to lure people who want to go to a nightclub (there are three, including a burlesque club), see a concert (Beyoncé just added a fourth show in May), bask in a spa (this one is 32,000-square-feet and has a co-ed bath house), swim or surf at the beach (now being replenished by the Corps of Engineers), or lounge by a pool (with cocktail girls and pool boys with misting bottles). They want people to visit their 14 restaurants and "curated collection of Iron Chefs, Michelin chefs and James Beard Award winners." Instead of gaming credits or slot dollars, they're offering a $30 "tasting credit" toward foodie-friendly eats as part of their preview package. Gone are the bland buffets, replaced by trendy tapas, "food truck" style tacos and churros (with spicy Valrhona chocolate dipping sauce to help ease some of those losses at the blackjack table), Belgian beers, and a "1920s-era zinc cocktail bar."[43]

Yet even at a total cost of $2.4 billion, the property that opened was scaled down from the original vision. To get the tax breaks, they had to open. One tower with slightly under 2,000 rooms was built instead of the original two, and some of the interior floors were not completed. The beach area in front of the hotel, renamed "Revel Beach," was unfinished and marred by construction cranes.

The flashy opening attracted a media blitz that soon fizzled out. The casino floor itself was relatively small because high rollers gamble in more secluded spaces. The layout of the property made it difficult to find things, unlike at Borgata, where shops and restaurants are laid out in a circle surrounding the casino floor. The size and multi-level design presented structural difficulties for seniors and others with limited mobility.[44] There were no affordable food and beverage options. Even chef Jose Garces's taco truck was costly. Pondering the menu at one restaurant, a patron complained to a reporter, "I'm not getting that [a $30 lobster burger]. That's completely out of my price range."[45] The entire Revel property was smoke free—a radical departure from the common industry assumption that addictive personalities both gamble and smoke cigarettes. DeSanctis was proud of bucking conventions, confiding to one reporter, "I think smoking is so yesterday."[46]

In their effort to appeal to wealthy overnight guests who didn't regularly gamble, Revel management made middle-income day trippers feel unwelcome and intimidated. Casino regulars and even locals related that the place was stuffy. When the initial revenue numbers indicated that Revel ranked eighth out of the twelve casinos in gaming revenue in its early months, more and more observers began to doubt that the project would live up to its hype. (Measured by GGR, Revel hovered in the lower third of the Atlantic City rankings throughout 2012 and 2013.) Within six months, adjectives used to describe Revel included "lackluster, disappointing, underwhelming, and even abysmal."[47] Seeming to confirm the concerns of labor leaders that Revel would simply cannibalize gamblers from other properties rather than grow the Atlantic City market, DeSanctis admitted in July 2012 that gambling is a "market-share game." Yet he continued to defend Revel's three-prong demographic approach—gamblers, conventioneers, and leisure-seeking tourists—maintaining that its success would be grounded in the third group.[48]

Revel was also offering a different kind of labor-management relations than its predecessors. The casino refused to sign the pattern
contract with Local 54 or even to recognize union representation for its
hotel and restaurant employees. All frontline employees are offered
short-term appointments of four to six years, and are expected to reapply for their jobs, competing against other candidates, at the end of
each cycle. The lack of job security makes it difficult to buy a home,
take out a car loan, start a family, or plan for the future. Almost immediately after it opened, Local 54 began a quiet campaign to organize the
Revel staff. Sympathetic employees were identified and they began to
talk union with their coworkers. The process was initially slow, but
critical. Labor leaders feared the example of a union-busting Revel
might inspire other casinos to take a more aggressive stance.

Total Atlantic City casino employment rose temporarily when Revel
opened, but the numbers fell off again after the initial opening summer.
The property never delivered anywhere close to the promised job creation. By October of the same year, Revel had lost over $110 million,
measured as gross operating profit. Borgata, number one in operating
profit in 2012, earned roughly the arithmetic reverse, or $119 million.
DeSanctis started looking for an additional infusion of credit. Though
Revel, the casino that was supposed to help save Atlantic City, was
struggling, the venture was not a complete failure. What Revel did for
the industry was help boost hotel room occupancy, measured in room
nights booked/occupied. It also helped increase sales by third-party
restaurants, owned independently from the casino properties. These
successes increased luxury and sales tax collections.

Still, less than one year after opening, Revel filed for bankruptcy.
CEO DeSanctis was ousted. An interim crisis team was brought in to
usher the property through bankruptcy. Revel emerged from bankruptcy protection under a new ownership structure, a holding company
owned by the casino's creditors. A key stake in this holding company (28
percent) is held by hedge fund Chatham Asset Management; the CCC
awarded Chatham a license to operate the casino in June 2013. The
State Investment Council subsequently approved a controversial $300
million investment of public sector pension monies in Chatham. To
avoid state pension money being indirectly invested in Revel, Chatham
is supposed to be divested of its shares of the casino before this investment is implemented. According to news reports, New Jersey Treasury

Department staff told the Investment Council members who questioned the investment that "they expect Chatham to be out of Revel by the time the state provides the money."[49]

The resort switched decks following the bankruptcy reorganization. One of the first things to be tossed was the no-smoking policy. Revel reversed the ban as it opened for the 2013 summer season over Memorial Day weekend. The new head of marketing said even his mother complained about the smoking ban; quoting his mother, he claimed "It doesn't feel like a casino unless you smell smoke in the air."[50] Outside observers had jumped on the smoking ban as a key reason for the casino's problems, but the employees we spoke with who actually work there (both nonsmokers) disagree. In his interview, Keith, a part-time waiter, told us that "what I remember is guests saying to me 'This air is remarkable.'" Isiah, a dealer at both Borgata and Revel, thought that management did not promote the benefits of the smoke-free environment aggressively enough. He felt that people could get used to smoke-free casinos just as they have adjusted to smoke-free restaurants. Looking for a quick fix and a symbol that they wanted middle-income gamblers, Revel made room for the largest contiguous smoking section of any Atlantic City casino, 30,000 square feet.[51] What an about-face.

Another high priority was to cut costs in all areas, from big-ticket items and staffing to supplies. For example, Revel successfully renegotiated its tax assessment to $1.15 billion, only half of the $2.4 billion construction cost. Other cost-cutting measures followed. Keith noticed a drastic decrease in the number of security staff patrolling the floors and other reductions in service. Isiah indicated that many of his full-time coworkers were offered a choice between losing their jobs (with some kind of severance package) or being "demoted" to part-time status. The company announced that it was stopping contributions to employee 401(k) accounts in August 2013.

The property was also renamed the Revel Casino-Hotel. "If you want gamblers to feel wanted, then you need to let them know you're a casino," said Randall Fine, a representative of the Las Vegas firm charged with marketing the new brand.[52] An aggressive campaign sought to attract gamblers from across the northeast region. A new billboard for Revel along the Atlantic City Expressway proclaimed simply, "Gamblers Wanted."

It might have said "Buyers Wanted." As of 2014, the property was once again for sale. Employees' jobs were threatened. Revel's hotel and restaurant staff, however, had a card to play. The organizing campaign went public. Local 54 started a media campaign advocating speedy union recognition in order to protect jobs and avoid another wave of job losses like the ones when Sands and Atlantic Club closed. Without a contract, the hotel and restaurant workers would not have the same protections as their compatriots in other casinos, the protections described by Keith in the opening of chapter 6—job security, but also access to health benefits and a pension. The employees voiced fears that a new owner could suspend operations during renovations, laying off most of the staff and forcing them to reapply for their positions. Dealers like Isiah had no similar recourse. He fretted about the possibility of losing his job. Although it was only one of three jobs he and his wife held, they needed the income to support their family.

Public pressure was applied to political leaders and state administrators to lean on Revel's managers to recognize the union and preserve jobs. The State Investment Council, Local 54 argued, could exert its leverage over Chatham (Revel's largest shareholder). Local 54 President Bob McDevitt observed, "From the outset, the state has justified its interest in Revel with the promise of jobs, but has shown little regard for the workers who filled those jobs, or for the workers who lost their jobs, in part, due to Revel's unwelcome contribution to overcapacity in the Atlantic City market." Some political leaders from both parties agreed that the state needed to monitor the sale, if only by using the remaining licensing power of the CCC, in order to prevent another wave of job losses.

The internal organizing combined with public pressure was partially effective. The hotel and restaurant employees overwhelmingly voted for union representation in an election held in June 2014: approximately 80 percent in favor. In a press release issued by the union, a Revel employee said, "I want the same job security and benefits for me and my son that Local 54 members have."[53] Revel president Scott Kreeger agreed not to contest the election. Negotiations would be in conjunction with the other ten casinos since the Local 54 contracts expire at the same time in September of 2014. However, the Revel employees—both unionized and nonunion—still face an uncertain future. Shortly after agreeing to recognize the union, the casino entered Chapter 11 bank-

This is only the beginning . . .

Esto es sólo el principio . . .

UNITE**HERE!**
LOCAL **54**

1014 Atlantic Avenue • Atlantic City, NJ 08401 • 609-344-5400

ruptcy for the second time and was put up for auction. Without an imminent buyer, the casino was slated to close before contract negotiations started, meaning Keith, Isiah, and their coworkers would have no job protection.

So what did the state get in exchange for its assistance to Revel? Had its innovative model been successful, public intervention to facilitate financing and sacrifice of tax revenue could have been defended as an investment in a less gambling-centric future for the city. Twenty years of tax credits might be a steep price, but the Revel hype promised to return Atlantic City to its former glory as a tourist destination. The reality is that Revel has not redeemed or rejuvenated tourism in Atlantic City. Instead, it seems to be a case study of taxpayers assuming economic risks for a private venture—one that lowered job quality standards instead of creating good jobs. Ironically, while CRDA takes aim at blight in the community surrounding Revel, the biggest potential blight may be the casino itself if it closes. All of the economic development initiatives in what has been renamed the Revel Beach neighborhood are dependent on that fifty-seven-story building—the second largest in the state—not being empty.

As the casino gaming industry has matured and the market for gambling as entertainment has become saturated, the private institutions with vested interests in maintaining their economic status have pursued three strategies, sometimes with the assistance of public policy makers. In chapter 3, we focused on the first strategy, that is, efforts to maintain an oligopoly position through product differentiation by branding Atlantic City as a destination resort for a younger, hipper, and more well-to-do clientele. In chapters 4 and 5, we discussed cost-cutting measures as a means of restoring profitability and their impact on the working lives of the employees. We also noted how, but there is a backlash against these cost-cutting strategies by organized labor, including efforts of union members to express their voices at work. This response was addressed in chapter 6.

The third managerial strategy, socializing (or externalizing) risk using public funds, was covered in this chapter. Profits are private, but when ventures fail, the taxpayers are expected to chip in. We addressed the relationship between public and private sectors, especially the ways in which private interests are supported by public initiatives. Governor Christie championed four interrelated measures in order to reshape the casino gaming market in New Jersey: (1) deregulation to enable the casinos to cut costs; (2) restructuring of the regulatory authorities that disempowered the relatively independent Casino Control Commission; (3) usurpation of democratically elected government in favor of bureaucratic administration under state control; and (4) tax breaks for a struggling new casino that ultimately could not deliver on its promises. Taken together, they represent the approach of big government conservatism—a far cry from the fairy tales of swashbuckling entrepreneurs operating in deregulated markets that conservatives like to tell. Instead, it brings us back to Galbraith's definition of predation: using public sector resources for private gain.

Most of these moves are often justified by referring to the vision of Atlantic City as an upscale vacation destination, though some are clearly responsive to the industry's calls for lower costs. Whether or not the architects of the 2011 legislation that engineered the takeover and the policy makers who supported development subsidies envisioned themselves as advancing the public interest in pursuing these initiatives is beyond our scope. Our focus is on impact. What is concerning for the future is that scant attention is being paid to what we consider the core issue in economic development: good jobs. The casino economy needs to be more than a place to party. It needs to provide sustainable livelihoods and meaningful work for the people of Atlantic City and surrounding communities, as well as other localities tied to casino gaming.

LENA'S STORY

We met Lena after work on a hot summer evening. We sat comfortably in three chairs in her newly decorated business. The shop had just closed and a few employees were packing up and saying goodbye. The display cases looked immaculate, and even after a long work day, Lena's clothing looked fresh and she did not have one hair out of place. Her old friend, Gloria, was also there. They have known each other for years. Gloria helped watch Lena's children when they were young; she seemed like more of an aunt than an older friend. "I was the nanny," she exclaims. Several times during the interview, Gloria interjects with interesting prompts to encourage Lena not to forget certain experiences as she described her employment in the Atlantic City gaming houses.

Lena has worked hard in several jobs at five casinos—cashier, cocktail waitress, marketing assistant, casino host, and poker dealer. As with other workers we spoke with, working in the industry was a family affair. Her parents first settled in New York City after they emigrated

In New York, she felt they had a normal family life, with weekends off to spend together. It was different once her parents worked in the casinos. "And just coming here . . . weekends were spent alone with your brothers and your sisters babysitting, cleaning, and doing chores." In her mind, a "normal family structure" was "almost nonexistent" in Atlantic City because of the shift work: "I think that's what I struggled with the most for twenty years working in the casinos." Traveling to visit relatives in Colombia from time to time, she envied how extended families would help each other, how "everybody takes care of everybody's kids."

Like many other employees we met, Lena's entrée into the casino workforce was by default. "[T]hat was my last option in life when I was younger . . . to end up in the casinos. . . . I ended up getting pregnant my senior year in high school, having a child, and I was forced to work in the casinos." She started out as a cashier, "in the cage," as it was called then, making change for the slot machines and issuing chips for gaming tables. That job did not last long. Lena recalls: "I was fired because I was short money. Or I had too much money. My accounts were never even. I was the worst cashier ever." Watching the money was just not her thing. She was only twenty years old then. Hard to imagine that she would eventually watch over pots worth multiple thousands of dollars while dealing poker. Even harder to imagine that she would one day own her own business.

Lena is very warm and outgoing. She smiles easily. Called a "nice girl" by her coworkers and superiors, she sought something that would more fit her personality. She landed a job as a cocktail server at Trump Plaza. But she was very low in seniority, so she had to take the assignment and shift that was offered. It was a Chinese restaurant off the gaming floor. Lena called it an "executive pit stop" for one drink after work, and the executives "didn't tip." "I was making $4.00 an hour and I was just like 'How am I going to support my child?'" She relished the cue, lucky Saturday nights when another server called out or went home early and she could be reassigned to a station with more business and better tips. Earning more money was a priority. Then an opportunity came along to serve cocktails at a local nightclub. The decision was a "no brainer," she says, adding, "I went from making $7.00 a night to making $250.00 a night!"

Lena's satisfaction with her nightclub job lasted about two years. She wanted to go to college, to stop working nights in the club. She rose early to see her children (she now had two, the second with her eventual husband) before they were passed into Gloria's capable hands. In the warm weather, they would all go to the beach for the day and Lena would sit and do her homework, asking for as quiet an environment as possible. Unfortunately, she suffered a steep loss in income during the July 1990–March 1991 recession. Nightclubs in town had fewer customers and, as a result, were not making money. This forced Lena to look elsewhere for work.

As Atlantic City casino employment rose from 1991 to 1997, it was relatively easy to cycle in and out of the industry. Lena was able to secure a position in casino marketing at the Atlantic City Hilton—the property that once housed the famous Golden Nugget and eventually became the now-closed Atlantic Club. Marketing was a remarkably small, two- or three-person department at most casinos, thus a low-level worker handling reservations would also be included in meetings with a director or executive. As a woman, especially a Latina, Lena struggled to have her voice heard at marketing meetings. She had ideas, brilliant ones in retrospect, but they were overlooked. At one meeting, she urged the casino president to open up a beach bar, pressing "You know, you have this whole area right here in front of the beach. Why don't you make a club there?" She continues: "And they all looked at me and laughed. I said, 'I am telling you, if you put a club in one corner right on the beach, this place would be jam-packed on a daily basis. People want to come here to party.' [Management replied], 'People don't come to Atlantic City to party. People come to Atlantic City to eat and gamble and that is what we focus on.' And I said, 'No, no, no, no, no, no! You are missing a whole crowd; you are missing a big piece.'" They treated her like a little girl, as if saying "hush up." That was circa 1994. The Atlantic City Hilton beach bar opened in 2003, nine yea~

The marketing department was tough. Lena ta⅃⅃
game. If you are not willing to play the ga
progress. And it was a boy's game. "You li
the casino industry [in marketing]. The
turn yourself into a man and you got to ι
be bold like the boys, or you have to sleep
gumption, but she stressed to us that she was ull∖

After two years just booking reservations, Hilton
reward her with a slight promotion as a casino host. Sh   a working as a host because she dealt with the public. Hosts cater to customer needs, especially high rollers. They give out show tickets, dinner vouch-

ers, and other comps. In her words, "Everything went through marketing." She was stretched thin, running around at all hours of the day and night, picking up the phone constantly, taking requests from executives, plus making quick decisions. One big gambler wants a bottle of Hennessey XO in his room at 3:00 in the morning. No requests went unheeded and few were turned down. Lena felt she was earning $20,000 per year doing virtually the same job as executives earning $100,000 per year. And her hours got longer and more erratic. She witnessed "ridiculous favoritism" among managers toward employees. The demands and the work schedule became impossible when she had a new baby. In short, she was "taking care of everybody" except her own family. She needed a change.

She switched to the marketing department at the Trump Taj Mahal because she was promised a day schedule and more regular hours. She worked for a female manager who served as a mentor. While the mentor was capable and considerate, the entire upper management operation at the Taj appeared unorganized, scattered, "one big mess." At the Taj, Lena confirmed to herself that marketing was a dead-end job for women. Two casinos. Two marketing positions. Unfulfilled promises and dreams. She gave up college for this?

Lena got very depressed about what to do next. She used to hang around the poker room with her then boyfriend (now ex-husband) while he played poker. The poker boom was just starting to take off. The game was viewed by a new generation of gamblers as more skilled than the usual table games where you play against the house and the house always has the edge. The manager of the poker room offered to pay for her casino license and train her. Lena was enticed with the offer and the paycheck potential of $150–$200 in cash per night. She dealt poker for over ten years, rotating among all shifts—grave, swing, and day. To try to best balance dealing poker with her family responsibilities as her children grew from infants to young adulthood.

Dealing poker requires skills. Cards have to be shuffled low to the table felt. The cards need swift, steady wrist action, also low to the table. You have to be intelligent, with strong math skills. Ironically, the young woman who was fired for being the worst cashier wound up counting and handling correctly hundreds of thousands of dollars in poker chips. Plus, you need people skills, moving the game along, handling the customers, and entertaining them. On a good night, Lena would deal twenty to twenty-five poker hands in just 30 minutes, averaging in tips $10 to $20 per hour. One night, however, she "pushed" a $135,000 pot, meaning she pushed the chips to the winning player. The player's tip was a measly $3.00. This equaled .0022 percent, a tiny fraction less than 1 percent. The hand took about fifteen minutes to deal, and $3.00 is fairly insulting. Sometimes, Lena adds, it's "demoralizing" because no one talks to you, you're "just a machine there." But poker helped her feed her family.

It was the smoking in the poker room that made her quit after she got pregnant with her last child. She let her husband support her while she stayed home with her children. She returned two years later to the poker room at the Borgata because she heard dealers were "making crazy money." When Borgata opened in 2003, the game was surging in popularity, fueled by young players who learned the game online and wanted to experience the live version. The poker room kept growing in size to accommodate more tables, and yet the dealer staff remained essentially the same size, resulting in more tips, shared by roughly the same number of dealers. Lena would do seven or eight table deals—meaning management would shift her to different tables—without a break. Or work eight hours straight with one break. The special situation about dealing poker is this: When your shift is over, your shift is *not* over. Not in the middle of a hand. "You're not done until they say you can go," said Lena. There is no walking out. Overtime can be mandatory.

The tips hit $60 per hour, but the work was physically and mentally demanding. According to Lena:

> Your brain's gotta go; you have to be aware. The deck has to be accounted for every single hand. So as you're counting pots, as you're checking, you know, keeping track of the cards that are going out, you also got to keep track of your cards, where your cards are. If there is a card missing at any particular point and at the time we didn't have . . . deck counters, machines that shuffle for us. Back then there was no shufflers. So we had to hand shuffle count the decks every three hands. We had to count the decks. It was, it was a demanding job. I mean the money was excellent, I'm not complaining. I just couldn't deal with it.

The repetitive motion of dealing caused injuries to the wrist, the arm, the shoulder, and sometimes the back. She and her fellow dealers were prescribed pain medications, physical therapy treatments, and endured multiple surgeries. "Every day there is somebody on medical leave or injury. Head injury, elbow surgery. Every day there is prescription drug abuse to the max." That's what it takes to get through a shift, Lena confesses.

In high limit games, when players were losing money—on tilts as it is called in poker—some would throw cards at her. The crisp, sharp edges would cut her hands. One time a player smacked her in the back of the head, even though casinos frown upon the physical harassment of dealers. If you make a mistake in the deal, she says, they will eat you alive. Other customers would swear at her—names like bitch, slut, scum, dirty "spic" (a racial slur), and even cunt (a slur for females). The f-bomb was hurled at her regularly. It got to the point where the pressure of the job and the anger inside of her in anticipation of the next shift overcame Lena. She would get sick to her stomach nearly every day. It not only affected her. It affected her husband and her children. At first, she took half a Xanax to calm down in order to cook dinner and share a meal with her family before swing shift. Then she eventually learned and practiced self-hypnosis that she integrated into her shower and makeup and dressing routine. This bought her another few years on the job.

Even though Lena loved her regular clients, estimating that she knew about 80 percent of them on a personal level, ultimately, the work intensification and the injuries, along with the player abuse and the depression of seeing people lose money every night or every week, forced her to look for something else to do in life. Lena was stuck, without hope, and feeling at the end of the line, a "pressure time bomb" as she called it, both at work and at home. To survive, she needed to walk away. And so she did.

Except now her adult son is dealing poker to eke out a living. Just like his mother, the industry offered him a life preserver when it was needed. Lena clearly frets about his future, observing that "at the time he barely got his high school degree and he just didn't know what to do with his life so I had to make the choice." Dealing cards was better than dealing drugs. Only for him casino work is part-time, with no benefits. The once-booming business is now shrinking, and full-time jobs as rare as hen's teeth. It remains to be seen if her two younger children, who are still in school, will also be drawn in.

She bemoans the limited options for young men in the local economy, viewing technical schools as "aimed for a female kind of situation," meaning mostly focused on careers in female-dominated industries such as health care, cosmetology, and massage therapy. Even the casinos offered fewer options for her son than for her: "As far as from housekeeping to cleaning, most all you see is female staff. Cocktail waitressing. Food and beverage. Mostly an all-female staff unless you go into the high, high-end restaurants where the only thing you see is male management and the waiters themselves. Other than that, it's all female. You walk into a club, it's mostly female staff. Everywhere you go, it's a big female market." In response to our probing for more information, she indicates that even dealing is increasingly feminized, especially in poker. The reason is clear. "I just think it's a big tipping industry and they're more interested [in bringing in male gamblers]. So you gotta keep the place full of females."

Lena is now an entrepreneur, a sole proprietor. She recently opened a small business in a health care field. She says she owes a lot of money to her investors who believe in her and the business plan she developed. She works hard every day, but loves being her own boss. "Having a business is like having a child," Lena laughs. "It's like taking care of a baby." As we have seen, Lena is a dedicated mother.

8

THE FUTURE OF THE CASINO ECONOMY

Gamblers know that it is important not to stay at the tables too long. Your best chances of winning are when you start playing the game. But it is hard to walk away. You keep thinking, "Just one more hand." Atlantic City and the State of New Jersey also keep betting on casino gaming, and they, too, are trying to hang on for one more hand. Early on, the wager on casinos seemed to pay off. The tourists came back to the city built on sand. Jobs were plentiful and the wages and benefits were decent. The surrounding neighborhoods and small businesses did not always benefit from the boom, but the bust has been even tougher. Casino profits are down and some are losing money. Tax revenues are declining. Employees are feeling squeezed. Nevertheless, policy makers and business leaders keep hoping that the next hand they play will be a winner. A new destination resort—Revel—was supposed to be their ace in the hole. The State of New Jersey used its own chips—tax credits—to sweeten the pot. Not a winner. A tourism district was carved out of the city and taken over by the state to be run by a private-public partnership instead of local government. It has proven slow to pay out and, when it does, the major beneficiaries are likely to be financial speculators investing in real estate ventures instead of members of the local community. The newest bets are on Internet gaming and sports betting. As suggested by a February 10, 2013, headline in the *Press of Atlantic City*: "Web Wagers Seen as A.C.'s Savior, Ruin," not everyone sees these gambits as winners either.[1]

Meanwhile, employees are also trying to keep in the game as long as possible. When we began this project in 2006, Atlantic City casinos employed over 40,000 people and the economy was still strong. We wanted to know if casino jobs were good jobs. Thirty-five interviews and eight years later, approximately one-fifth of those jobs are gone. More will disappear soon. Showboat, Zoe's employer, is closing at the end of the summer of 2014, putting most of their 2,100 employees out of work. Even though the property still has gross operating profits, Caesars Entertainment (the company that helped close Atlantic Club) determined that it was in its business interest to shut the property down. Presumably, as the owner of three other properties in the city, Caesars believes that they can absorb most of Showboat's customers themselves rather than lose market share to competitors. Rumors abound about whether the property will have a second life as an entertainment venue with little to no gambling. Revel also announced that it will close at the end of the summer of 2014, though a new buyer could reopen the property. And the struggling Trump Plaza is also scheduled to close, with little hope of reopening.

Those frontline jobs that remain are not providing new employees the same opportunities as the Day-Oners who opened the casinos in the 1970s and 1980s. Employees in a wide variety of jobs loved the early days in the casino industry. Work was fun. Management knew you and valued you. Opportunities were available for workers right out of high school. Employees found they could build their lives and provide for themselves and their families. Yes, there was smoking (even to this day, on parts of the casino floors) and drinking and rude behavior. Working swing shift or grave shift made it hard to coordinate schedules with friends and family. Each job posed specific health challenges due to standing, repetitive motions, carrying heavy objects, or second-hand smoke. Female employees working as cocktail servers and entertainment dealers were expected to use their bodies as marketing ploys. The negatives were always there. But they were offset by the monetary rewards as well as the sense that staff and management were collectively bringing amusement to the lives of their customers.

These days, the bonds among employers, workers, and customers have frayed. With new owners coming and going through mergers and bankruptcies, greater responsiveness to debt-holders and other financial investors focused on short-term gains, and managers who move from casino to casino in a global labor market, employees feel they are treated like numbers on an accounting spreadsheet. One employee working at Atlantic Club when it was for sale opined that the reason management was closing most of the restaurants was to make the property look more "desirable" for prospective buyers, by simply lowering costs on the corporate balance sheet.

Throughout the city, wages have been frozen, benefits cut, and in some casino houses the work has been reorganized to remove individual autonomy and skill. There are fewer opportunities to get to know the customers as cutbacks impinge on service. More and more employees are working part-time, income-packaging with multiple jobs. As Bernice, a former gaming inspector, shared: "Almost everybody at the casinos now are part-time workers. That's sad. Because that was a reason why New Jersey thirty years ago wanted casinos here. They wanted them here so people can build up their family life. Now they got people that can't even maintain their family life." If casinos survive but the employees don't thrive, the promise of sustainable economic development cannot be achieved.

This kind of economic insecurity is not unique to Atlantic City or to the casino industry. The industry is in a particularly difficult position because it now operates in a saturated market in many parts of the country. Each new gambling venue has to draw most of its convenience gamblers from a smaller geographic radius before bumping into the territory of the next closest town with a casino. Amid this backdrop, Atlantic City and some other localities have been trying to transition from convenience gambling centered on slots and maybe some table games to destination resorts for overnight guests. Success depends upon standing out in a crowd. It's not easy to do. A good analogy would be sports teams. Most sports franchises primarily appeal to fans in their local media market. Very few teams are able to sustain a premier position of national popularity year after year. Las Vegas, in this analogy, is the New York Yankees of gambling destinations (despite some lean years in the wake of the Great Recession). Atlantic City, with its beaches, boardwalk, and new investments in other amenities, has a lot to offer tourists as well. But locations that have little besides casinos are unlikely to compete beyond convenience gambling. Most casino markets, just like most sports franchises, will have to settle for a smaller, local fan base. But this means policy makers and voters need to pause before betting the farm on casinos to bring in fresh revenue.

Yet the betting on a gambling comeback continues in Atlantic City (and elsewhere). Aided by less regulation with the state takeover, casino moguls and political leaders are taking actions to enter the market for Internet gambling, potentially a multi-billion-dollar industry.[2] Competition among U.S. states for a share of online gaming is fierce. Delaware was the first state to do so in June of 2012. In February of 2013, Nevada and New Jersey both rushed to legalize online gambling originating from their states. New Jersey governor Chris Christie signed a bill authorizing e-gambling for a ten-year trial period. The initiative was constructed to augment the revenue of the brick-and-mortar casinos while bringing in tax revenue for the state. Currently, Internet wagering on blackjack, slots, and poker can only be offered by New Jersey casinos, though most have partnered with other companies with expertise in online gambling (who must be approved by the Division of Gaming Enforcement). The computer servers must be physically in Atlantic City. Bettors must be physically present anywhere in the state and have to register to verify that they are also at least twenty-one years old.[3]

Proponents echoed their mantra from the original 1978 referendum: jobs, tax revenue, and investment. Rosy scenarios prior to going live predicted anywhere from hundreds to thousands of new jobs, mostly for information technology specialists.[4] These IT jobs may be good jobs—at least at first. And some laid-off slot technicians may have the skill set to take advantage of the opportunities provided.[5] New Jersey Internet gross gambling revenue (GGR) is taxed at 15 percent, more than the 8 percent for onsite revenue; mandated CRDA investment rates are higher as well. Eventually, leaders envision legalized e-gambling might be able to cross state lines, allowing New Jersey to once again garner income from outsiders.

Critics contend that when customers gamble from home rather than venturing into casinos, it further decimates non-gaming revenue. What about the frontline service workers (described in chapter 5) in food and beverage service and hotel operations? How are businesses in the tourism district (chapter 7) supposed to take advantage of Internet gambling? Even if the casino houses themselves will profit from e-gambling, the impact on jobs, and therefore the local economy, is questionable. Since New Jersey casinos are owned by large corporations, holding companies, or private equity firms, there is no reason to believe that any added profits will be reinvested locally in Atlantic City—or even New Jersey. Further, as often happens with technological innovation, the new jobs may require very different skills than many of the lost jobs, making smooth transitions between labor markets difficult. Tending to a computer server is not the same as interacting with customers. Sliding down a slippery slope, one can imagine virtually empty casinos alongside warehouses full of computer servers tended by a small group of electronics specialists. If e-gambling is the next Schumpeterian innovation, it may eventually crowd out the older industry and many of the existing casinos with them. While the whales and other high rollers would continue to visit a few select resorts that combine gambling with lavish restaurants, clubs, shows, shops, and other attractions, the middle and low end of the market could be hollowed out.

So far, the critics' pessimism is warranted. Tax revenue has been far lower than expected. Consequently, the investment bank Morgan Stanley has already lowered its projections about the profitability of Internet gambling.[6] And the industry itself is battling over a bill introduced in the U.S. Congress to outlaw e-gambling completely, with members of the American Gaming Association falling on both sides of the debate.

New Jersey has also sought entry into sports betting, but this venture is in legal limbo. Federal law—the 1992 Professional and Amateur Sports Protection Act (PASPA)—only permits states with a history of sports betting to continue the practice: Nevada, Delaware, Montana, and Oregon.[7] New Jersey also had the opportunity to be "grandfathered in," with a special loophole, designed explicitly with Atlantic City in mind, giving states with a ten-year history of casino gambling up to a year to jump in and authorize sports wagering. Meeting the 1993 deadline would have required an amendment to the state constitution, but the effort was stalled in the State Assembly. Exactly why is unclear.[8]

As other gaming revenue declined, interest was revived. Advocates maintain that sports betting on events such as the National Collegiate Athletic Association's (NCAA's) "March Madness" basketball tournament would bring tourists to the city during the cooler months.[9] So the legislature passed an authorizing amendment to the state constitution in 2010, and it was ratified by New Jersey voters in 2011. The legislature followed up by amending the Casino Control Act to permit sports betting, thus directly challenging PASPA. New Jersey's law was taken to court by the four major professional sports leagues and the NCAA. In 2014, the U.S. Supreme Court refused to hear the case, leaving the provisions of PASPA in place.

Undeterred, some political leaders continue to look for ways around the ban, pointing to states that ignore federal laws against marijuana use.[10] As a stopgap measure, New Jersey's Division of Gaming Enforcement published temporary regulations allowing fantasy sports tournaments, effective April 22, 2013. Fantasy sports are technically not considered gambling, and any income from fantasy sports wagers would not be subject to the state gambling (luxury) tax but rather the ordinary corporate income tax.[11]

Sports betting, if allowed to stand by the courts, probably cannot single-handedly turn around the prognosis for any one locale. Even if New Jersey succeeds in exploiting a loophole in PASPA, other states will follow quickly, so any advantage would be short-lived.

Just as a gambler looks to one hand, one pull on the slot handle, one spin of the wheel, or one toss of the dice to change his or her luck, the temptation for industry analysts and policy makers is to latch onto a quick fix to turn around the local economy. But we all know that we would probably be better off with diversified investments in our retirement portfolio rather than taking our savings to a casino. The same is true for economic development. A diversified strategy that includes but does not fully rely upon gambling—or even the broader leisure and hospitality sector—makes more sense than quick fixes. Economist Oliver Cooke, editor of the *South Jersey Economic Review*, has studied the economic performance of thirteen similarly sized U.S. metropolitan areas between 1990 and 2012. Nine of them diversified their economies during this period, becoming less reliant on a few key industries; these diversifying local economies demonstrated much better growth in employment and personal income than Atlantic City—which was the least diversified at both the start and the end of the period in question.[12] His findings support previous economic research indicating that cities with diversified economies provide space for "knowledge spillovers" between industries and thereby encourage growth.[13]

Another important characteristic of diversified economies is that they can rely upon internal markets, meaning that local businesses provide goods and services to local residents. This dynamic is reminiscent of the virtuous circle in the high road approach to economic development identified by David Gordon (see chapter 3). Professional and business services, currently underrepresented in Atlantic City compared with faster-growing metropolitan areas, include several industries that could potentially expand in the local market. Personal services, particularly those designed to assist people working nonsocial hours, would also make promising investments. Imagine if CRDA designated casino resources toward projects to provide affordable child care and elder care 24/7 for shift workers. Employees would not have to pass their children back and forth between caregivers.

Exports are also critical. Tourism, as an industry, is technically an "export," drawing external money to the local economy. So can labor-intensive light manufacturing, done on a small scale.[14] Southern New Jersey, for example, has a strong history of yacht manufacturing; the industry struggled during the economic downturn but could rebound. In another article, Cooke suggests that targeting economic development funds toward small business start-ups is an effective way to pursue diversification: "Incubating new businesses (especially ones that lie outside the hospitality and gaming sector) will prove vitally important to Atlantic City's economic future."[15]

From its early history, Atlantic City has prospered when it has used the comparative advantage of its beachfront location to promote tourism. These days, however, its location provides a potential new edge in renewable energy. The Atlantic Ocean's off-shore wind—and its waves and tides—can be harnessed to provide electricity, according to environmental advocates. Wind power, for example, is one of six areas recommended for job-creating "green economy investments" by the University of Massachusetts's Political Economy Research Institute (PERI). Researchers there identify a range of jobs stimulated by the wind power industry, from electrical engineers to metal workers to electronics assembly.[16] Power generation can generate backward linkages to manufacturing turbines. Former casino workers would need retraining to take advantage of such opportunities, thus programs should be developed to assist with this process. Unlike many casino jobs, the occupations listed by PERI are primarily gendered male. On the one hand, such job opportunities would alleviate the concerns expressed by former poker dealer Lena that there are few opportunities in

Atlantic City for young men like her son. On the other, training women for these occupations would give them the chance to break down barriers.

In 2010, New Jersey passed the Off-Shore Wind Economic Development Act. The organization Environment New Jersey contends, however, that there has been little follow-through by the administration of Governor Christie in implementing the wind power initiative.[17] One proposal to build a wind farm three miles off the Atlantic City coast failed to get approval of the New Jersey Board of Public Utilities in early 2014—to the dismay of wind power advocates.[18] The state Court of Appeals has ordered the board to reconsider the project (with a new pricing structure). Southern New Jersey has the chance to lead in the next "wave" of economic innovation and benefit from the spillover effects of new technologies by nurturing green energy industries, in addition to focusing on leisure and hospitality.

Once gamblers can play blackjack, slots, and poker legally from home, the normalization of gambling that Atlantic City helped initiate will be entrenched. With legal e-gambling on the horizon, every home will potentially be a casino—which seems to us a perfect metaphor for the current state of our economic lives. As we said in the opening of the book, risk is becoming a way of life. Those at the top of the income distribution knowingly make big bets but have the resources to recover from losses. Hence, in the years since the Great Recession of 2008–2009, economic recovery has been much faster for the wealthy one-percenters on Wall Street than for small businesses and working families on Main Street. Increasingly strapped working families are assuming risks without intending to gamble. Many families who bought homes that have plunged in value, many students who took out loans in the belief that they were investing in their future, many retirees (including those in the public sector) who were promised pensions, and many employees who have given years of their lives to their employers and their customers are realizing that what once seemed like prudent choices have turned out to be gambles.

While economist Joseph Schumpeter and today's libertarians glorify risk as the engine of innovation, too much risk undermines the fabric of our social and economic lives. Risk means lives characterized by insecurity and instability. The erosion of job quality that our participants described in their casino jobs are echoed throughout the global economy. The expansion of part-time, temporary, and contract labor that started incrementally several decades ago has surged during the so-called recovery from the Great Recession. Companies that once hired full-time workers with benefits now utilize more contingent labor. This means that people who lost full-time jobs during the recession sometimes find themselves working for their old employers once more, but now without any long-term job security or benefits. The ability to build a life, one of the crucial elements of a good job and one of the functions a successful economy needs to fulfill, is slipping away for too many people, generating fear, anxiety, and anger. Economist Guy Standing terms this process *precariatization*.[19] And not just because of all the cost cutting that diminishes the ability of employees to sustain themselves and their families. Precariatization also destabilizes a secure, work-based identity, our sense of ourselves.

An economy is not simply a machine that produces goods and services. We live there. Living in the casino economy—one that is an endless stream of short-term financial transactions—is undermining the well-being of workers, their families, and their communities. But a sustainable economy needs to be about more than short-term gains. As political economists, we agree with Nobel Prize winner Amartya Sen, who argues that human flourishing should actually be the metric for economic success. Flourishing (or well-being), according to Sen, is dependent upon both meeting basic needs and having meaningful choices about how to live.[20] Our research on casinos, along with this view of the economy, has informed our definition of a good job as one that helps you create a life and reinforces a positive sense of identity. Isiah, who worked his way from kitchen runner to dealer to supervisor and back to part-time dealer, reflected on what makes a job a good job: "Respect. Most people would say money but if you're being respected I think that's what makes the most important part."

Good jobs, therefore, provide access to resources that enable people to achieve well-being as they define it. But well-being is also dependent upon whether the experience of work enhances one's dignity and sense of purpose or undermines these human needs. For example, a major research project by Gallup on the conditions that contribute to well-being identifies "career well-being" or, more broadly, "purpose" (to include unpaid activities) as one of five critical dimensions. Positive relationships with managers and engaged collaboration with coworkers, Gallup finds, are the most important determinants of career well-being.[21] Gallup's research is insightful, but we should not conclude that well-being at work is simply a function of winning the "boss lottery." As we have seen, the larger institutional structures of the contemporary economy make it difficult for individuals to be good bosses. Better public policies and institutions can help promote well-being at work.[22] Good jobs, therefore, need to be a central goal of our economic and development policies in order to meet peoples' needs for sustainable livelihoods and meaningful work.

In chapter 1, we quoted a part-time floorperson, Graciela, who compared casinos to other entertainment venues: "The truth of the exchange is less clear." She was thinking about customers who gamble in the expectation of getting comps from the casino. When they feel they are not being treated fairly, they lash out—usually at an employee who does not have discretion over ratings and rewards. Graciela's phrase resonates with us. The truth of the exchange seems to have disappeared from many of the implicit social contracts that are necessary for a healthy economy. This trend has important implications for the casino economy and its workers. The truth of the exchange between employer and employee or between management and worker is less clear as casinos and other businesses themselves become products exchanged on global markets by hedge funds, private equity managers, and other financial interests. This financialized economy is not conducive to long-term time horizons. Instead, it is all about the next hand.

APPENDIX I

Atlantic City Casinos Timeline

(Openings of new properties are indicated by *italics* with their current names in **bold** brackets.)

1978

- *May 26: Resorts International opens Resorts International Casino, the first casino in Atlantic City.* [**Resorts Casino Hotel**]

1979

- *June 26: Boardwalk Regency opens in a renovated Howard Johnson's property.* The Casino Control Commission permitted it to add Caesars to the name in 1983. [**Caesars Atlantic City**]
- *December 29: Bally's Park Place opens a new casino at the location of the former Marlborough-Blenheim Hotel, which was largely demolished to make way for it.* [**Bally's Atlantic City**]

1980

- February: Harrah's Hotel Casino Company is acquired by Holiday Inns, Inc.

- *August 31: The Brighton Hotel and Casino opens a new property under the ownership of Greate Bay Casino Corporation.* [**Sands Casino Hotel, no longer in operation**]
- *November 23: Harrah's Hotel Casino is opened.* [**Harrah's Resort Atlantic City**]
- *December 12: Golden Nugget Atlantic City is opened as a partnership of Golden Nugget Companies (Steve Wynn, owner) and Michael R. Milken.* [**Atlantic Club Casino, no longer in operation**]

1981

- February: The Brighton Hotel and Casino is purchased by Inns of America; the resort is renamed Sands Casino Hotel.
- *April 4: Playboy Enterprises (in a partnership with the Elsinore Corporation) receives a temporary gaming permit and opens the Playboy Hotel and Casino.* The property is no longer in operation.
- *November 26: Ramada Inns opens the Tropicana Atlantic City.* [**Tropicana Casino & Resort Atlantic City**]
- *July: The Del Webb Corporation purchases the Claridge Hotel and turns it into a casino with the name Del Webb's Claridge Hotel and Casino.* [**The Claridge Tower, part of Bally's Atlantic City until 2013**]

1984

- *May 26: Harrah's at Trump Plaza opens as a new property, a joint venture by Trump Entertainment Resorts and Harrah's.* [**Trump Plaza Hotel and Casino**]
- Playboy Hotel and Casino becomes Atlantis Hotel and Casino under partnership with the Elsinore Corporation following Playboy Enterprises' licensure denial in 1982. Playboy ultimately sells its shares to Elsinore.
- The Casino Reinvestment Development Authority (CRDA) is formed to channel a portion of casino revenue to urban redevelopment in Atlantic City.

1985

- *June 19: Trump Castle opens as a new property, owned by Trump Entertainment Resorts.* [**Golden Nugget Atlantic City**]
- November 15: Atlantis Hotel and Casino files for bankruptcy.

1986

- Trump Entertainment Resorts purchases Harrah's shares of Harrah's at Trump Plaza and renames the casino Trump Plaza Hotel and Casino.

1987

- *April 2: Showboat Inc. opens the Showboat Casino.* [**Showboat Atlantic City**]
- Caesars Boardwalk Regency's name is changed to Caesars Atlantic City.
- Bally's Entertainment Corporation purchases Golden Nugget Atlantic City from Steve Wynn; the resort is renamed Bally's Grand Casino/Hotel.

1988

- Resorts International Casino is bought by Merv Griffin (Griffin Gaming & Entertainment Company) and is renamed Resorts Atlantic City.
- Tropicana Atlantic City is renamed TropWorld Casino and Entertainment Resort after Tivoli Pier is built.

1989

- Ramada Inns spins off their gaming properties (Tropicana) into Aztar Corporation, a division of the company.
- May 22: Atlantis Casino closes and reopens several months later under new ownership as the Trump Regency Hotel.
- December 22: Resorts Atlantic City files for bankruptcy.

1990

- January: Holiday Inn transfers Harrah's and their other hotel brands into the Promus Companies.

- *April 2: Trump Taj Mahal opens under ownership of Trump Entertainment Resorts, financed by high-interest "junk bonds."* **[Trump Taj Mahal]**

1991

- July 16: Trump Taj Mahal files for bankruptcy one year after opening.

1992

- Trump Hotel and Casino Resorts, owner of both Trump Castle and Trump Plaza, files for bankruptcy. Donald Trump gives up 49 percent of ownership stake to lenders.

1995

- June: The Promus Companies spins off its non-casino hotel brands and creates a separate corporation renamed Harrah's Entertainment, Inc.

1996

- April 15: Trump Regency is reopened as a casino-hotel named Trump World's Fair at Trump Plaza Hotel and Casino.
- Summer: TropWorld Casino and Entertainment Resort is renamed Tropicana Casino and Resort upon completion of its expansion.
- Bally's Grand is renamed Atlantic City Hilton after its acquisition by the Hilton Hotels Corporation.

1997

- Wild Wild West is opened as an additional casino gaming area connected to Bally's Casino while under the ownership of Hilton Hotels Corporation.
- July: Trump Castle is renamed Trump Marina.

1998

- January 5: The Sands Casino Hotel files for bankruptcy.
- June: Showboat, Inc. is acquired by Harrah's Entertainment Inc.
- Griffin Gaming & Entertainment Company, owner of Resorts, is purchased by Sun International Hotels.
- Hilton Hotels Corporation spins off its casino properties into a new company called Park Place Entertainment.

1999

- August 16: Claridge Casino Hotel files for bankruptcy.
- October: Trump World's Fair is permanently closed and torn down one year later.

2000

- Carl Icahn purchases the Sands Casino Hotel.
- Sun International sells Resorts Atlantic City to Colony Capital LLC, creating Resorts International Holdings.
- Park Place Entertainment purchases Caesars properties (in Las Vegas and Atlantic City). The company is renamed Caesars Entertainment, Inc. in 2003.

2001

- June 1: Park Place Entertainment, owner of Bally's, acquires the Claridge Casino Hotel.

2003

- *July 2: Borgata Hotel Casino and Spa opens, owned by Marina District Development LLC, a joint venture between Boyd Gaming, Vornado Realty Trust, and MGM Resorts International.* **[Borgata Hotel Casino and Spa]**

2004

- November 21: Trump Hotels and Casino Resorts, owner of Trump Castle and Trump Plaza, files for bankruptcy a second time. Trump's personal stake is reduced to 25 percent.

2005

- June: Harrah's Entertainment completes its acquisition of Caesars Entertainment, Inc., the largest merger in the history of the gaming industry. As a part of this merger, all Bally's casinos and hotels are owned by Harrah's.
- Resorts International Holdings manages Atlantic City Hilton as well as Resorts.

2006

- May: Aztar, owner of Tropicana, is acquired by Columbia Sussex Corporation.
- September: Pinnacle Entertainment Inc. purchases the Sands Casino from Carl Icahn and closes it permanently two months later.

2007

- October 18: The Sands Casino is imploded, the first-ever casino implosion on the East Coast.

2008

- January: Harrah's Entertainment is acquired by Apollo Global Management and Texas Pacific Group, private equity interests.

2009

- February: Donald Trump resigns as chairman of Trump Entertainment Resorts (Taj) as the company files for bankruptcy.
- June 12: Columbia Sussex's Tropicana Casino and Resort loses its license and goes bankrupt.
- December 10: Resorts International Holdings (owned by Colony Capital LLC) is unable to pay the mortgage for the Resorts Atlantic City. Both Resorts and Atlantic City Hilton are surrendered to Resorts Atlantic City Holdings LLC.

2010

- March 8: Tropicana Entertainment Inc., led by Carl Icahn, becomes the new owner of Tropicana Casino and Resort as it emerges from Chapter 11 bankruptcy.
- August 23: Resorts is purchased by DGMB Casino LLC and operated by Gomes Gaming. Dennis Gomes is named CEO.
- November 23: Harrah's Entertainment changes it corporate name to Caesars Entertainment, Inc.

2011

- February 14: Landry's Restaurants purchases Trump Marina from Trump Entertainment Resorts. Trump Marina is renamed Golden Nugget of Atlantic City.
- July 1: Atlantic City Hilton is given temporary name of ACH because Hilton Hotels ends its licensing agreement with Colony Capital LLC, withdrawing permission to use the Hilton name.

2012

- February 7: ACH is rebranded as the Atlantic Club Casino Hotel, owned by Colony Capital LLC doing business as RIH Acquisitions NJ, LLC.
- *April 2: Revel Atlantic City opens for preview; official grand opening is Memorial Day weekend.* The owner is Revel Entertainment Group LLC, now Revel AC, Inc. **[Revel Casino Hotel]**

2013

- March 25: Revel files for bankruptcy for the first time and is taken over by its creditors.
- November 6: Atlantic Club files for bankruptcy.
- December: Atlantic Club is sold to two competitors, Caesars and Tropicana, after filing for bankruptcy. The new owners intend to close the casino and sell or utilize its assets.

2014

- January 13: Atlantic Club, born as the original Golden Nugget in Atlantic City, closes.

- February: Claridge Hotel is sold by Bally's and is renovated to become a stand-alone hotel, without a gaming floor.
- June 19: Revel files for bankruptcy for the second time.
- June 27: Caesars announces that it is closing Showboat Casino on August 31.
- Summer: Impending closures are approved for Showboat, Revel, and the Trump Plaza.

Sources: Atlantic City Library, *Press of Atlantic City*, and corporation websites and annual reports.

NOTES

PREFACE

1. The description of this job fair and the text of this statement are from Jennifer Bogdan, "Golden Nugget Job Fair: Work-Seekers Pack Casino," *Press of Atlantic City*, February 27, 2014.

2. The school of macroeconomic theory based on the work of John Maynard Keynes views demand for goods and services as the primary driver of economic growth. Price adjustments will not self-regulate an economy out of a recession because oligopolistic industries tend to cut production and jobs rather than lowering prices. This creates a downward spiral as consumers with lower incomes continue to reduce their spending. Since it is rational for businesses and consumers to tighten their belts, government spending is needed to revive the economy. Government stimulus creates an upward spiral known as the multiplier effect. Greater income leads to increased consumer spending in the private sector. Thus, government spending is not viewed as competing with private investment, but as a way of boosting it.

3. Wayne A. Lewchuk, "Men and Monotony: Fraternalism as a Managerial Strategy at the Ford Motor Company," *Journal of Economic History* 53, no. 4 (1993): 824–56.

4. Arthur MacEwan and John Miller, *Economic Collapse, Economic Change: Getting to the Roots of the Crisis* (Armonk, NY: Sharpe, 2011); and Timothy Noah, *The Great Divergence: America's Growing Inequality Crisis and What We Can Do About It* (New York: Bloomsbury, 2012).

5. This is, of course, an allusion to the 1939 film version of *The Wizard of Oz*.

6. Robin Greenwood and David Scharfstein, "The Growth of Finance," *Journal of Economic Perspectives* 27, no. 2 (2013): 3–28.

7. Christopher Palmeri, "Casinos Know When to Fold 'Em," *Bloomberg Businessweek*, April 7–14, 2014, 25–26.

8. Guy Standing, *The Precariat: The New Dangerous Class* (London: Bloomsbury, 2011).

1. STORIES FROM A CASINO ECONOMY

1. American Gaming Association, *2013 State of the States: The AGA Survey of Casino Entertainment* (Washington, DC: AGA, 2013).

2. Harold L. Vogel, *Entertainment Industry Economics: A Guide for Financial Analysis*, 8th ed. (Cambridge, UK: Cambridge University Press, 2011), 424.

3. The U.S. share is based on our calculations using industry market value as estimated by Datamonitor. Industry data is from Datamonitor, *Global Casinos & Gaming*, Reference Code 0199-2019 (New York: Datamonitor USA, May 2011), and *Casinos & Gaming in the United States*, Reference Code 0072-2019 (New York: Datamonitor USA, May 2011).

4. American Gaming Association, *2011 State of the States*, 2.

5. American Gaming Association, *2013 State of the* States, 18.

6. See Deborah M. Figart, "Social Responsibility for Living Standards: Presidential Address, Association for Social Economics, 2007," *Review of Social Economy* 65, no. 4 (2007): 391–405; and Deborah M. Figart and Ellen Mutari, "Work: Its Social Meanings and Role in Provisioning," in *The Elgar Companion to Social Economics*, ed. John B. Davis and Wilfred Dolfsma (Aldershot, England: Edward Elgar, 2008), 287–301.

7. William M. Dugger, "Redefining Economics: From Market Allocation to Social Provisioning," in *Political Economy for the 21st Century: Contemporary Views on the Trend of Economics*, ed. Charles J. Whalen (Armonk, NY: Sharpe, 1996), 36.

8. Neoclassical labor economists have made many amendments and modifications of this core concept. The disutility argument, however, remains the theoretical starting point.

9. For a more detailed review of this literature, see Figart and Mutari, "Work: Its Social Meanings and Role in Provisioning," 287–301.

10. Peter B. Doeringer and Michael J. Piore, *Internal Labor Markets and Manpower Analysis* (Lexington, MA: Heath, 1971).

11. Chris Tilly, "Arresting the Decline of Good Jobs in the USA?" *Industrial Relations Journal* 28, no. 4 (1997): 269–74.

12. Randy Albelda and Robert Drago, *Unlevel Playing Fields: Understanding Wage Inequality and Discrimination*, 4th ed. (Boston: Economic Affairs Bureau, 2013).

13. Chris Warhurst, Françoise Carré, Patricia Findlay, and Chris Tilly, *Are Bad Jobs Inevitable? Trends, Determinants and Responses to Job Quality in the Twenty-First Century* (London: Palgrave Macmillan, 2012).

14. Julie A. Nelson, *Economics for Humans* (Chicago: University of Chicago Press, 2006).

15. Joseph Schumpeter, *Capitalism, Socialism, and Democracy* (1942; repr., New York: Harper Perennial Modern Classics, 2008).

16. Paul Sweezy, in fact, was a student of Schumpeter's at Harvard University.

17. For an excellent summary and update of this work, see John Bellamy Foster, "Monopoly Capital at the Turn of the Millennium," *Monthly Review* 51, no. 11 (2000): 1–18.

18. American Gaming Association, *U.S. Commercial Casino Industry: Facts at Your Fingertips* (Washington, DC: AGA, 2009).

19. John Lyman Mason and Michael Nelson, *Governing Gambling* (New York: Century Foundation, 2001).

20. National Gambling Impact Study Commission, *NGISC Report Recommendations* (Washington, DC, 1999), accessed January 20, 2006, http://govinfo. library.unt.edu/ngisc/. See also Mason and Nelson, *Governing Gambling*.

21. William R. Eadington, "Preface," in *The Business of Gaming: Economic and Management Issues*, ed. William R. Eadington and Judy A. Cornelius (Reno, NV: Institute for the Study of Gambling and Commercial Gaming, 1999), xviii.

22. Dual rate jobs are transitional positions between steps in the career ladder. Dual rates may work partly as regular dealers and partly as floor supervisors each week, being paid at different rates for the hours in each position. There are also dual rates, like Ken, who rotate between two supervisory positions: floor supervisor and pit boss.

23. Social practices are patterns of behavior that express norms and beliefs, especially about collective identities such as gender, race, ethnicity, and class. Anthropologist Sherry Ortner refers to them as "motivated, organized, and socially complex ways of going about life in particular times and places." Social theorists are attentive to social practices because they reveal the meaning behind institutionalized behavior. Prevailing social practices are embedded in social structures, but are also contested and altered by the collective behavior of different social groups. See Sherry B. Ortner, *Making Gender: The Politics and Erotics of Culture* (Boston: Beacon, 1996), 12.

24. Three members of one family were interviewed in 2009.

25. The research process and instrument was approved by the Richard Stockton College of New Jersey Institutional Review Board and followed the practices and recommendations of the federal Collaborative Institutional Training Initiative.

26. Note that ours is a study of jobs and job quality, not a broader study of the quality of life of casino employees. A larger study would include additional variables such as health care, crime, poverty rates, arts and recreation, access to transportation, and education, as well as jobs.

27. National Gambling Impact Study Commission, *Final Report*, 7–1.

28. National Gambling Impact Study Commission, *Final Report*, 7–4.

29. National Gambling Impact Study Commission, *Final Report*, 7–8.

30. NJ Department of Labor and Workforce Development, *County Community Fact Book: Atlantic County Edition* (Trenton, 2013), 8, accessed March 1, 2014,http://www.nj.gov/oag/ge/index.html.

2. A CITY BUILT ON SAND

1. Nelson Johnson, *Boardwalk Empire: The Birth, High Times, and Corruption of Atlantic City* (Medford, NJ: Plexus, 2002), 34. *Boardwalk Empire*, and the HBO television series upon which it is based, highlight the days before legal gambling, with corruption in politics and organized crime.

2. Johnson, *Boardwalk Empire*, 21–22; Bryant Simon, *Boardwalk of Dreams: Atlantic City and the Fate of Urban America* (New York: Oxford University Press, 2004), chap. 3.

3. Simon, *Boardwalk of Dreams*, chap. 4.

4. For an overview and evaluation of various theories of Atlantic City's decline, see Simon's *Boardwalk of Dreams*, chap. 5.

5. Michael Pollock, "From Divestment to Reinvestment: Atlantic City Addresses Core Issues," in *Casino Gaming in Atlantic City: A Thirty Year Retrospective, 1978–2008*, ed. Brian J. Tyrrell and Israel Posner (Margate, NJ: ComteQ, 2009), 13–21.

6. Jane Jacobs, *The Death and Life of Great American Cities* (New York: Vintage, 1961).

7. Larry Sawers and William K. Tabb, *Sunbelt/Snowbelt: Urban Development and Regional Restructuring* (New York: Oxford University Press, 1984).

8. Simon, *Boardwalk of Dreams*, 127.

9. George Sternlieb and James W. Hughes, *The Atlantic City Gamble* (Cambridge, MA: A Twentieth Century Fund Report from Harvard University Press, 1983), 81.

10. The image and reality of the industry in Nevada had been improved in the 1960s and 1970s by the entrance of mainstream businessmen like Howard Hughes and major hospitality and entertainment corporations such as Hilton, Hyatt, and MGM. See Denise von Herrmann, *The Big Gamble: The Politics of Lottery and Casino Expansion* (Westport, CT: Praeger, 2002), 12–13.

11. One of the prime architects of the pro-casino campaign, then-Assembly-man Steven Perskie, recently reminisced that their original intent was to confine gaming to Atlantic City, but they had to insert the local option to get enough votes in the State Senate to put the initiative on the ballot. Steven P. Perskie, "The Political and Economic Background of Atlantic City in the 1970s," in Tyrrell and Posner, *Casino Gaming in Atlantic City*, 3.

12. Michael Pollock, *Hostage to Fortune: Atlantic City and Casino Gambling* (Princeton, NJ: Center for Analysis of Public Issues, 1987), 11. Pollock was a reporter for the *Press of Atlantic City* at the time of publication in 1987. He later went on to work for the Casino Control Commission and then became an industry consultant.

13. Ovid Demaris presents a skeptical view of the motives and connections of those promoting gaming that contrasts with other locally based writers. Ovid Demaris, *The Boardwalk Jungle* (Toronto: Bantam, 1986), 52–59.

14. Sternlieb and Hughes, *Atlantic City Gamble*, 81.

15. Sternlieb and Hughes, *Atlantic City Gamble*, 79.

16. Johnson, *Boardwalk Empire*, 221.

17. Other space requirements are detailed in Nick Casiello Jr., "The Adoption and Development of the Casino Control Act," in Tyrrell and Posner, *Casino Gaming in Atlantic City*, 84–85.

18. Casiello, "Adoption and Development of the Casino Control Act," 81–82; emphasis in original.

19. See John Froonjian, "Special Report: Coming to Atlantic City," *Press of Atlantic City*, December 28, 29, and 30, 2003.

20. Pollock, *Hostage to Fortune*, 18–19.

21. This figure comes from Sternlieb and Hughes, *Atlantic City Gamble*, 10.

22. Oliver Cooke, "The Economic Impact of Gaming in Atlantic City," in Tyrrell and Posner, *Casino Gaming in Atlantic City*, 135.

23. New Jersey Casino Control Commission, *Casino Gambling in New Jersey: A Report to the National Gambling Impact Study Commission* (Atlantic City: NJCCC, January 1998).

24. An often-quoted study was Michael Pollock's book, *Hostage to Fortune*. Sternlieb and Hughes's 1983 study for the Twentieth Century Fund, *The Atlantic City Gamble*, raised early concerns about the lack of spillover effects.

25. Sternlieb and Hughes, *Atlantic City Gamble*, 82–94.

26. Joseph Rubenstein, "Casino Gambling in Atlantic City: Issues of Development and Redevelopment," *Annals of the American Academy of Political and Social Science* 474 (July 1984): 69.

27. Cooke, "Economic Impact of Gaming in Atlantic City," 143.

28. David Listokin and Candice A. Valente, "Public Finance and Atlantic City Casinos," in Tyrrell and Posner, *Casino Gaming in Atlantic City*, 89–133.

29. Harriet Newberger, with Anita Sands and John Wackes, *Atlantic City: Past as Prologue* (Philadelphia: Federal Reserve Bank of Philadelphia, 2009), 21.

30. Anthony Marino, "Transportation in Atlantic City," in Tyrrell and Posner, *Casino Gaming in Atlantic City*, 45.

31. Datamonitor, *Global Casinos & Gaming*, reference code 0199-2019 (New York: Datamonitor USA, May 2011).

3. GOING UPSCALE IN AN ERA OF INCOME POLARIZATION

1. See Anthony Marino, "Transportation in Atlantic City," in *Casino Gaming in Atlantic City: A Thirty Year Retrospective, 1978–2008*, ed. Brian J. Tyrrell and Israel Posner (Margate, NJ: ComteQ, 2009), 45.

2. Gary Rivlin, "Atlantic City Aiming Higher As Casinos Slip," *New York Times*, March 19, 2007.

3. Harold L. Vogel, *Entertainment Industry Economics: A Guide for Financial Analysis*, 8th ed. (Cambridge, UK: Cambridge University Press, 2011). See also Rivlin, "Atlantic City Aiming Higher."

4. Christopher Palmeri, "Casinos Know When to Fold 'Em," *Bloomberg Businessweek*, April 7–13, 2014, 25–26.

5. Brian J. Tyrrell and Jeffrey Vasser, "Marketing Atlantic City as a Destination," in Tyrrell and Posner, *Casino Gaming in Atlantic City*, 174–92.

6. See Jim Landers, "What's the Potential Impact of Casino Tax Increases on Wagering Handle: Estimates of the Price Elasticity of Demand for Casino Gaming," *Economics Bulletin* 8, no. 6 (2008): 1–15.

7. American Gaming Association, *U.S. Commercial Casino Industry: Facts at Your Fingertips* (Washington, DC: AGA, 2009).

8. Naomi Klein, *No Logo: Taking Aim at the Brand Bullies* (New York: Picador, 2002).

9. Robert H. Frank, *Luxury Fever: Money and Happiness in an Era of Excess* (Princeton, NJ: Princeton University Press, 1999).

10. The declining emphasis on bus patrons and focus on upscale customers is described by *Press of Atlantic City* reporter Donald Wittkowski in a May 16,

2010, article entitled "Atlantic City Casinos Relying Less on Bus Patrons, More on Overnight Stays."

11. For an analysis of increased pressures on management by financial markets, see David Weil, *The Fissured Workplace: Why Work Became So Bad for So Many and What Can Be Done to Improve It* (Cambridge, MA: Harvard University Press, 2014), 44–45.

12. Similarly, Jeffrey Sallaz's study of a Nevada casino notes that "over the past decade, corporate management has cut employee wages and benefits, often through forcing out full-time, veteran dealers and replacing them with young, usually immigrant, women." See Jeffrey J. Sallaz, "The House Rules: Autonomy and Interests Among Service Workers in the Contemporary Casino Industry," *Work and Occupations* 29, no. 4 (2002): 404.

13. Dean Baker, *Taking Economics Seriously* (Cambridge, MA: MIT Press, 2010), 2–3.

14. David M. Gordon, *Fat and Mean: The Corporate Squeeze of Working Americans and the Myth of Managerial Downsizing* (New York: Free Press, 1996), 144.

15. Donald Wittkowski, "Borgata Stands Out 10 Years On," *Press of Atlantic City*, July 1, 2013.

16. Donald Wittkowski, "MGM to Delay Start of Atlantic City Casino Project until 2009," *Press of Atlantic City*, August 30, 2008.

17. UNLV Center for Gaming Research, Caesars Entertainment Corporation Company Profile, accessed July 30, 2013, http://gaming.unlv.edu/abstract/fin_het.html.

18. Michael Clark, "Atlantic City Council May Impose Construction Deadlines in Light of Pinnacle Delays," *Press of Atlantic City*, September 15, 2008.

19. The private equity firms that own Caesars Entertainment (TPG Capital and Apollo Global Management) both describe a wide range of investments on their web sites, from financial services to media, from chemicals to health care, and from retail to technology. Landry's, which recently acquired the property rechristened as the Golden Nugget, is concentrated in seafood restaurant chains. But it also owns the Downtown Aquarium in Houston, an entertainment complex with amusement rides and midway games. In contrast, Boyd Gaming, owner of the successful Borgata, operates casinos in Las Vegas, Illinois, Indiana, Iowa, Kansas, Louisiana, and Mississippi, as well as New Jersey.

20. Eileen Appelbaum and Rosemary Batt, *Private Equity at Work: When Wall Street Manages Main Street* (New York: Russell Sage Foundation, 2014), 81, 98, and 266.

21. This is confirmed by two key industry profiles by a private consulting firm, Datamonitor. See *Casinos & Gaming in the United States* and *Global Casinos & Gaming*.

22. Timothy Noah, *The Great Divergence: America's Growing Inequality Crisis and What We Can Do About It* (New York: Bloomsbury, 2012), 3.

23. According to the Congressional Budget Office, the threshold for being in the top 1 percent of households was a pre-tax annual income of $347,421 in 2007. See Congressional Budget Office, *Trends in the Distribution of Household Income Between 1979 and 2007* (Washington, DC: CBO, October 2011), 3.

24. Noah, *The Great Divergence*, 23–25; emphasis in original.

25. For an overview of these trends, see Arthur MacEwan and John Miller, *Economic Collapse, Economic Change: Getting to the Roots of the Crisis* (Armonk, NY: Sharpe, 2011) and Paul Krugman, *The Conscience of a Liberal: Reclaiming America from the Right* (New York: Norton, 2009).

26. Frank, *Luxury Fever*, 18–19 and 33.

27. Juliet Fletcher, "Nightclubs in Atlantic City Casinos Not Just Hot on Weekends," *Press of Atlantic City*, August 16, 2009.

28. See Donald Wittkowski, "New Ways to Play," *Press of Atlantic City*, August 27, 2012.

29. Rivlin, "Atlantic City Aiming Higher." As of 2012, Atlantic City's slogan is the equally suggestive "DO AC."

30. Dennis Hevesi, "Dennis Gomes, Operator of Casino in Atlantic City, Dies at 68," *New York Times*, February 25, 2012.

31. M. V. Lee Badgett, *Money Myths, and Change: The Economic Lives of Lesbians and Gay Men* (Chicago: University of Chicago Press, 2001).

32. Jennifer Bogdan, "Margaritaville to be Only One for 200 Miles," *Press of Atlantic City*, August 14, 2012.

33. Quoted in Donald Wittkowski, "Theme Change Boon to Resorts," *Press of Atlantic City*, September 16, 2013.

34. Donald Wittkowski, "Atlantic City Casinos Look Closer to Home for New Customers," *Press of Atlantic City*, April 11, 2010.

35. Wittkowski, "Atlantic City Casinos Look Closer to Home." The marketing vice president quoted in the article quickly added, "Obviously, all customers have value to us."

4. DEALING WITH CHANGE

1. Wanda M. Costen, Christian E. Hardigree, and Michael A. Testagrossa, "Glass Ceiling or Saran Wrap™? Women in Gaming Management," *UNLV Gaming Research & Review Journal* 7, no. 2 (2003): 1–12.

2. Marc Linder and Ingrid Nygaard, *Void Where Prohibited* (Ithaca, NY: ILR, 1998).

3. Other methodologies use a multiple of the poverty line.

4. See the University of Washington's Center for Women's Welfare work on self-sufficiency standards, accessed May 28, 2014, http://www. selfsufficiencystandard.org/pubs.html. We used the Excel chart for New Jersey in 2011.

5. American Gaming Association, *2007 State of the States: The AGA Survey of Casino Entertainment* (Washington, DC: AGA), 32.

6. Work sharing policies have been implemented in many developed countries, but usually focus on male workers in manufacturing and construction industries. But a study by the Center for Economic and Policy Research indicates that the leisure and hospitality sector could benefit greatly from such a policy. See Dean Baker, *Work Sharing: The Quick Route Back to Full Employment* (Washington, DC: Center for Economic and Policy Research, June 2011).

7. American Gaming Association, *2013 State of the States*, 35.

8. Calculated from New Jersey Division of Gaming Enforcement, "DGE Announces December 2012 Casino Win Results," January 13, 2013, accessed March 3, 2014, http://www.nj.gov/oag/ge/financialandstatisticalinfo.html.

9. Atlantic City's casinos have purchased machines from a local company founded in 1978 to coincide with gaming in the city, AC Coin and Slot. In 2009, this local company signed an amended agreement with one of the world's leaders in gaming equipment manufacturing, International Game Technology (IGT). It allows IGT to distribute machines and games in Atlantic City and allows AC Coin and Slot to tap into IGT's global distribution network.

10. Jane Bokunewicz, "The Evolution of Casino Technology Atlantic City," in *Casino Gaming in Atlantic City: A Thirty Year Retrospective, 1978–2008*, ed. Brian J. Tyrrell and Israel Posner (Margate, NJ: ComteQ, 2009), 23.

11. One of Atlantic City's earliest slot machines is on display in the lobby of the hotel at Resorts Casino.

12. Bokunewicz, "Evolution of Casino Technology in Atlantic City," 24.

13. In one interview, we received quite a detailed lesson in the wiring of the older and new generation of slot machines from Terrence, a slot technician.

14. Cameron Lynne Macdonald and Carmen Sirianni, eds., *Working in the Service Society* (Philadelphia: Temple University Press, 1996), 25.

15. Ronnie J. Steinberg and Deborah M. Figart, eds., *Emotional Labor in the Service Economy*, The Annals of the American Academy of Political and Social Science, 561 (Thousand Oaks, CA: Sage, 1999).

16. Harriet B. Presser, *Working in a 24/7 Economy: Challenges for American Families* (New York: Russell Sage Foundation, 2003).

17. Israel Posner and Lewis Leitner, "Front Line Careers," *Casino Connection* magazine, June 2007. The paper magazine was discontinued in 2011 and is replaced by a website at http://www.casinoconnectionac.com/.

18. Dena C. Wittmann, "A Day in the Night of a Casino Worker: Shift Work Culture of Mississippi Dockside Gaming Employees," in *Resorting to Casinos: The Mississippi Gaming Industry*, ed. Denise von Herrman (Jackson: University of Mississippi Press, 2006), 121–42.

19. Child Care Aware of America, *Parents and the Cost of Child Care: 2013 Report*, Arlington, VA, accessed March 3, 2014, http://naccrra.org/costofcare.

20. This brief history is from Derek Harper, "Total Ban on Smoking has Life in Legislature," *Press of Atlantic City*, February 26, 2009.

21. Paul A. Pilkington, Selena Gray, and Anna B. Gilmore, "Health Impacts of Exposure to Second Hand Smoke (SHS) Amongst a Highly Exposed Workforce: Survey of London Casino Workers," *BMC Public Health* 7, no. 257 (2007): 1–8.

22. Melanie Wakefield, Melissa Cameron, Graeme Inglis, Tessa Letcher, and Sarah Durkin, "Second-hand Smoke Exposure and Respiratory Symptoms among Casino, Club and Office Workers in Victoria, Australia," *Journal of Occupational and Environmental Medicine* 47, no. 7 (2005): 698–703.

23. Billy Bai, K. Pearl Brewer, Gail Simmons, and Skip Swerdlow, "Job Satisfaction, Organizational Commitment, and Internal Service Quality: A Case Study of Las Vegas Hotel/Casino Industry," *Journal of Human Resources in Hospitality & Tourism* 5, no. 2 (2006): 37–54; Donald M. Peppard Jr. and Frances A. Boudreau, "Job Quality and Job Satisfaction among Casino Workers: The Case of Foxwoods," *Gaming Research & Review Journal* 2, no. 2 (1995): 31–42; and Zhonglu Zeng, David Forrest, and Ian G. McHale, "Happiness and Job Satisfaction in a Casino-Dominated Economy," *Journal of Gambling Studies* 29, no. 3 (2013): 471–90.

5. THE SQUEEZE ON SERVICE

1. Evelyn Nakano Glenn, "From Servitude to Service Work: Historical Continuities in the Racial Division of Paid Reproductive Labor," *Signs* 18, no. 1 (1992): 1–43. See also Deborah M. Figart, Ellen Mutari, and Marilyn Power, *Living Wages, Equal Wages: Gender and Labor Market Policies in the United States* (New York: Routledge, 2002), chap. 2.

2. Glenn, "From Servitude to Service Work," 20.

3. Saru Jayaraman, *Behind the Kitchen Door* (Ithaca, NY: Cornell University Press, 2013), 105 and 116–17.

4. Philip Moss and Chris Tilly, *Stories Employers Tell: Race, Skill, and Hiring in America* (New York: Russell Sage Foundation, 2001).

5. Gregory J. Kamer and Edwin A. Keller Jr., "Give Me $5 Chips, a Jack and Coke—Hold the Cleavage: A Look at Employee Appearance Issues in the Gaming Industry," *Gaming Law Review* 7, no. 5 (2003): 335–46.

6. Amel Adib and Yvonne Guerrier, "The Interlocking of Gender with Nationality, Race, Ethnicity and Class: The Narratives of Women in Hotel Work," in *Global Perspectives on Gender and Work*, ed. Jacqueline Goodman (Lanham, MD: Rowman & Littlefield, 2010), 251.

7. Jennifer Bogdan, "Borgata Can Make 'Babes' Watch Weight," *Press of Atlantic City*, July 25, 2013. A study of Reno casino cocktail servers found a racial preference for white servers; an Eastern European immigrant with limited language skills could easily be hired while Latinas were not. See Lorraine Bayard de Volo, "Service and Surveillance: Infrapolitics at Work among Casino Cocktail Waitresses," *Social Politics* 10, no. 3 (2003): 354.

8. See, for example, Doris Weichselbaumer, "Discrimination in Gay and Lesbian Lives," in *Handbook of Research on Gender and Economic Life*, ed. Deborah M. Figart and Tonia L. Warnecke (Cheltenham, UK: Edward Elgar, 2013), 236–54.

9. M. V. Lee Badgett and Mary C. King, "Lesbian and Gay Occupational Strategies," in *Homo Economics*, ed. Amy Gluckman and Betsy Reed (New York: Routledge, 1997), 73–86.

10. Koji Ueno, Teresa Roach, and Abráham E. Peña-Talamantes, "Sexual Orientation and Gender Typicality of the Occupation in Young Adulthood," *Social Forces* 91, no. 1 (2013): 81–108.

11. Judith Lorber, "'Night to His Day:' The Social Construction of Gender," in *Global Perspectives on Gender and Work*, ed. Jacqueline Goodman (Lanham, MD: Rowman & Littlefield, 2010), 15–32.

12. Yvonne Stedham and Merwin C. Mitchell, "Sexual Harassment in Casinos: Effects on Employee Attitudes and Behaviors," *Journal of Gambling Studies* 14, no. 4 (1998): 381–400.

13. Stedham and Mitchell, "Sexual Harassment in Casinos," 387. Similarly, the workers in a participant observation study conducted at a national chain restaurant with the pseudonym "Bazooms" regarded sexual harassment and sexual joking as endemic to the job. They wished they knew how to manage it better. See Meika Loe, "Working at Bazooms: The Intersection of Power, Gender, and Sexuality," in *Mapping the Social Landscape: Readings in Sociology*, ed. Susan J. Ferguson (New York: McGraw-Hill, 2010), 330–45.

14. A participant observation study in three Reno casinos also found touching was rare. See Bayard de Volo, "Service and Surveillance," 357–59.

15. Kamer and Keller, "Give Me $5 Chips, a Jack and Coke—Hold the Cleavage."

16. Jennifer Bogdan, "A.C. Does Sexy," *Press of Atlantic City*, February 17, 2013.

17. Bogdan, "Borgata Can Make 'Babes' Watch Weight."

18. Lynda Cohen, "New Sexual Harassment Suits Go Beyond the Pool, Allege Harrah's Knew and Covered Up," *Press of Atlantic City*, February 9, 2010; Jennifer Bogdan, "Harrah's Waitress Settles Sex-Harassment Suit," *Press of Atlantic City*, May 22, 2012.

19. Ann C. McGinley, "Babes and Beefcake: Exclusive Hiring Arrangements and Sexy Dress Codes," *Duke Journal of Gender Law and Policy* 14, no. 1 (2007): 273–74.

20. Derek Harper, "Automated Casino Booze Irks Servers," *Press of Atlantic City*, September 13, 2013.

21. Barbara Ehrenreich and Arlie Russell Hochschild, *Global Woman: Nannies, Maids, and Sex Workers in the New Economy* (New York: Holt, 2004).

22. Wayne A. Lewchuk, "Men and Monotony: Fraternalism as a Managerial Strategy at the Ford Motor Company," *Journal of Economic History* 53, no. 4 (1993): 824–56.

6. COLLECTIVE VOICE IN TURBULENT TIMES

1. J. Staas Haught, "Question Vexes Unions: Dealers, or No Dealers? *Press of Atlantic City*, December 10, 2006.

2. The full name of the UAW is the International Union, United Automobile, Aerospace and Agricultural Implement Workers of America.

3. See Benjamin F. Blair, R. Keith Schwer, and C. Jeffrey Waddoups, "Gambling as an Economic Development Strategy: The Neglected Issue of Job Satisfaction and Nonpecuniary Income," *Review of Regional Studies* 28, no. 1 (1998): 47–62.

4. The PATCO strike and its aftermath is described in Steve Babson, *The Unfinished Struggle* (Lanham, MD: Rowman & Littlefield, 1999).

5. The AFL-CIO is a federation of international and national unions that resulted from the merger of the American Federation of Labor, a federation of craft unions, and the Congress of Industrial Organizations, a federation of industrial unions, in 1955.

6. You may have heard the stories that the unionized Broadway musicians insist on a minimum size orchestra for a musical performance or show; the stagehands' union requires a minimum stage crew; or that sheet metal workers may not lay bricks and that bricklayers may not perform simple carpentry tasks.

These are union work rules: influencing the structure of the work process or the production process to save union jobs or protect health and safety, for example.

7. Richard B. Freeman and James L. Medoff, *What Do Unions Do?* (New York: Basic, 1984), 7–8.

8. Freeman and Medoff, *What Do Unions Do?*, 19.

9. See Jake Rosenfeld, *What Unions No Longer Do* (Cambridge, MA: Harvard University Press, 2014). "Card-check" is a proposal that would allow a union to be certified without a secret ballot election provided that a majority of workers at a site sign an authorization card indicating they wish to be represented by the union organizing the bargaining unit.

10. A split within UNITE HERE occurred in 2009 when UNITE's Bruce Raynor resigned and broke off most of formerly UNITE workers into a new union called Workers United, affiliating instead with the Service Employees International Union (SEIU). UNITE HERE retained food service workers in many industries while SEIU would organize them in health care, prisons, and government buildings. The split is covered in C. Jeffrey Waddoups and Vincent H. Eade, "Hotels and Casinos: Collective Bargaining During a Decade of Instability," in *Collective Bargaining Under Duress: Case Studies of Major North American Industries*, ed. Howard R. Stanger, Paul F. Clark, and Ann C. Frost (Champaign, IL: Labor and Employment Relations Association annual research volume, 2013). An excellent history of UNITE HERE is in Julius G. Getman's *Restoring the Power of Unions: It Takes a Movement* (New Haven: Yale University Press, 2010).

11. Bryant Simon, *Boardwalk of Dreams: Atlantic City and the Fate of Urban America* (New York: Oxford University Press, 2004), 215.

12. Susan Chandler and Jill Jones, "Because a Better World Is Possible: Women Casino Workers, Union Activism and the Creation of a Just Workplace," *Journal of Sociology and Social Welfare* 30, no. 4 (2003), 57–78; and Susan Chandler and Jill B. Jones, *Casino Women: Courage in Unexpected Places* (Ithaca, NY: Cornell University Press, 2011).

13. "Margaret" is a pseudonym, quoted in Chandler and Jones, "Because a Better World Is Possible," 65.

14. Security and fire command officers at Bally's also voted for union representation in June 2007.

15. John Logan, "The Union Avoidance Industry in the United States," *British Journal of Industrial Relations* 44, no. 4 (2006), 651–75.

16. Martin Jay Levitt with Terry Conrow, *Confessions of a Union Buster* (New York: Crown, 1993).

17. Quoted in Maya Rao, "Timing Benefited Union's A.C. Push," *Press of Atlantic City*, April 8, 2007.

18. Joe Ashton, "UAW Leader: Blame Harrah's, Not Union," *Press of Atlantic City*, October 10, 2009.

19. Ashton, "UAW Leader." In Las Vegas, Caesars Entertainment also played hardball, and negotiations were as protracted as they were in Atlantic City. The first dealer contract in Las Vegas was inked in 2010 at Wynn Las Vegas, followed by Caesars Palace in 2012. As of 2014, three more Caesars Entertainment properties in Vegas have union representation and new contracts: Paris Las Vegas, Bally's, and Harrah's.

20. Erik Ortiz, "Union, Casinos Waging War in Multimedia/UAW Runs Ad Blitz, Threatens Strike, Harrah's Prepares to Replace Workers," *Press of Atlantic City*, July 21, 2009.

21. Quoted in Ortiz, "Unions, Casinos Waging War."

22. Walter M. (his real name) was quoted in Erik Ortiz, "600 Rally in Atlantic City for UAW Contracts at Bally's, Caesars," *Press of Atlantic City*, August 30, 2009.

23. J. Carlos Tolosa, "Voice of the People/Harrah's: We Don't Want a Public Battle, but UAW Does," *Press of Atlantic City*, July 28, 2009.

24. Erik Ortiz, "Dealers Frustrated with Trump and UAW," *Press of Atlantic City*, September 18, 2009.

25. Levitt with Conrow, *Confessions of a Union Buster*.

26. Quoted in Erik Ortiz, "Dealers Clinch First Contract/UAW Waited Out Tropicana," *Press of Atlantic City*, August 29, 2010.

27. Quoted in Erik Ortiz and Donald Wittkowski, "UAW Has Tentative Deal with Trop/Dealers Voting on Contract that Would Be First of Its Kind in Resort," *Press of Atlantic City*, August 19, 2010.

28. Donald Wittkowski, "Union Forges Friendlier Relationship with Casinos," *Press of Atlantic City*, July 30, 2012.

29. Wittkowski, "Union Forges Friendlier Relationship with Casinos."

30. C. Jeffrey Waddoups, "Wages in Las Vegas and Reno: How Much Difference Do Unions Make in the Hotel, Gaming, and Recreation Industry?" *UNLV Gaming Research & Review Journal* 6, no. 1 (2001), 16.

31. C. Jeffrey Waddoups, "Wage Inequality and Collective Bargaining: Hotels and Casinos in Nevada," *Journal of Economic Issues* 36, no. 3 (2002): 617–34.

32. Waddoups and Eade, "Hotels and Casinos," 81–117.

33. Michael D. Yates, *Why Unions Matter*, 2nd ed. (New York: Monthly Review Press, 2009), 11.

7. PUBLIC INVESTMENT OR SOCIALIZED RISK?

1. Barbara A. Lee and James Chelius, "Government Regulation of Labor Management Corruption: The Casino Industry Experience in New Jersey," *Industrial and Labor Relations Review* 42, no. 4 (1989): 536–48; Robert Goodman, *The Luck Business* (New York: Free Press, 1995).

2. DGE staff increased from 270 to around 340 following the reorganization, according to an interview with the new director, David Rebuck. See Israel Posner, "Interview with David Rebuck," *LIGHT'S ON* 2, no. 2 (2012): 1–3, accessed May 29, 2014, http://intraweb.stockton.edu/eyos/page.cfm?siteID=150&pageID=72.

3. Philip Mattera and Kasia Tarczynska, with Greg LeRoy, *Megadeals: The Largest Economic Development Subsidy Packages Ever Awarded by State and Local Governments in the United States* (Washington, DC: Good Jobs First, 2013).

4. Between February 1, 2010, and January 31, 2013, New Jersey development agencies have awarded $2.1 billion in tax credits and grants to 170 projects throughout the state; the average monthly subsidy increased by 400 percent during the Christie years. John Whiten, *New Jersey's Subsidy Surge Has Not Subsided* (Trenton: New Jersey Policy Perspectives, 2013), accessed May 29, 2014, http://www.njpp.org/reports/new-jerseys-subsidy-surge-has-not-subsided.

5. The pier was originally converted to a mall in the 1980s, with small shops owned by local business owners. These business owners lost their shops during the conversion to the Pier.

6. Good Jobs First, "Beginner's Guide," accessed May 29, 2014, http://www.goodjobsfirst.org/accountable-development/beginners-guide.

7. Edward A. Morse and Ernest P. Goss, *Governing Fortune: Casino Gambling in America* (Ann Arbor: University of Michigan Press, 2007).

8. Casinos technically have the option of paying a 2.5 percent investment alternative tax instead. Now that online gaming has been introduced (see chapter 8), there is a higher rate of 2.5 percent in investments or a 5 percent investment alternative tax on online GGR.

9. Funds from the luxury tax support marketing the resort as a tourist destination and debt service on the Atlantic City Convention Center. The source of data for casino taxes and fees is "DGE Announces 4th Quarter and Year-End 2013 Results," April 7, 2014, Press Release, accessed April 10, 2014, http://www.nj.gov/oag/ge/docs/Financials/QuarterlyFinRpt2013/4thQTR2013PressRelease.pdf.

10. Karl Polanyi, *The Great Transformation: The Political and Economic Origins of Our Time* (1944; repr., Boston: Beacon, 2001).

11. Rent-seeking behavior is defined as the effort to obtain economic benefits in the political arena. For a discussion of the propensity for rent seeking by
casinos, see Alan Mallach, "Economic and Social Impact of Introducing Casino
Gambling: A Review and Assessment of the Literature," Discussion Paper
(Philadelphia: Federal Reserve Bank of Philadelphia, March 2010), 16.

12. Dean Baker, *Taking Economics Seriously* (Cambridge, MA: MIT Press,
2010), 14. See also Pietra Rivoli, *The Travels of a T-Shirt in the Global Economy*, 2nd ed. (Hoboken, NJ: Wiley, 2009).

13. James K. Galbraith, *The Predator State* (New York: Free Press, 2007),
xiii.

14. Goodman, *Luck Business*, 135–37.

15. Jesse McKinley and Charles V. Bagli, "Success of Cuomo's Plan for
More Casinos Relies on His Power of Persuasion," *New York Times*, June 17,
2013.

16. Douglas M. Walker, *Casinonomics* (New York: Springer, 2013), 88.

17. Morse and Goss, *Governing Fortune*.

18. Suzette Parmley, "Casino Closure Means Tax-Revenue Drop for A.C.,"
Philadelphia Inquirer, December 31, 2013; Suzette Parmley, "New A.C. May-
or Vows to Dig City Out of 'Mess,'" *Philadelphia Inquirer*, January 14, 2014;
Suzette Parmley, "Fiscal Pain from Atlantic City's Decline is Countywide,"
Philadelphia Inquirer, March 30, 2014.

19. Randall Chase, "$8M Bailout Proposed for Del. Casinos," *Press of At-
lantic City*, June 18, 2013.

20. Nick Casiello Jr., "The Adoption and Development of the Casino Control Act," in *Casino Gaming in Atlantic City: A Thirty Year Retrospective,
1978–2008*, ed. Brian J. Tyrrell and Israel Posner (Margate, NJ: ComteQ,
2009), 82.

21. Posner, "Interview with David Rebuck."

22. Michael Clark, "Gov. Christie's Plan for A.C. Takeover: Christie's Plan
is a Partnership, Mayor Lorenzo Langford Says," *Press of Atlantic City*, July 22,
2010.

23. Anthony Marino, "Crime in Atlantic City," in Tyrrell and Posner, *Casino
Gaming in Atlantic City*, 54–62.

24. Casino Reinvestment Development Authority, *Tourism District Master
Plan*, February 1, 2012, accessed May 27, 2014, http://www.njcrda.com/ac-
tourism-district/master-plan/.

25. Juliet Fletcher, "Blunt Talk and Atlantic City are Highlights of Chris
Christie's First Year as New Jersey Governor," *Press of Atlantic City*, January
2, 2011.

26. Juliet Fletcher, "Gov. Christie, Senate President Sweeney Coming Closer to Agreement on Atlantic City," *Press of Atlantic City*, August 22, 2010.

27. Interview with William Cheatham, quoted in Michael Clark, "Overhaul Leaves Atlantic City Feeling Weak," *Press of Atlantic City*, February 6, 2011.

28. Other concessions included an amendment that insisted that the state commander overseeing public safety would have to coordinate with the mayor and city police officials. Michael Clark and Juliet Fletcher, "Atlantic City 'Renaissance' Awaits Christie's Pen," *Press of Atlantic City*, January 11, 2011.

29. Casino Reinvestment Development Authority, *Tourism District Master Plan*, 1-1.

30. The Benton Harbor story is described in Jonathan Mahler, "Now That the Factories are Closed, It's Tee-time in Benton Harbor, Mich.," *New York Times Magazine*, December 15, 2011, and Roger Bybee, "Democracy vs. Profit is Central Issue in Takeover of Benton Harbor, Mich.," *In These Times*, April 26, 2011.

31. Pew Charitable Trusts, *The State Role in Local Government Financial Distress*, 2013, accessed June 10, 2014, http://www.pewstates.org/research/reports/the-state-role-in-local-government-financial-distress-85899492075.

32. Donald Wittkowski, "Gov. Christie's Plan for A.C. Takeover: Gaming Industry Welcomes Atlantic City Plan, but Others Skeptical that NJ Can Do Better," *Press of Atlantic City* , July 22, 2010.

33. Jennifer Bogdan, "Clock Ticking for Results in State's Five-Year Experiment," *Press of Atlantic City*, January 26, 2014.

34. Casino Reinvestment Development Authority, *2012 Annual Report: The Five Year Master Plan, 1 of 5*, accessed May 27, 2014, http://www.njcrda.com/applications-and-public-notices/reports/annual-reports/.

35. CRDA, *2012 Annual Report*, 13.

36. Donna Weaver and Wallace McKelvey, "Mission in Crisis," *Press of Atlantic City*, September 23, 2012.

37. Braden Campbell, "Landowners Fight CRDA," *Press of Atlantic City*, May 21, 2014.

38. Jennifer Bogdan, "Growth Ahead in A.C.," *Press of Atlantic City*, March 19, 2014.

39. See "Revel Casino Timeline," in Donald Wittkowski, "Revel in Atlantic City May Have Deal with Chinese Bank to Finish Casino," *Press of Atlantic City*, March 31, 2010.

40. Michael Clark, "Casino Union Local 54 Sues Atlantic City to Force Referendum on $300 M. Revel Tax Break," *Press of Atlantic City*, March 9, 2010.

41. Additional subsidies for road improvements, worker training, and other items were promised, leading to a total estimated subsidy of $323,000,000 according to some accounts. More information can be found in the Good Jobs First subsidy tracker database.

42. Emily Previti, "Revel's Original Estimate of 5,500 Full-time Employees Will Now Be 38 Percent Part-Timers," *Press of Atlantic City*, February 15, 2012.

43. Kelly Bennett, "Can Revel Save Atlantic City?" *The Atlantic* blog, accessed August 27, 2012, http://www.theatlanticcities.com/arts-and-lifestyle/2012/05/can-revel-save-atlantic-city/2057/.

44. "Casino Chat with Chuck Darrow and Suzette Parmley," June 13, 2012, Philly.com, accessed July 16, 2012, http://www.philly.com/philly/business/158459365.html.

45. Donald Wittkowski, "Revel Falling Short," *Press of Atlantic City*, October 21, 2012.

46. Kitty Bean Yancey, "Could New Megaresort Revel Be Atlantic City's Game-Changer?" *USA Today*, March 8, 2012.

47. Wittkowski, "Revel Falling Short."

48. Amy Brittain, "3 Months After Opening, Atlantic City's Revel Casino Still Has Some Kinks—Like an Unfinished Beach," *Star-Ledger*, July 16, 2012.

49. John Appezzato, "N.J. Casino Commission Approves Restructuring Plan for Revel," *Star-Ledger*, June 1, 2013, and Jean Mikle, "State Takes $300 Million Pension Gamble on Revel Casino Owner," *Courier-Post*, August 12, 2014.

50. Randall Fine, quoted in Donald Wittkowski, "Revel Lifts Smoking Ban, Hopes Gamblers Light Up," *Press of Atlantic City*, May 29, 2013.

51. Jennifer Bogdan, "Revel Goes All In with Slot-Loss Refunds for July," *Press of Atlantic City*, June 21, 2013.

52. Quoted in Jennifer Bogdan, "Revel Switches Gear, Name to Market to Gamblers," *Press of Atlantic City*, June 20, 2013.

53. W. F. Keogh and Vincent Jackson, "Revel Workers Vote to Unionize," *Press of Atlantic City*, June 8, 2014.

8. THE FUTURE OF THE CASINO ECONOMY

1. The article is by Donald Wittkowski and Hoa Nguyen.

2. Michael Cooper, "Casino Boom has States Looking to the Internet for Gambling Dollars," *New York Times*, August 3, 2012, and Wayne Parry, "Wall St. Cuts Its Outlook for Internet Gambling," *Press of Atlantic City*, March 25, 2014.

3. Jennifer Bogdan, "Internet Gambling: It's Here to Stay," *Press of Atlantic City*, November 17, 2013.

4. Donald Wittkowski, "Analysts See 100s of Jobs in E-Betting," *Press of Atlantic City*, October 13, 2013.

5. We spoke with one frequent gambler and software entrepreneur who is developing and marketing a program to track the betting habits of online poker players. Such small businesses do benefit from the spillover of e-gambling, but the employment potential of such cottage industries is limited.

6. Parry, "Wall St. Cuts Its Outlook for Internet Gambling," and Angela Della Santi, "Internet Gambling Revenue a Bust for State Budget," *Press of Atlantic City*, April 2, 2014.

7. The latter three have offered sports lotteries. In Delaware, for example, customers can buy tickets at lottery outlets to wager on the outcomes of professional football games. Oregon eliminated their sports lottery in 2005, and Montana focuses on fantasy sports.

8. Christopher L. Soriano, "The Efforts to Legalize Sports Betting in New Jersey—A History," *New Jersey Lawyer* no. 281 (April 2013): 22–25.

9. Steven Lemongello and Jennifer Bogdan, "Officials: A.C. Would Thrive on Madness," *Press of Atlantic City*, March 20, 2014.

10. Brent Johnson, "U.S. Supreme Court Allows Sports Betting Ban in NJ to Remain," *New Jersey Star Ledger*, June 24, 2014, and Reuben Kramer, "Court Upholds Sports Bet Ban," *Press of Atlantic City*, June 24, 2014.

11. Hoa Nguyen, "A.C. Casinos to Make Sports Bettors' Fantasy a Reality," *Press of Atlantic City*, March 19, 2013.

12. Oliver Cooke, "The Diversification Premium," *South Jersey Economic Review* (Winter 2014): 3–7, accessed May 29, 2014, http://intraweb.stockton. edu/eyos/office_of_academic_affairs/content/docs/SJER%20winter%202014. pdf.

13. Edward L. Glaeser, Hedi D. Kallal, José A. Scheinkman, and Andrei Shleifer, "Growth in Cities," *Journal of Political Economy* 100, no. 6 (1992): 1126–52.

14. Cooke, "The Diversification Premium."

15. Oliver Cooke, "Economic Update," *LIGHT'S ON*, 2, no. 1 (2012): 8–9, accessed May 29, 2014, http://intraweb.stockton.edu/eyos/page.cfm?siteID= 150&pageID=72.

16. Robert Pollin and Jeannette Wicks-Lim, *Job Opportunities for the Green Economy*, June 2008, accessed June 10, 2014, http://www.peri.umass. edu/fileadmin/pdf/other_publication_types/Green_Jobs_PERI.pdf.

17. See Environment New Jersey, "Report Highlights Environmental Benefits of Wind, but New Jersey Off-Shore Wind Program Stuck in Neutral," News Release, December 5, 2013, accessed June 11, 2014, http://www. environmentnewjersey.org/news/nje/report-highlights-environmental-benefits-wind-new-jersey-shore-wind-program-stuck-neutral and Michael Miller, "N.J.'s Economic Pearl Seen in Ocean's Power," *Press of Atlantic City*, June 6, 2014.

18. Wallace McKelvey, "State Rejects Wind Farm Plan," *Press of Atlantic City*, March 20, 2014.

19. Guy Standing, *The Precariat: The New Dangerous Class* (London: Bloomsbury, 2011), 16.

20. Amartya Sen, *Development as Freedom* (New York: Anchor, 1999).

21. Tom Rath and Jim Harter, *Wellbeing: The Five Essential Elements* (New York: Gallup, 2010). For additional information about the Gallup project, see the Gallup-Healthways Solutions website, accessed June 26, 2014, http://www.healthways.com/solution/default.aspx?id=1125.

22. For a starting point on how to create such an institutional context, see the International Labour Organization's preconditions for decent work. International Labour Organization, "Decent Work Agenda," accessed June 26, 2014, http://www.ilo.org/global/about-the-ilo/decent-work-agenda/lang--de/index.htm.

BIBLIOGRAPHY

Adib, Amel, and Yvonne Guerrier. "The Interlocking of Gender with Nationality, Race, Ethnicity and Class: The Narratives of Women in Hotel Work." In *Global Perspectives on Gender & Work*, edited by Jacqueline Goodman, 245–59. Lanham, MD: Rowman & Littlefield, 2010.

Albelda, Randy, and Robert Drago. *Unlevel Playing Fields: Understanding Wage Inequality and Discrimination*. 4th ed. Boston: Economic Affairs Bureau, 2013.

American Gaming Association. *State of the States: The AGA Survey of Casino Entertainment*. Washington, DC: AGA, various years.

———. *U.S. Commercial Casino Industry: Facts at Your Fingertips*. Washington, DC: AGA, 2009.

Appelbaum, Eileen, and Rosemary Batt. *Private Equity at Work: When Wall Street Manages Main Street*. New York: Russell Sage Foundation, 2014.

Babson, Steve. *The Unfinished Struggle*. Lanham, MD: Rowman & Littlefield, 1999.

Badgett, M. V. Lee. *Money, Myths, and Change: The Economic Lives of Lesbians and Gay Men*. Chicago: University of Chicago Press, 2001.

Badgett, M. V. Lee, and Mary C. King. "Lesbian and Gay Occupational Strategies." In *Homo Economics: Capitalism, Community, and Lesbian and Gay Life*, edited by Amy Gluckman and Betsy Reed, 73–86. London: Routledge, 1997.

Baker, Dean. *Taking Economics Seriously*. Cambridge, MA: MIT Press, 2010.

———. *Work Sharing: The Quick Route Back to Full Employment*. Washington, DC: Center for Economic and Policy Research, June 2011.

Bai, Billy K., Pearl Brewer, Gail Simmons, and Skip Swerdlow. "Job Satisfaction, Organizational Commitment, and Internal Service Quality: A Case Study of Las Vegas Hotel/Casino Industry." *Journal of Human Resources in Hospitality & Tourism* 5, no. 2 (2006): 37–54.

Bayard de Volo, Lorraine. "Service and Surveillance: Infrapolitics at Work among Casino Cocktail Waitresses." *Social Politics* 10, no. 3 (2003): 346–76.

Blair, Benjamin F., R. Keith Schwer, and C. Jeffrey Waddoups. "Gambling as an Economic Development Strategy: The Neglected Issue of Job Satisfaction and Nonpecuniary Income." *Review of Regional Studies* 28, no. 1 (1998): 47–62.

Bokunewicz, Jane. "The Evolution of Casino Technology in Atlantic City." In *Casino Gaming in Atlantic City: A Thirty Year Retrospective, 1978–2008*, edited by Brian J. Tyrrell and Israel Posner, 23–30. Margate, NJ: ComteQ, 2009.

Casiello, Nick Jr. "The Adoption and Development of the Casino Control Act." In *Casino Gaming in Atlantic City: A Thirty Year Retrospective, 1978–2008*, edited by Brian J. Tyrrell and Israel Posner, 80–87. Margate, NJ: ComteQ, 2009.

Chandler, Susan, and Jill Jones. "Because a Better World Is Possible: Women Casino Work-
ers, Union Activism and the Creation of a Just Workplace." *Journal of Sociology and
Social Welfare* 30, no. 4 (2003): 57–78.
Chandler, Susan, and Jill B. Jones. *Casino Women: Courage in Unexpected Places*. Ithaca,
NY: Cornell University Press, 2011.
Child Care Aware of America. *Parents and the Cost of Child Care: 2013 Report*. Arlington,
VA. Accessed March 3, 2014. http://naccrra.org/costofcare.
Congressional Budget Office. *Trends in the Distribution of Household Income Between 1979
and 2007*. Washington, DC: Congressional Budget Office, October 2011.
Cooke, Oliver. "The Economic Impact of Gaming in Atlantic City." In *Casino Gaming in
Atlantic City: A Thirty Year Retrospective, 1978–2008*, edited by Brian J. Tyrrell and
Israel Posner, 134–72. Margate, NJ: ComteQ, 2009.
Costen, Wanda M., Christian E. Hardigree, and Michael A. Testagrossa. "Glass Ceiling or
Saran Wrap™? Women in Gaming Management." *UNLV Gaming Research & Review
Journal* 7, no. 2 (2003): 1–12.
Datamonitor. *Casinos & Gaming in the United States*. Reference Codes 0072-2019 and
0199-2019. New York: Datamonitor USA, May 2011.
———. *Global Casinos & Gaming*. Reference Code 0199-2019. New York: Datamonitor
USA, May 2011.
Demaris, Ovid. *The Boardwalk Jungle*. Toronto: Bantam, 1986.
Doeringer, Peter B., and Michael J. Piore. *Internal Labor Markets and Manpower Analysis*.
Lexington, MA: Heath, 1971.
Dugger, William M. "Redefining Economics: From Market Allocation to Social Provision-
ing." In *Political Economy for the 21st Century: Contemporary Views on the Trend of
Economics*, edited by Charles J. Whalen, 31–43. Armonk, NY: Sharpe, 1996.
Eadington, William R. "Preface." In *The Business of Gaming: Economic and Management
Issues*, edited by William R. Eadington and Judy A. Cornelius, xv–xx. Reno, NV: Institute
for the Study of Gambling and Commercial Gaming, 1999.
Ehrenreich, Barbara, and Arlie Russell Hochschild, eds. *Global Woman: Nannies, Maids,
and Sex Workers in the New Economy*. New York: Holt, 2004.
Figart, Deborah M. "Social Responsibility for Living Standards: Presidential Address, Associ-
ation for Social Economics, 2007." *Review of Social Economy* 65, no. 4 (2007): 391–405.
Figart, Deborah M., and Ellen Mutari. "Work: Its Social Meanings and Role in Provision-
ing." In *The Elgar Companion to Social Economics*, edited by John B. Davis and Wilfred
Dolfsma, 287–301. Aldershot, England: Edward Elgar, 2008.
Figart, Deborah M., Ellen Mutari, and Marilyn Power. *Living Wages, Equal Wages: Gender
and Labor Market Policies in the United States*. London: Routledge, 2002.
Foster, John Bellamy. "Monopoly Capital at the Turn of the Millennium." *Monthly Review*
51, no. 11 (2000): 1–18.
Frank, Robert H. *Luxury Fever: Money and Happiness in an Era of Excess*. Princeton, NJ:
Princeton University Press, 1999.
Freeman, Richard B., and James L. Medoff. *What Do Unions Do?* New York: Basic, 1984.
Galbraith, James K. *The Predator State: How Conservatives Abandoned the Free Market and
Why Liberals Should Too*. New York: Free Press, 2008.
Getman, Julius G. *Restoring the Power of Unions: It Takes a Movement*. New Haven: Yale
University Press, 2010.
Glaeser, Edward L., Hedi D. Kallal, José A. Scheinkman, and Andrei Shleifer. "Growth in
Cities." *Journal of Political Economy* 100, no. 6 (1992): 1126–52.
Glenn, Evelyn Nakano. "From Servitude to Service Work: Historical Continuities in the
Racial Division of Paid Reproductive Labor." *Signs* 18, no. 1 (1992): 1–43.
Goodman, Robert. *The Luck Business*. New York: Free Press, 1995.
Gordon, David M. *Fat and Mean: The Corporate Squeeze of Working Americans and the
Myth of Managerial "Downsizing."* New York: Free Press, 1996.
Greenwood, Robin, and David Scharfstein. "The Growth of Finance." *Journal of Economic
Perspectives* 27, no. 2 (2013): 3–28.
Jacobs, Jane. *The Death and Life of Great American Cities*. New York: Vintage, 1961.

Jayaraman, Saru. *Behind the Kitchen Door*. Ithaca, NY: Cornell University Press, 2013.

Johnson, Nelson. *Boardwalk Empire: The Birth, High Times, and Corruption of Atlantic City*. Medford, NJ: Plexus, 2002.

Jones, Jill B., and Susan Chandler. "Connecting Personal Biography and Social History: Women Casino Workers and the Global Economy." *Journal of Sociology and Social Welfare* 28, no. 4 (2001):173–93.

Kamer, Gregory J., and Edwin A. Keller Jr. "Give Me $5 Chips, a Jack and Coke—Hold the Cleavage: A Look at Employee Appearance Issues in the Gaming Industry." *Gaming Law Review* 7, no. 5 (2003): 355–46.

Klein, Naomi. *No Logo: Taking Aim at the Brand Bullies*. New York: Picador, 2002.

Krugman, Paul. *The Conscience of a Liberal: Reclaiming America from the Right*. New York: Norton, 2009.

Landers, Jim. "What's the Potential Impact of Casino Tax Increases on Wagering Handle: Estimates of the Price Elasticity of Demand for Casino Gaming." *Economics Bulletin* 8, no. 6 (2008): 1–15.

Lee, Barbara A., and James Chelius. "Government Regulation of Labor-Management Corruption: The Casino Industry Experience in New Jersey." *Industrial and Labor Relations Review* 42, no. 4 (1989): 536–48.

Levitt, Martin Jay. *Confessions of a Union Buster*. With Terry Conrow. New York: Crown, 1993.

Lewchuk, Wayne A. "Men and Monotony: Fraternalism as a Managerial Strategy at the Ford Motor Company." *Journal of Economic History* 53, no. 4 (1993): 824–56.

Linder, Marc, and Ingrid Nygaard. *Void Where Prohibited*. Ithaca, NY: ILR, 1998.

Listokin, David, and Candice A. Valente. "Public Finance and Atlantic City Casinos." In *Casino Gaming in Atlantic City: A Thirty Year Retrospective, 1978–2008*, edited by Brian J. Tyrrell and Israel Posner, 88–133. Margate, NJ: ComteQ, 2009.

Loe, Meika. "Working at Bazooms: The Intersection of Power, Gender, and Sexuality," in *Mapping the Social Landscape: Readings in Sociology*, edited by Susan J. Ferguson, 330–45. New York: McGraw-Hill, 2010.

Logan, John. "The Union Avoidance Industry in the United States." *British Journal of Industrial Relations* 44, no. 4 (2006): 651–75.

Lorber, Judith. "'Night to His Day': The Social Construction of Gender." In *Global Perspectives on Gender & Work*, edited by Jacqueline Goodman, 15–32. Lanham, MD: Rowman & Littlefield, 2010.

Macdonald, Cameron Lynne, and Carmen Sirianni, eds. *Working in the Service Society*. Philadelphia: Temple University Press, 1996.

MacEwan, Arthur, and John Miller. *Economic Collapse, Economic Change: Getting to the Roots of the Crisis*. Armonk, NY: Sharpe, 2011.

Mallach, Alan. "Economic and Social Impact of Introducing Casino Gambling: A Review and Assessment of the Literature." Discussion Paper. Philadelphia: Federal Reserve Bank of Philadelphia, Community Affairs Department, March 2010.

Marino, Anthony. "Crime in Atlantic City." In *Casino Gaming in Atlantic City: A Thirty Year Retrospective, 1978–2008*, edited by Brian J. Tyrrell and Israel Posner, 54–62. Margate, NJ: ComteQ, 2009.

———. "Transportation in Atlantic City." In *Casino Gaming in Atlantic City: A Thirty Year Retrospective, 1978–2008*, edited by Brian J. Tyrrell and Israel Posner, 44–53. Margate, NJ: ComteQ, 2009.

Mason, John Lyman, and Michael Nelson. *Governing Gambling*. New York: Century Foundation, 2001.

Mattera, Philip, and Kasia Tarczynska. *Megadeals: The Largest Economic Development Subsidy Packages Ever Awarded by State and Local Governments in the United States*. With Greg LeRoy. Washington, DC: Good Jobs First, 2013.

McGinley, Ann C. "Babes and Beefcake: Exclusive Hiring Arrangements and Sexy Dress Codes." *Duke Journal of Gender Law and Policy* 14, no. 1 (2007): 257–82.

Morse, Edward A., and Ernest P. Goss. *Governing Fortune: Casino Gambling in America*. Ann Arbor: University of Michigan Press, 2007.

Moss, Philip I., and Chris Tilly. *Stories Employers Tell: Race, Skill, and Hiring in America*. New York: Russell Sage Foundation, 2001.

National Gambling Impact Study Commission. *NGISC Report Recommendations*. Washington, DC, 1999. Accessed January 20, 2006. http://govinfo.library.unt.edu/ngisc/.

Nelson, Julie A. *Economics for Humans*. Chicago: University of Chicago Press, 2006.

Newberger, Harriet. *Atlantic City: Past as Prologue*. With Anita Sands and John Wackes. Philadelphia: Federal Reserve Bank of Philadelphia, 2009.

New Jersey Casino Control Commission. *Casino Gambling in New Jersey: A Report to the National Gambling Impact Study Commission*. Atlantic City: NJCCC, January 1998.

NJ [New Jersey] Department of Labor and Workforce Development. *County Community Fact Book: Atlantic County Edition*. Trenton, 2013. Accessed March 1, 2014. http://www.nj.gov/oag/ge/index.html.

Noah, Timothy. *The Great Divergence: America's Growing Inequality Crisis and What We Can Do About It*. New York: Bloomsbury, 2012.

Ortner, Sherry B. *Making Gender: The Politics and Erotics of Culture*. Boston: Beacon, 1996.

Palmeri, Christopher. "Casinos Know When to Fold 'Em." *Bloomberg Businessweek*, April 7–13, 2014, 25–26.

Peppard, Donald M. Jr., and Frances A. Boudreau. "Job Quality and Job Satisfaction Among Casino Workers: The Case of Foxwoods." *Gaming Research & Review Journal* 2, no. 2 (1995): 31–42.

Perskie, Steven P. "The Political and Economic Background of Atlantic City in the 1970s." In *Casino Gaming in Atlantic City: A Thirty Year Retrospective, 1978–2008*, edited by Brian J. Tyrrell and Israel Posner, 1–8. Margate, NJ: ComteQ, 2009.

Pilkington, Paul A., Selena Gray, and Anna B. Gilmore. "Health Impacts of Exposure to Second Hand Smoke (SHS) Amongst a Highly Exposed Workforce: Survey of London Casino Workers." *BMC Public Health* 7, no. 257 (2007): 1–8.

Polanyi, Karl. *The Great Transformation: The Political and Economic Origins of Our Time*. 1944. Reprint, Boston: Beacon, 2001.

Pollock, Michael. "From Divestment to Reinvestment: Atlantic City Addresses Core Issues." In *Casino Gaming in Atlantic City: A Thirty Year Retrospective, 1978–2008*, edited by Brian J. Tyrrell and Israel Posner, 12–21. Margate, NJ: ComteQ, 2009.

———. *Hostage to Fortune: Atlantic City and Casino Gambling*. Princeton, NJ: Center for Analysis of Public Issues, 1987.

Posner, Israel, and Lewis Leitner. "Front Line Careers," *Casino Connection* magazine, June 2007.

Presser, Harriet B. *Working in a 24/7 Economy: Challenges for American Families*. New York: Russell Sage Foundation, 2003.

Rath, Tom, and Jim Harter. *Wellbeing: The Five Essential Elements*. New York: Gallup, 2010.

Rivoli, Pietra. *The Travels of a T-Shirt in the Global Economy*. 2nd ed. Hoboken, NJ: Wiley, 2009.

Rosenfeld, Jake. *What Unions No Longer Do*. Cambridge, MA: Harvard University Press, 2014.

Rubenstein, Joseph. "Casino Gambling in Atlantic City: Issues of Development and Redevelopment." *Annals of the American Academy of Political and Social Science* 474 (July 1984): 61–71.

Sallaz, Jeffrey J. "The House Rules: Autonomy and Interests Among Service Workers in the Contemporary Casino Industry." *Work and Occupations* 29, no. 4 (2002): 394–427.

Sawers, Larry, and William K. Tabb. *Sunbelt/Snowbelt: Urban Development and Regional Restructuring*. New York: Oxford University Press, 1984.

Schumpeter, Joseph. *Capitalism, Socialism, and Democracy*. 1942. Reprint. New York: Harper Perennial Modern Classics, 2008.

Sen, Amartya. *Development as Freedom*. New York: Anchor, 1999.

Simon, Bryant. *Boardwalk of Dreams: Atlantic City and the Fate of Urban America*. New York: Oxford University Press, 2004.

Soriano, Christopher L. "The Efforts to Legalize Sports Betting in New Jersey—A History." *New Jersey Lawyer* no. 281 (April 2013): 22–25.

Standing, Guy. *The Precariat: The New Dangerous Class*. London: Bloomsbury, 2011.

Stedham, Yvonne, and Merwin C. Mitchell. "Sexual Harassment in Casinos: Effects on Employee Attitudes and Behaviors." *Journal of Gambling Studies* 14, no. 4 (1998): 381–400.

Steinberg, Ronnie J., and Deborah M. Figart, eds. *Emotional Labor in the Service Economy*. The Annals of the American Academy of Political and Social Science 561. Thousand Oaks, CA: Sage, 1999.

Sternlieb, George, and James W. Hughes. *The Atlantic City Gamble*. Cambridge, MA: A Twentieth Century Fund Report from Harvard University Press, 1983.

Tilly, Chris. "Arresting the Decline of Good Jobs in the USA?" *Industrial Relations Journal* 28, no. 4 (1997): 269–74.

Tyrrell, Brian J., and Jeffrey Vasser. "Marketing Atlantic City as a Destination." In *Casino Gaming in Atlantic City: A Thirty Year Retrospective, 1978–2008*, edited by Brian J. Tyrrell and Israel Posner, 174–92. Margate, NJ: ComteQ, 2009.

Ueno, Koji, Teresa Roach, and Abráham E. Peña-Talamantes. "Sexual Orientation and Gender Typicality of the Occupation in Young Adulthood." *Social Forces* 91, no. 1 (2013): 81–108.

UNLV Center for Gaming Research, Caesars Entertainment Corporation Company Profile. Accessed July 30, 2013. http://gaming.unlv.edu/abstract/fin_het.html.

Vogel, Harold L. *Entertainment Industry Economics: A Guide for Financial Analysis*. 8th ed. Cambridge, UK: Cambridge University Press, 2011.

von Herrmann, Denise. *The Big Gamble: The Politics of Lottery and Casino Expansion*. Westport, CT: Praeger, 2002.

Waddoups, C. Jeffrey. "Wage Inequality and Collective Bargaining: Hotels and Casinos in Nevada." *Journal of Economic Issues* 36, no. 3 (2002): 617–34.

———. "Wages in Las Vegas and Reno: How Much Difference Do Unions Make in the Hotel, Gaming, and Recreation Industry?" *UNLV Gaming Research & Review Journal* 6, no. 1 (2001): 7–21.

Waddoups, C. Jeffrey, and Vincent H. Eade. "Hotels and Casinos: Collective Bargaining During a Decade of Instability." In *Collective Bargaining Under Duress: Case Studies of Major North American Industries*, edited by Howard R. Stanger, Paul F. Clark, and Ann C. Frost, 81–117. Champaign, IL: Labor and Employment Relations Association annual research volume, 2013.

Wakefield, Melanie, Melissa Cameron, Graeme Inglis, Tessa Letcher, and Sarah Durkin. "Second-hand Smoke Exposure and Respiratory Symptoms among Casino, Club and Office Workers in Victoria, Australia." *Journal of Occupational and Environmental Medicine* 47, no. 7 (2005): 698–703.

Walker, Douglas M. *Casinonomics: The Socioeconomic Impacts of the Casino Industry*. New York: Springer, 2013.

Warhurst, Chris, Françoise Carré, Patricia Findlay, and Chris Tilly. *Are Bad Jobs Inevitable? Trends, Determinants and Responses to Job Quality in the Twenty-First Century*. London: Palgrave Macmillan, 2012.

Weichselbaumer, Doris. "Discrimination in Gay and Lesbian Lives." In *Handbook of Research on Gender and Economic Life*, edited by Deborah M. Figart and Tonia L. Warnecke, 236–54. Cheltenham, UK: Edward Elgar, 2013.

Weil, David. *The Fissured Workplace: Why Work Became So Bad for So Many and What Can Be Done to Improve It*. Cambridge, MA: Harvard University Press, 2014.

Whiten, John. *New Jersey's Subsidy Surge Has Not Subsided*. Trenton: New Jersey Policy Perspectives, 2013. Accessed May 29, 2014. http://www.njpp.org/reports/new-jerseys-subsidy-surge-has-not-subsided.

Wittmann, Dena C. "A Day in the Night of a Casino Worker: Shift Work Culture of Mississippi Dockside Gaming Employees." In *Resorting to Casinos: The Mississippi Gaming Industry*, ed. Denise von Herrman, 121–42. Jackson: University of Mississippi Press, 2006.

Yates, Michael D. *Why Unions Matter*. 2nd ed. New York: Monthly Review Press, 2009.

Zeng, Zhonglu, David Forrest, and Ian G. McHale. "Happiness and Job Satisfaction in a Casino-Dominated Economy." *Journal of Gambling Studies* 29, no. 3 (2013): 471–90.

INDEX

ABOUT THE AUTHORS

Ellen Mutari is professor of economics at the Richard Stockton College of New Jersey. She is coauthor of *Living Wages, Equal Wages: Gender and Labor Market Policies in the United States* (2002), *Women and the Economy: A Reader* (2003), and *Gender and Political Economy: Incorporating Diversity into Theory and Public Policy* (1997). She was the editor for the Routledge IAFFE Advances in Feminist Economics book series from 2008–2013.

Deborah M. Figart is professor of education and economics at the Richard Stockton College of New Jersey. She is the author or editor of sixteen books or monographs. Her edited volumes include *Handbook of Research on Gender and Economic Life* (2013), *Living Standards and Social Well-Being* (2011), and *Working Time: International Trends, Theory, and Policy Perspectives* (2000). She is coauthor of *Living Wages, Equal Wages: Gender and Labor Market Policies in the United States*, with Ellen Mutari and Marilyn Power (2002). She is a former president of the Association for Social Economics and served as coeditor of the *Review of Social Economy* from 2005–2013.